interests in conflict, the stability of conflict settlements, the purposes beyond strategic interaction that are served by conflict strategies, the flexibility of strategies, the nature of political choices, and the basis for compromise. Using these fundamental components of the political bargaining process, Lockhart offers insight into settlement prediction—examining what resources are useful in severe international conflicts, how those resources are transformed into usable options, and when various strategies (adaptation, coercion, accommodation) are appropriate and when they are counter-productive.

Charles Lockhart is assistant professor at Texas Christian University where he teaches international and comparative politics.

D1526366

Bargaining in International Conflicts

Bargaining in International Conflicts

Charles Lockhart

New York   Columbia University Press   1979

Library of Congress Cataloging in Publication Data
Lockhart, Charles, 1944–
  Bargaining in international conflicts.

  Bibliography: p.
  Includes index.
  1. Pacific settlement of international disputes.
2. Diplomatic negotiations in international disputes.
I. Title.
JX4473.L62   327'.11   78-23334
ISBN 0-231-04560-3

Columbia University Press
New York and Guildford, Surrey

Contents

Preface

This is an essay on bargaining among the great powers in severe international conflicts. The book grows out of my work during 1968–71 as a graduate assistant with the Crisis Bargaining Project, Center for International Conflict Studies, State University of New York at Buffalo. The research behind this book was supported in part by National Science Foundation Grant GS3227. Several colleagues on this project were kind enough to continue to include me in their activities while I spent three long and otherwise largely isolated years in the army (1971–74). As an outgrowth of the Crisis Bargaining Project this book bears the mark in some fashion of everyone who contributed to the larger enterprise. I would like particularly to mention the Project Director, Glenn H. Snyder, and also Kenneth Fuchs, Clark Murdock, and Charles Planck. And the guidance of Paul Diesing, to whom I owe an intellectual debt I can never repay, has been essential to every aspect of this book. Beyond those on the Crisis Bargaining Project at Buffalo I want to thank Terry Nardin and Harry Wilker for their help.

I have continued to receive support from numerous sources in my present position. Among my colleagues at Texas Christian University, Steve Brown, Michael Dodson, Don Jackson, and Gordon Smith have offered valuable advice. The Texas Christian University Research Foundation has provided support for the completion of the manuscript. Susan Butler, Lynn Dally, Flynt Leverett, John Lovell, Clark Murdock, Jerry Slater, and Henry Tom offered various kinds of assistance at crucial points. Paul Diesing and Glenn H. Snyder read the entire manuscript and offered many useful suggestions for improvement. Alexander L. George and Bob Jervis also read the entire manuscript, and I am particularly grateful to them for their helpful comments and encouragement. The comments of these four scholars have improved the book, but I am responsible for any weaknesses that remain in it. I want to thank Princeton University Press for permission to use some short passages that are virtually identical to material that appeared previously in *World Politics* (Lockhart, 1977a). The staff of Columbia University Press, particularly Karen Mitchell, has been accessible and helpful. Annette Dodson typed (and sometimes edited) the manuscript in a manner refreshing beyond my expectations.

Bargaining in International Conflicts

PART 1

BARGAINING THEORIES

Although bargaining is a common aspect of political life and constitutes a central political activity, theoretical analyses of bargaining have not generally been pursued by students of politics. Scholars focusing on international politics (Zartman, 1971; Iklé, 1964) have been more interested in bargaining than their colleagues who study domestic politics, but most theorizing on bargaining has been done by economists, administrative theorists, and psychologists. While some of their works deal directly with bargaining in politics (Schelling, 1966; Olson, 1965) and others can be related to political life (Rapoport and Chammah, 1965; Boulding, 1962), much of the work on bargaining done in economics, administrative theory, and psychology is difficult to apply to international conflicts. However, a review of some of the work these theorists have already done will help to formulate a conceptualization of bargaining appropriate for severe international conflicts. This review will not constitute an exhaustive survey of bargaining research in these fields. Rather, it will analyze selected prominent works with respect to two specific issues: first, the form that bargaining theory takes in these works, and second, their appropriateness for analyzing bargaining in severe international conflicts. The focus of these bargaining theories in some respects reduces their applicability to the study of bargaining in severe international conflicts, and clearly delineating the inappropriate characteristics will facilitate the task of constructing a more useful conceptualization.

1.

Formal Models of Bargaining:

Bargaining Theory in Economics & Administrative Theory

Much economic theory has taken the form of simple formal models; so it is not surprising that most early treatments of bargaining in economics appeared in this format. In Coleman's (1964: 34–50) terminology these are synthetic models. Synthetic models are simple, elegant creations, such as the normal curve (Gaussian distribution), that exist abstractly apart from their relevance to any particular empirical referent. They may be contrasted with more complicated models that approximate the dynamics or structure of a particular empirical instance (a computer simulation of a presidential election). These latter models are designed to explain specific cases—Coleman calls them explanatory models; and in acquiring a particular complex form in order to explain the dynamics or structure of a specific case, they lose their simplicity and elegance. In short, they lose any general meaning. The central question to ask about an explanatory model is how accurately it reflects the dynamics or structure of its empirical referent, for this is the key to its usefulness. In contrast, the major question in assessing the usefulness of a model of the synthetic type for analyzing particular empirical cases is whether the model is an appropriate representation of the instance under consideration (Rapoport and Perner, 1974: 114; Diesing, 1971: 48–62). Do the elements of the abstract model correspond to the crucial aspects of the empirical process or structure? If so, the model is appropriate; if not, the model is not inaccurate, for it has an existence independent of the particular case at hand. The normal curve is not inaccurate if a particular variable—personal income in Peru—follows a different distribution pattern. Instead the model is simply inappropriate for this case. It retains its general meaning, however, and may be useful for analyzing other instances. Some synthetic models have been used for analyzing bargaining in international conflicts (Ellsberg, 1968), although they have sometimes been put to use in ways unanticipated by their creators (Snyder, 1971a).

Recently, however, economists and administrative theorists have sometimes sought to relax the rigorous assumptions of the early formal models and to develop less elegant theories that focus on a variety of aspects crucial to bargaining in everyday life, including international conflicts. The work of Simon (1955), Schelling (1960), Cyert and March (1963), and Walton and McKersie (1965) offers fine examples of research in this vein. Efforts such as these have tended to work back from particular empirical phenomena—Coleman's explanatory models—and have created conceptualizations of bargaining far more complex than the early synthetic theories.

Synthetic Models of Bargaining: The Search for Saliency

For many of the economists initially engaged with bargaining, the topic posed a problem of specifying principles from which rational solutions could be deduced. That is, the problem was to elucidate the criteria a rational pair of antagonists would consider in arriving at an agreement. Once the criteria were specified thoroughly enough so that a solution range or point could be identified, the particular bargaining case at hand, or preferably the class of cases the current instance represented, was solved. Since the theorists engaged in these efforts were highly sophisticated mathematicians, the hypothetical antagonists they constructed shared their sophistication. In terms of Schelling (1960) their theories represent the criteria prominent or salient to mathematicians. While the criteria are certainly arbitrary in that they represent idiosyncratic selections of rational characteristics, they often impart an intuitive soundness to the layman when expressed in everyday as opposed to mathematical terms.

Rapoport (1966: 104–22) provides a convenient summary and comparison of several important theories of this nature; so it would be superfluous to scrutinize the specific internal dynamics of various examples in this category. A brief description of Nash's (1950, 1953) solution to the bargaining problem, however, will provide a useful basis for further discussion of theories of this type. First, Nash presupposes an environment similar to that of simple games. In particular, each bargainer is aware of both parties' stable preferences, and each bargainer's preferences are arranged along a single homogeneous dimension: utility. Then Nash assumes that rational bargainers will require four characteristics of a solution. First, there can be no interpersonal comparison of utilities. If, for instance, the bargainers differ in their stockpiles of utility so that one is far wealthier than the other, Nash assumes that this will have no impact on their evaluation of further units of utility. An additional unit will not be more valuable to the poor bargainer than to the wealthy one. Second, Nash assumes Pareto optimality. That is, an outcome is not acceptable as a solution if one bargainer can improve his payoff without hurting the other's payoff. Third, Nash assumes the solution to be independent of "irrelevant" alternatives. By this he means that if a new alternative is added to the existing options without changing the disagreement point, the new option either provides the solution or it has no impact whatsoever. Fourth, a solution point has the quality of symmetry. That is, if an outcome offers a solution, then reversing the positions of the bargainers so that each now stands in the other's shoes will make no difference; the outcomes will still be a solution. Nash (1950) was able to show mathematically that only a single possibility meets these four criteria. This solution is the point which maximizes the product of the difference between each player's payoff and his status quo position. Nash later (1953) refined the method of ascertaining status quo positions by basing it on the payoff levels at which each bargainer could threaten to hold the other.

Many arguments have been raised as to the specifics of Nash's theory. For instance, Schelling (1960) makes a persuasive argument against symmetry. Riker and Ordeshook (1973: 109–14) raise questions about independence from irrelevant alternatives. Shapley (1953) disagrees with the mechanism for determining the status quo point. Raiffa (1953) and Braithwaite (1955) advocate a different procedure for placing the solution point. This list of arguments is hardly complete, but it does give an indication of the arbitrariness of the specifics of Nash's theory. For the purposes of this book, Nash's theory will serve nicely as an example of synthetic bargaining theories; and rather than dispute specifics, the effort here will be to examine the strengths and weaknesses of this genre of theory for analyzing bargaining in international conflicts.

Political Applications of Synthetic Models

Several scholars have applied synthetic models similar to Nash's to international conflicts and related situations. Considerable ingenuity has been used in the application of these models, and the original theorists would surely be surprised at the heuristic purposes their efforts have served. One example of an application of this nature is Ellsberg (1968). Ellsberg applies Zeuthen's (1968) model and develops thereby the concept of "critical risk." This concept can be discussed more adequately with the help of diagram 1.1. In the diagram Challenger, a hypothetical nation that desires to control a small piece of territory now controlled by another, is pressing its claims against the other nation, Target. If Target

DIAGRAM 1.1. CRITICAL RISK

		Target	
		Comply	Resist
Challenger	Acquiesce	0, 0	−1, 1
	Advance	2, −2	−3, −3

The numbers represent an interval scale. That is, the difference between 1 and 2 is the same as the difference between 2 and 3; 2 and 1 are the most desired payoffs for Challenger and Target, respectively, and − 3 is the least desired payoff.

resists with a show of force before which Challenger withdraws its demands, there will be a modest gain and loss of reputation, respectively. If

Challenger succeeds in wresting control from Target, it gains territory and reputation, which are both lost by Target. The issues at stake in this conflict are not important enough for either nation to warrant a military struggle.[1]

Target would like to resist and improve its reputation while holding the territory (1) rather than complying and losing both reputation and territory (-2). But if it resists *and* Challenger advances, it finds itself in a war it does not desire (-3). For Ellsberg, Target's choice here depends on the probabilities that it attaches to Challenger's alternatives. If Target feels Challenger is apt to advance, Target complies (thus receiving -2 rather than -3). If Target thinks Challenger will acquiesce, Target resists. The probability at which Target shifts from comply to resist is the critical risk. In the example in diagram 1.1, its value is .75.[2] If Target perceives the probability that Challenger will advance to be .75 or higher, it will comply. If it feels the probability of a challenge is less than .75, it will resist. Actually Ellsberg does not engage in calculating specific probabilities. Instead he demonstrates from a variety of actual occurrences, primarily bank robberies, that a perception of a high probability of receiving punishment is often sufficient to yield compliance.[3] Ellsberg then goes on to discuss methods for creating perceptions of high probability of punishment among targets.

Snyder (1972) uses the Zeuthen model in an even more imaginative fashion. Snyder utilizes the logical base of the Zeuthen formula for critical risk to generate a typology of conflict tactics. That is, given the Zeuthen conceptualization of bargaining, a bargainer's efforts should fall neatly into one of five categories. First, Target in diagram 1.1 can attempt to reduce its cost of war. Increasing its capabilities or indicating to Challenger that it anticipates a quick and easy victory are possible tactics

[1] The upper left-hand corner of this matrix is not defined by the model. For convenience the payoffs are labeled as zero, and a possible interpretation is the status quo.

[2] Zeuthen's formula for critical risk is: (utility of successful resistance) − (utility of challenged compliance) / (utility of successful resistance) − (utility of war).

[3] Ellsberg's shift from calculating the specific probabilities for which the model was designed to simply estimating whether the chance of the target's receiving punishment is high or low is well advised. Statements about the probability of adversaries' adopting particular strategies are rare in international politics. In one of the few instances in recent history President Kennedy could do no better than "somewhere between one out of three and even" (Sorensen, 1965: 795) for the probability that the Soviet Union would follow a hard-line strategy in the Cuban crisis.

here. Second, Target can raise its evaluation of the issues at stake. Target can signal Challenger that it perceives the current struggle to be an indicator of future relations between the two parties, so that the immediate issue appears as a part of a much larger problem. Or the domestic costs of yielding to the foreign adversary may be stressed. Both possibilities serve essentially to reduce the reluctance to risk war and thus increase Target's critical risk level. Third, tactics that influence the adversary's perception of Target's strategy choice may be invoked. Schelling's (1966, 1960) tactics of irrevocable commitment are examples of this option. If Target can credibly signal that it is unable to yield, Challenger is forced to choose between a mild setback (-1) and war (-3). Fourth, Target can work directly on its adversary's utilities. It can try to increase Challenger's perceived costs of war by increasing or even exaggerating Target's own capabilities. Fifth, Target can try to reduce the issues at stake for Challenger. Target can provide a loophole so that Challenger can back down without humiliation, or Target can indicate that its intransigence on this issue does not mean a disinclination to work out compromises in other areas of disagreement between the two parties. Both of these last two categories are designed to reduce the adversary's desire to press the conflict. In terms of the model, they depress Challenger's critical risk level. The point here is that once Zeuthen's conceptualization is accepted, bargaining entails these five processes. Other activities are irrelevant to the bargaining problems as defined by the model. So the model either ignores other activities or prompts attempts to interpret other activities in terms of one of these five categories.

Ellsberg, Snyder, and others [4] take synthetic formulations such as Nash's or Zeuthen's out of the realm of abstract mathematics and modify them so that they relate to actual examples of conflict in international politics. Their efforts have surely met with some success, but they do not come to grips with the central problem the models pose. By accepting the conceptualizations of bargaining encapsulated in these formal models, theorists miss several processes that are crucial to bargaining in actual international conflicts. For Ellsberg and for Snyder (1972) bargaining

[4] For example, Kent (1967) develops some applications of Nash's conception of the bargaining problem that focus on creating threat strategies appropriate for a variety of specific conditions.

amounts to effectively lowering the adversary's critical risk. Their theories either fit other activities into this central concern or ignore them.

Form and Focus of Synthetic Models

Nash and others who use synthetic models of bargaining (England, 1973; Cross, 1969) view bargaining as an integrated process. While the specifics of their conceptions differ, all these theories share the advantage that the various elements included in their processes fit neatly into a model that provides an internally consistent and logically complete interpretation of all the aspects of bargaining activity on which the model focuses. The elements that comprise these models focus attention on selected aspects of bargaining activity. Collectively the elements define what bargaining is and what questions about bargaining are important. Scholars following the vein of a particular model fill in the answers to these questions, but for the most part filling in the answers is drab work; it entails working out conclusions that flow logically from the premises of the model. The interesting as well as the crucial aspects of such theories are these initial premises. Accepting a set of premises leads to the concomitant acceptance of a conception of what bargaining is and of what questions a theory of bargaining should answer.

While for Nash's and other similar theories, strengths of internal consistency and logical completeness flow from their general form, weaknesses, particularly from the standpoint of analyzing severe international conflicts, arise from the character of the premises that determine a model's focus. The problem is *not* that the premises are unrealistic, although many are. Downs (1957) and Friedman (1953: 16–23) have argued persuasively that a model can be useful when its assumptions are unrealistic or even contrary to what is known to be empirically accurate. Rather, the problem arises from shunting to the sideline by assumption or presupposition materials that are crucial to the bargaining processes in actual international conflicts. Synthetic models of bargaining are appropriate to the degree that their elements correspond to the crucial aspects of the empirical cases for which they are used as abstract representations. And difficulties in applying these models to international conflicts stem from discrepancies between these crucial processes and the processes on which many synthetic models focus. These models assume that information is complete, preferences are completely ranked and stable, and strategies of utility maximation appropriate for these conditions are followed. The models then focus on the process of calculating a solution. In actual conflicts among nations, gathering and interpreting information, discovering the criteria for an acceptable solution, and constructing a viable strategy are processes that occupy a considerable proportion of statesmen's attention. And these factors, so integral to bargaining in international conflicts, should not be shunted to the sideline. For in some instances, such as the 1962 Cuban missile affair, the recent Southeast Asian conflict, or the 1948–49 Berlin crisis, the interaction *among* nations is certainly no more important than the information processing, solution definition, and strategy search that occur *within* the parties to the conflicts. So while the conception of bargaining as an *integrated process* common to the synthetic models offers a valuable precedent about the form bargaining theory for international conflicts can take, these specific models are not appropriate to actual international conflicts.

Broader Conceptualizations of Bargaining

Some economists have turned their efforts toward developing conceptual frameworks that admit more and different processes into the bargaining problem rather than toward refining the narrow conceptualizations of the early synthetic models. The impetus for complexity has stemmed in part from dissatisfaction with the unrealistic assumptions of the synthetic models. Schelling (1960: 267–90) has mounted a sophisticated argument against one assumption of the synthetic models: he argues that symmetry is not a feasible assumption if the participants can communicate before choosing strategies. Consider the following situation. Two men have to agree on a method of splitting $100. They are in a negotiating room with a combination witness, referee, and purse-holder, who is to witness the proceedings, assure that the rules are observed, and arrange for subsequent payment if a settlement is reached within the rules. The rules are that each of the two bargainers must write a statement expressing an identical solution on a chalkboard visible to all three, and that once a player has left the negotiating room he has left the game. Now, if no hidden asymmetries characterize this bargaining pair from their relations in the world outside the negotiating room, a prominent solution and a solution meeting the criterion of mathematical symmetry would be a 50–50 split. But suppose one bargainer suddenly writes a solution that grants him the favorable end of a 90–10 split on the chalkboard and races out of the room. This is a commitment that alters the situation irrevocably. The man remaining in the room now has the choice of $10 or nothing—a choice not acceptable to the first bargainer.

Actual conflict situations are full of asymmetries. Some of these exist apart from the strategies of the parties to the conflicts. For instance, in the Cuban crisis the United States enjoyed the advantage of several asymmetries arising from the fact that Cuba was far closer to the United States than to the Soviet Union. The proximity of Cuba to the United States facilitated the United States claim that Cuba lay within a United States sphere of influence. The nearness of Cuba gave the United States advantages in mounting and supplying conventional military operations. Other asymmetries—those that form the focus of Schelling's work—stem from the strategies of the antagonists. In the 1948–49 Berlin crisis, for example, the surprising success of the airlift forced on the Soviets the choice of initiating violence or accepting a Western enclave in their sphere of influence. The airlift relieved United States leaders from the onus of initiating violence. Conditions of asymmetry such as these are common in actual conflicts and lead Schelling to urge reconsideration of the symmetry principle. For Schelling mathematical symmetry is simply a single example of prominence that was particularly salient to the mathematicians who developed the early synthetic theories. Actual conflicts offer numerous other sources of prominence, and many of the solutions prominent to the participants violate the assumption of mathematical symmetry. Schelling then broadens the scope of bargaining theory by focusing attention on the development and use of prominence in bargaining.

A more important impetus behind the broadened conceptualization of bargaining found in some research is the realization that early conceptualizations ignored or disfigured processes important to bargaining in actual conflicts. For instance, Simon (1955) and Cyert and March (1963) have dealt extensively with the information conditions and objectives that characterize actual conflicts, and the account here follows their work. The man—business executive or statesman—who struggles in the maze of everyday life faces insurmountable information obstacles. He cannot visualize all potential solutions to his problems, nor can he accurately foresee all the consequences of the various alternatives he does recognize. He is plagued with limited and often misleading patterns of perception (Steinbruner, 1974; Jervis, 1968). The vast obstacles confronting the decision maker's limited resources force him to channel his efforts toward the construction of a single adequate solution. Developing any satisfactory solution sufficiently taxes the limited or bounded rationality of the everyday decision maker; so the process models of everyday decision theory concentrate on defining adequacy and delineating the procedure used to achieve it.

The nature of the objectives sought in everyday decisions creates additional difficulties. The decision maker must reconcile various independent and possibly conflicting objectives rather than dealing with a homogeneous measure such as utility. For example, two common objectives in international conflicts are coercing the adversary to give up something he desires or already holds and avoiding war. Succeeding in one of these objectives does not necessarily entail accomplishing the other. In fact, these two objectives are often contradictory, inasmuch as wresting from the adversary what he holds and/or desires may carry a grave risk of war. The statesman has to weigh the various criteria that define a satisfactory solution and must tread a difficult path among these distinct and often conflicting guides. In short, Simon's bargainer pursues a different set of activities that Nash's. Bargaining is simply not the same activity for these two theorists.

Information deficiencies and difficulties in deciding among independent, even conflicting, objectives generally leave the everyday decision maker unable to pick a *best* solution, and rigorous decision standards such as the minimax criterion of game theory are inapplicable to his world. The decision maker, beset by the hassles of everyday life, responds by trying to sustain satisfactory levels of achievement with regard to several different objectives. Important deficiencies—existent or threatening—in the situations confronting him create guidelines for action. The decision maker strives to regain satisfactory levels of achievement in deficient areas without jeopardizing other essential considerations in the process. So critical deficiencies of the existing state of affairs furnish general criteria for a successful strategy. They give the statesman guidance as to where he must go.

In the context of severe international conflicts, emphasis on achieving an acceptable solution ("satisficing") as opposed to maximizing sometimes takes the specific form of concern with avoiding disaster rather than obtaining optimal outcomes. In Boulding's terms, statesmen in international conflicts are like blindfolded men on a mesa. Their essential concern is not for the tiny hillocks here and there but for the cliffs; avoiding a great fall is considerably more important than finding the highest spot on the mesa. Concern for disaster avoidance focuses attention almost exclusively on achieving a satisfactory situation rather than on choosing an optimal solution from several moderately varying favorable conditions. The statesman then directs his attention toward alleviating *intolerable* shortcomings of existing circumstances and avoiding impending disasters. International conflicts pose for the statesman an array of critical violations of satisfactory conditions. The foreign adversary's insufferable position on crucial issues, an increasingly successful challenge by domestic competitors who claim their policies and leadership would better secure national values, and a seemingly inexorable drift toward war are sample problems that create or threaten deficiencies between actual conditions and an acceptable minimum. The minimally acceptable state of affairs defines for the statesman critical standards that he *must* achieve: certain crucial values must be preserved by whittling away the foreign adversary's position, the basis for governing must be reinforced by tailoring policy changes to dissident domestic interests, and war must be avoided.

Walton and McKersie (1965) provide a fitting final example of efforts to broaden the processes considered integral to the bargaining problem. Their work not only attempts to integrate some of the foregoing examples, but also leads into the concern of the next chapter. Walton and McKersie visualize the bargaining problem as a series of four often contradictory and yet ultimately complementary processes. One process is distributive bargaining. The focus here is on division of spoils. A second process that both contradicts and complements the first is integrative bargaining. Integrative bargaining deals with upgrading the common interest, or increasing the size of the pie as opposed to dividing a given pie. These two processes are complementary in that many bargaining situations, even specific issues, provide opportunities for both activities. That is, they are examples of mixed bargaining. But reconciling the contradictory demands of these processes creates severe dilemmas for action. The famous mixed bargaining situation of Prisoner's Dilemma is shown in diagram 1.2. Analyses of this game are common, and the discussion here will serve only to outline the distributive-integrative dilemma. Both Row and Column in diagram 1.2 have at least two incentives to choose their dominant strategies, "compete" in each case. Each has a positive in-

DIAGRAM 1.2. PRISONER'S DILEMMA

Column

		Cooperate	Compete
Row	Cooperate	3, 3	1, 4
	Compete	4, 1	2, 2

The numbers represent quantities of utility at the ordinal level of measurement. That is, 4 is the most desired outcome and 1 is the least desired outcome. The differences between outcomes—for instance, the difference between 1 and 2 or between 3 and 4—are unknown and are not assumed to be equal.

centive to obtain 4 and a negative incentive to avoid 1. However, by following this distributive concern, they both achieve a poorer payoff (2 rather than 3) than they would receive if they cooperated and agreed to a compromise. Movement from the lower right-hand corner of the matrix to the upper left-hand corner lies along a line of integrative bargaining. The problem this game presents is how to mutually overcome the distributive incentives and upgrade the interests of all parties.

Attitudinal structuring is the third process Walton and McKersie consider. This is largely a matter of influencing the perceptions of the opponent. For instance, if Row in diagram 1.2 suggests that it will choose cooperation if Column will agree to do the same, its statement may be a sincere attempt to reach a compromise or it may be an attempt to trick Column into choosing cooperation while Row chooses competition. Column's interpretation of Row's offer depends in large measure on its image of Row, and attitudinal structuring for Walton and McKersie deals with influencing this image. There is a limited contradiction between distributive bargaining and developing a positive image in the eyes of bargaining opponents. Developing positive attitudes does not conflict with integrative bargaining.

The fourth bargaining process for Walton and McKersie is intraparty disagreement. In contrast to most of the other conceptualizations discussed so far, Walton and McKersie include as part of the bargaining problem disagreements within the negotiating parties that alter interparty relations. Intraparty disagreement provides difficulties for distributive bargaining. Intraparty disagreement may make commitments fuzzy or may make them virtually impossible. Also, to the degree that the intraparty dispute of one bargainer is known to the other, the latter can plan a strategy to strengthen the internal position of those in the divided party most favorable to him. Intraparty disagreement can also hinder integrative bargaining. For instance, disagreement between the President and Congress about United States policy toward the plight of Soviet dissidents recently hampered an international trade agreement that would have benefited both the United States and the Soviet Union. The relationship between attitudinal structuring and intraparty disagreement is complex and varies across different bargaining contexts. The relationship is often more obvious in labor-management negotiations than in international conflicts. One factor here is that the intraparty conflict has to be recognized by the interparty opponent before it can influence images. Governments tend to seek largest-common-denominator compromise strategies that reduce the chances for disagreement among officials to surface, whereas conflict between union officials and rank-and-file often rages openly. Also, the degree to which the actual negotiators are perceived as distinct from the organization they represent has an impact on interparty strategy. Thus the representatives of one nation might deal with the local ambassador of another nation who has "gone native" in a different way than they deal with the foreign or defense minister of the ambassador's nation.

Summary

Walton and McKersie define the bargaining problem much more broadly than any of the other scholars discussed so far. The breadth of their conceptualization gives their work relative advantages with respect to the others included in this review. Walton and McKersie share a conception of bargaining as a process (or an integrated set of processes) and thus benefit from a conception that integrates all aspects of interest into a single framework. In contrast to some of the other theorists discussed in this chapter, Walton and McKersie admit within their conceptualization a broad selection of processes, including processes that intensive case studies reveal to be important aspects of bargaining in everyday life. In short, their rough model focuses on processes that are important in actual bargaining situations. Their conceptual breadth holds drawbacks, however. With his narrow, abstract conceptualization Nash was able to pinpoint a solution. Walton and McKersie can do no such thing. In fact, their conception of bargaining does not even raise predicting a particular solution as an important task for bargaining theory. Instead their conception directs attention toward clarifying various dilemmas created by the conflicting and complementary processes that comprise bargaining. Their effort comes a good deal closer to explaining the problems that actual bargainers face than does Nash's, but the idea of closing on a solution range or point is lost.

Yet the notion that a theory of bargaining should contribute to locating settlement areas as well as specifying processes is appealing. Another group of bargaining researchers has addressed the settlement problem independently. Their focus has been on the impact that specific characteristics of the bargaining situation have on the settlement. And the discussion will now shift from processes to situational characteristics.

2.
Bargaining Experiments:
Bargaining Theory in Psychology

Not all psychological research on bargaining is experimental. One or two of the scholars cited in the preceding chapter were psychologists rather than students of economics or organizations. These psychologists and a few others for whom their work is representative were included in the previous discussion regardless of their institutional niches because of the nature of their theories. It is fair to say, however, that the bulk of the work on bargaining done by psychologists has been experimental; and the vastness of this experimental literature makes any review of it difficult. All that will be attempted in this chapter will be to examine the general theoretical form and some sample foci of experimental research and to discuss the appropriateness of experimental research on bargaining for analyzing bargaining in severe international conflicts.

Experimental Theory Form

Rather than conceptualizing bargaining in terms of a process entailing all aspects necessary and sufficient from the standpoint of the particular model at hand, most experimental research shares a concentration on specific independent variables, or predictors, that through their variation cause shifts in a dependent variable, or criterion. These predictors are the situation characteristics introduced at the end of the last chapter. This sort of theory provides a different form of explanation and a different con- . ception of bargaining than the models discussed in chapter 1. No longer is bargaining a process, either simple or complex; instead it becomes a series of relations between a criterion (the outcome) and several predictors (characteristics of the bargaining situation). The successful culmination of work of this nature might result in a complex equation of the form $y = ax + bz \ldots + e$; where y is the outcome and $x, z \ldots$ are the crucial predictors (Wyler, 1971, 1969). Experimental studies vary a good deal in the degree to which they attempt to specify the dynamic or causal patterns lying behind the observed relations (cf. Cann, Sherman, and Elkes, 1975; Deutsch and Krauss, 1960). In general over the last few years, however, experimenters have shown increased interest in the processes lying behind the relations they discover (Chertkoff and Esser, 1970). Whereas the theories in chapter 1 focused on a process and either ignored the specific characteristics of individual bargaining instances or used these specifics merely to illustrate the process, the theories in this chapter concentrate on the predictive power of one or more situational characteristics. While the contributions of other variables not included in a specific study to bargaining are recognized, there is generally no attempt to formulate a complete process model.[1]

Important Foci of Experimental Work

Bargaining experimenters have subjected a wide variety of variables to scrutiny in the course of their research. The criterion is usually the outcome. In economic scenarios (Druckman, Zechmeister, and Solomon, 1972) this often means the settlement point, although concession rates or other strategy choices are also used as the criterion in some studies. In experiments using matrix games the outcome is usually the criterion, although the nature of outcomes shifts from context to context. In Pris-

---

[1] Vinacke (1969) and in a more limited fashion Rapoport and Chammah (1965) are exceptions to this characterization. Also, Axelrod (1970) bridges the modeling and experimental communities.

oner's Dilemma games the rate of mutually cooperative responses is a common criterion. The level of coordination in coordination games and the degree of difference in difference maximization games are other possibilities. But strategy choices provide the criterion in some matrix games. The predictors in experimental bargaining situations are numerous. For convenience, most of these variables can be grouped into one of four categories: the players' personal characteristics, the payoff structure, the interaction patterns, and situational factors such as information conditions. These categories will be taken up in turn.

Characteristics of the Players

Much of the work done on the characteristics of players in experimental roles offers only limited insight for international conflicts. Variables such as sex (Wall, 1976; Bonoma and Tedeschi, 1973) or nationality (Druckman et al., 1976; Rapoport, Guyer, and Gordon, 1971) seem to be the least useful. First, group labels such as these do not offer powerful predictors for outcomes. Results of experiments using these variables show considerable differences across time and subtle nuances of the experimental situation (Vinacke et al., 1974). Second, labels of this variety are devoid of intrinsic explanatory value. If Danes act differently from Americans or men act differently from women, unspecified differences in the personality development and socialization processes common to these groupings are responsible for the differences (Kahn, Hottes, and Davis, 1971). Third, it is plausible that sex, nationality, and other similar labels are particularly inadequate for use in analyzing international conflicts since participants in these affairs are usually persons who have been successful in seeking positions of public power within their nations and who are familiar with and relatively competent at handling threats and other aspects of bargaining. Individuals who share these experiences may well share certain characteristics across lines of sex or nationality that are more useful in explaining their actions (Vinacke, 1969: 315).

Raser (1966) offers some preliminary thoughts on how national leaders may differ in their personality characteristics from populations at large, but his ideas have not prompted much experimental activity. More recently Barber's (1977) analysis introduces interesting constructs for differentiating political leaders that could provide the basis for useful experiments. The results of work actually done on individual personality characteristics appear in accordance with common sense. Deutsch (1960a) found F-scale scores inversely related to cooperation. McClintock et al. (1963) found internationalism to be positively associated with cooperation in gaming experiments. Other studies have produced similarly unstartling results (Baxter, 1973; Gillis and Woods, 1971; Pilisuk, Kiritz, and Clampitt, 1971), although occasional unanticipated insights have resulted from experimental studies of this nature (Kelley and Stahelski, 1970). These studies have not been designed specifically to analyze strategic interaction among national units. By and large they buttress common notions that exceptionally authoritarian or xenophobic persons will have difficulty in reaching compromises with members of other bargaining units (Bartos, 1967), but they are not particularly helpful for analyzing bargaining in international conflicts.

Payoff Structure

A great deal of work has been done on the impact of payoff patterns. The Prisoner's Dilemma game introduced in chapter 1 has captured the attention of many experimenters. Most of the manipulations have involved varying the payoff ratios among the various matrix squares in order to appeal to different motivational incentives contained within the game. Increasing the difference between the players' payoffs in each of the off-diagonal squares increases the competitive motivation. Increasing the mutual cooperation payoffs increases the cooperative motivation. Asymmetries have been introduced also. These have the effect of giving relative advantage to one of the players. Asymmetries have been particularly common in coordination games.

One interpretation of manipulations of the payoff structure is that they vary the effective capabilities of the players or the importance of the issues at stake. Following Harris (1972), three payoff structures particularly relevant to analogues of international conflicts may be ranked along a dimension of gradually increasing P, as in diagram 2.1. In the first of these

DIAGRAM 2.1. RELATED CONFLICT MODELS

	R, R	S, T	General Form
	T, S	P, P	

$T>R>S>P$ Player 2   Chicken

Player 1	cooperate	Player 2 cooperate 3, 3	Player 2 compete 2, 4
	compete	4, 2	1, 1

$T>R>P>S$ Player 2   Prisoner's Dilemma

Player 1	cooperate	cooperate 3, 3	compete 1, 4
	compete	4, 1	2, 2

$T>P>R>S$ Player 2   Deadlock

Player 1	cooperate	cooperate 2, 2	compete 1, 4
	compete	4, 1	3, 3

The numbers represent quantities of utility at the ordinal level of measurement; 4 is the most desired outcome, and 1 is the least desired outcome. R, S, T, and P follow the terminology of Rapoport and Chammah (1965: 33–34) and stand for reward, sucker's payoff, temptation, and punishment. These terms are applied most appropriately to the Prisoner's Dilemma matrix, but they are often used with other game matrices.

games, Chicken, P represents the poorest of the four payoff possibilities. This is Schelling's commitment game. From the standpoint of Schelling's prescriptive deductive logic, once either player has successfully communicated a credible commitment to play his second strategy, the other player will choose his first strategy. Experiments suggest that actual players understand this dynamic, although differences between their utility schedules and the matrix payoffs or situational factors different from the ones Schelling assumes may cause them to deviate from the prescribed action (Rapoport and Chammah, 1966). The middle game is the familiar Prisoner's Dilemma. The third game, Deadlock, has a stable equilibrium in the lower right-hand corner.[2]

[2] The term Deadlock comes from Snyder and Diesing (1977).

Chicken is a relevant analogue for international conflicts for which the issues at stake do not, in the eyes of the statesmen involved, merit the costs of defending them if the other side chooses escalation. This condition may arise from a negligible evaluation of the issues or from the high costs of the perceived conflict. In the Berlin crisis of 1948–49 both the United States and the Soviet Union felt that the costs of a military engagement outweighed the issues at stake in the Berlin situation (Murdock, 1971). When the issues at stake are perceived as meriting the costs of escalation, Prisoner's Dilemma is the appropriate analogue for the situation statesmen face. Since most international challenges do not threaten core values such as national existence, Prisoner's Dilemma might appear initially to characterize few international conflicts. The costs of war in a nuclear era contribute to this impression. However, highly valued intangible matters such as saving face or maintaining a reputation as a tough bargainer as well as equally important tangible domestic matters such as successfully fending off the attacks of domestic rivals are often threatened by modest international challenges. For instance, the Kennedy administration appears to have been willing to launch a military attack that might have escalated to nuclear war in order to remove Soviet strategic weapons from Cuba. And concerns such as international reputation and domestic position lay behind Kennedy's willingness to go to such lengths. Deadlock is not a fruitful experimental situation, but it does have analogues in international conflict. In the Fashoda crisis of 1898 the British preferred war over substantive—although not procedural—compromise with the French. Japanese relations with the United States prior to the Second World War approximate Deadlock as well. Some experimental situations and many international conflicts are asymmetrical mixtures of these structures. In the Fashoda crisis, while the British preferences were similar to Deadlock, the French faced a Chicken situation. And the Soviets appear to have held Chicken preferences in the Cuban affair of 1962, while the United States had a Prisoner's Dilemma preference structure. A United States military attack on the Soviet installations in Cuba, however, might well have engaged enough additional values for the Soviet leaders to push them over the threshold between Chicken and Prisoner's Dilemma.

Statesmen do tend to follow distinct and characteristic patterns of bargaining when confronted with these different payoff structures, and experimental work on related payoff structures may be relevant to bargaining in international conflicts. Differences in situational factors such as the specificity and nature of objectives create problems for the transfer of theory from one arena to the other, however. For example, actual bargainers satisfice among independent constraints, and adding several utility units to the payoffs for mutual cooperation holds no meaning for them. Nevertheless, some general principles appear to be applicable to both experimental games and international conflicts. For instance, high rewards for mutual cooperation are apt to be useful for avoiding particularly destructive forms of conflict activity in both the experimental and international realms.

Interaction Patterns

Strategy choice is sometimes the experimental criterion, but the concern at this point is with strategy as a predictor in the experimental situation. The usual context for this concern is the impact the strategy of one party will have on the subsequent strategy choices of the other. Some experiments with this focus use a programmed strategy as the predictor, with an experimental subject providing the criterion through his choices. Several experiments demonstrate a rough principle of reciprocity in the play of experimental subjects (Esser and Komorita, 1975; Wilson, 1969; Thibaut, 1968). Reciprocity as used here entails a willingness not only to return competitive strategy choices but to forego the temptation of competitive strategy and to respond in kind when the other player makes cooperative strategy choices. Reciprocity in this dual sense occurs with depressing irregularity in most experimental situations, however. Levels of mutual cooperation are often below 50 percent in experimental environments. A variety of factors normally outside the experimental focus— subject boredom (Shaw and Thorslund, 1975; Lieberman, 1960), subject indifference, and subject hostility (possibly latent) toward the experimenter, experimental situation, or both—probably contribute to the pervasive, perplexing result that one player's strategy has only a modest impact on his opponent's strategy.

Several specific conditions raise the level of strategic interaction (Oskamp, 1971; Bixenstine and Gaebelein, 1971). One situation in which reciprocity thrives includes experiments in which a large number of trials is run (Rapoport and Chammah, 1965). The effect of increased reciprocity often produced in these long sequences is attributed to opportunities for tacit communication that the long sequence of trials creates. This notion will be discussed further in the next section. Another situation associated with unusually high levels of reciprocity occurs when programmed or "stooge" strategies are run against a subject for the purpose of sensitizing the subject to interaction between the two parties. Reciprocity increases in computer-subject experiments when the programmed strategy changes dramatically, say from 90 percent competitive choices to 90 percent cooperative choices during the course of an experiment (Hartford and Solomon, 1967). In this instance an alert subject will notice a change in the pattern of the protagonist's responses. This perception of strategy change prompts the subject to consider the interaction of the two strategies more carefully. Also, having a stooge play "tit-for-tat"—that is, duplicate the subject's previous choice—has prompted high reciprocity in experimental subjects (Sermat, 1967). The tit-for-tat stooge has an impact similar to Hartford and Solomon's abrupt, dramatic change in strategy. Both create greater interest on the part of the subject in the interaction of the two strategies. Reciprocity also thrives in another condition studied by Miller (1967). In Miller's experiment the players were allowed a third option of not playing a particular trial. With the "no play" option a player who is dissatisfied with the strategy choices of his counterpart can signal his dissatisfaction. Under these conditions Miller found unusually high levels of mutual cooperation.

The results of many experiments focusing on strategy choices are discouraging from the standpoint of the incidence of mutual cooperation. Perhaps experimental subjects regularly find the game matrices too difficult.[3] Or they may simply not care about the experiment or may even try to sabotage the experiment out of hostility for the experimental situa-

[3] This comment is not facetious. Most of the experimental subjects reported in the literature are undergraduates—often in their first or second year. Efforts to explain the dynamics of simple games in the classroom to roughly equivalent groups are seldom universally successful. So, in a situation in which the student subjects have to learn the game themselves, it is reasonable to assume that some subjects fail to master the essence of Prisoner's Dilemma or other similar games. Shubik, Wolf, and Poon (1974) have reached similar conclusions.

tion. Yet the no-play option provides a particularly clear clue about the prerequisites for strategic interaction as opposed to blind individual play in gaming experiments. The no-play option—and also tit-for-tat stooges, abrupt computer strategy shifts, and experiments with particularly long trial sequences—all facilitate signaling between players. It is possible that mutual cooperation occurs so irregularly in many experimental situations at least in part because of the difficulty of effective communication between the subjects. The subject of signaling broaches the final category of experimental predictor variables.

Situational Factors

Situational factors include matters as prosaic and seemingly irrelevant to international conflicts as the sex of the experimenter (Skoto, Langmeyer, and Lundgren, 1974) as well as highly relevant factors affecting the subjects' information conditions such as opportunities for communication. The nature of the information available to the experimental subjects has considerable impact on their actions during the experiment. In general, increasing the information available to the players improves cooperation (Swingle and Santi, 1972; Wichman, 1970; Guyer and Rapoport, 1969). The preceding section introduced the notion that tacit communication increases cooperation. Experiments that offer opportunities for tacit communication—the no-play option, a large number of trials, tit-for-tat stooges, abrupt shifts in programmed strategies—all result in higher levels of mutual cooperation. Opportunities for explicit communication offered by a break in the experiment (Bixenstine, Levitt, and Wilson, 1966), also increase cooperation. Also, more experienced players tend to exhibit higher levels of cooperation (Conrath, 1970).

A related variable is the kind of information provided to the subjects when they are introduced to the experiment. For example, subjects can be given a motivational set—told to maximize joint payoffs or to maximize differences between the parties' payoffs (Deutsch, 1960b). One indication that subjects can master simple experimental games and that they are not universally indifferent or hostile to the experimental situation comes from the fact that attempts to set a motivational orientation regularly have an impact on the subjects' actions.[4] Groups instructed to play cooperatively regularly exhibit higher rates of mutual cooperation than do groups instructed to play competitively. Motivational set may be provided indirectly by providing information about the other party. Crow and Noel (1965) ran a clever experiment in which two groups of subjects were told the intentions of their counterparts. The "counterparts" were computer simulations programmed with the same strategy. One group was told they were facing a benevolent protagonist while the other group was told they were confronting a hostile adversary. These two groups of subjects then reacted differently to their opponent. Gruder (1971) has a similar finding; in response to identically programmed counterparts two groups with different descriptions about the nature of these counterparts acted in different yet predictable fashions. Each group used its information about the other party to draw dramatically different inferences from the same programmed strategy. Oskamp and Perlman (1966), among others, have found that similar effects occur among partners of varying familiarity. Mutual cooperation decreases from a high among friendly acquaintances through anonymous partners to pairs showing mutual antagonism.

Information about payoffs or the rules of play can be varied as well. Pruitt (1969) has altered the appearance of the Prisoner's Dilemma game by decomposing the matrix into individual strategies. In the decompositions shown in diagram 2.2 each player chooses a strategy from a matrix showing only his own alternatives, although each realizes that both players are shown the same matrix and that their payoffs are the result of the intersection of their choices. Once each player has chosen a strategy, the two choices are added. The two matrices in each decomposition add to form the Prisoner's Dilemma game shown at the top of the diagram. If, when dealing with Decomposition B, First Player chooses 2 and Second Player chooses 1, the result is 12 for First Player and 0 for Second Player, just as in the matrix at the top of the diagram. Any single Prisoner's Dilemma game can be decomposed in an infinite number of ways. Pruitt has found that strategy patterns for different decompositions differ from one another and from the pattern for the original matrix. Guyer, Fox, and Hamburger (1973) have found that subjects react to other types of format changes.

[4] Occasionally, however, the orientation the subjects pick up is not the one anticipated by the experimenter (Braver and Barnett, 1976).

DIAGRAM 2.2. DECOMPOSED PRISONER'S DILEMMA

Second Player

		1	2
First Player	1	8, 8	0, 12
	2	12, 0	4, 4

	Decomposition A: Your gains	Shown to each player Other player's gains
1	4	4
2	8	−4

	Decomposition B: Your gains	Shown to each player Other player's gains
1	0	8
2	4	0

Numbers represent an interval scale of utility.

Schelling (1960) has run a number of experiments in which the subjects develop the rules. These are normally coordination games in which the rule, common saliency, defines the solution. For instance, each of several New York commuters must independently choose the same place to meet the others: their common train station. Or each of several hikers must independently choose a common starting point from a map with a single dominant terrain feature.[5] Shubik (1961) has run related experiments with matrix games. Deutsch and Lewicki (1970), in an experiment with potentially profound implications for international conflicts, toyed with the rules for two groups of students in a Chicken game. One group was told the game was to be played once. The other group was told the game was to be played several times. Each group actually played only once, but the group told that several trials would be run had a higher incidence of competitive play.

Experiments dealing with the information players have about the situa-

[5] Eisenberg and Patch (1976) suggest that in order to be an effective coordinating device, saliency or prominence must be consistent with other norms, such as fairness.

tion confronting them holds a variety of interesting implications for conflicts among nations. Indeed, this area of research seems to be the most
fruitful from the standpoint of studying bargaining in international conflicts. Statesmen, like their subject counterparts, interpret the strategies of
opponents in terms of images formed largely prior to the conflicts in
which the strategies are used. Statesmen are often able to overcome uncertainty or misperception by picking up signals entailed in the opponent's strategy. Yet statesmen, like their experimental subject counterparts, often need to be jolted with sharp signals or other extraordinary
techniques in order to grasp the adversary's meaning. While there are
certainly difficulties in applying the experimental results of two individuals to the interaction of complex national units in which information is
processed by bureaucracies with parochial organizational interests, the
results of experiments in this area of research provide a rich basis for
heuristic probing into the impact of information conditions on conflicts
among nations.

Discussion of Experimental Research

Before turning to a discussion of the methodological strengths and
weaknesses of experimental research on bargaining for analyzing bargaining in international conflicts, we should briefly summarize the substantive significance of this research for the same purpose. Research into the
impact of personality characteristics on bargaining is potentially an im-
mensely interesting area. Unfortunately, the bulk of the experimental
research to date has not provided much help for analyzing international
conflicts (Terhune, 1970: 220). It would be interesting to know, for instance, the degree to which Eden's perception of a reincarnation of Hitler
in Nasser was due to personal idiosyncracy rather than to highly traumatic and generalizable diplomatic experiences during the Second World
War. The experiments conducted on personality variables give promise of
shedding light on issues of this nature, but they have not yet done so.[6]

[6] De Rivera (1968: 139–41) relates some fascinating and potentially relevant experimental
results on group risk taking. In essence, there is some evidence (Wallach, Kogan, and Bem,
1962; Marquis, 1962) that groups will take decisions involving higher risk than the constitu-

Research on payoff structure has isolated a variety of independent and conflicting approaches to specific games. If the payoff structure is altered to appeal to specific motives, the strategy choices can be shifted toward cooperation or competition. While principles such as appealing to mutual cooperation by raising the payoffs for this outcome are legitimately transferred from experimental situations to international conflicts, the complexity of international conflict episodes requires that the transfers be made with great care. For example, the Johnson administration developed the notion of a multinational "TVA" project in the Mekong River basin as an attempt to upgrade the benefits of a compromise settlement for the Southeast Asian conflict. As the Johnson administration saw the offer, acceptance by the North Vietnamese would channel some of their activity into a constructive project that entailed cooperation with other states on the Indochina peninsula, and the North Vietnamese would be able to draw on outside resources for their development. But the Vietnamese leadership saw the offer differently. Instead of an attempt to upgrade the value of a mutual compromise, the offer was perceived as a crass attempt to grasp control of the region by replacing the faltering program of military occupation with a more subtle program of economic domination. The Vietnamese wanted no part of such a program and did not cooperate. The seemingly sound policy of the Johnson administration failed then because the adversary perceived the effort in quite a different fashion than it was intended to.

To pick up clues as to the other's strategy, experimental subjects generally need help in the form of special options, long experimental sequences that build familiarity, or particularly blatant actions on the part of the protagonist. The effectiveness of explicit communication far surpasses that of tacit signaling through strategy choices in experimental situations, in contrast to international politics, where actions commonly speak louder than words. However, it would be easy to exaggerate the responsiveness of international actors to one another's strategy from the above statement. Constraints supplied by domestic politics and misperception may cause statesmen to cling to strategies that, in light of the adversary's responses, are clearly ineffective—although their reasons for not

---

ent members would be apt to take individually. However, these experiments were run outside of a bargaining context, and other experiments have produced contradictory results (Teger and Pruitt, 1967).

reacting to an adversary's strategy often differ from those common in experiments. But statesmen do share some rough analogues with experimental subjects in their interaction patterns. Sharp, unorthodox signals—the blockade of Cuba—are sometimes necessary to break through a statesman's misperception, just as abrupt strategy shifts capture the attention of experimental players. And much like Rapoport and Chammah's (1965) subjects, who learn from experience the costs of mutual competition, statesmen are often able to use experience with mutual escalation to generate compromise efforts. In chapters 4 and 5 below the results of experimental work on interaction patterns will occasionally be used to support arguments about bargaining in international conflicts. But this support is tentative at best, inasmuch as important differences in situational factors almost always distinguish experiments from international conflicts.

From the standpoint of analyzing international conflicts, the experimental literature on situational factors is currently the most enticing of the four areas surveyed. The impact of perceptions of the adversary or of motivational predispositions toward the bargaining process appear to have ready analogues in international affairs. Jervis (1976: 96–102) has long argued that much strategic debate takes place not around how a particular type of conflict should be treated but around what type of conflict a particular situation actually is. While disagreements as to how to deal with specific situations are sometimes simply masked by greater differences in opinions as to what the sitution is, Jervis' notion is supported by the repeated finding that various experimental groups that are shown different nuances of one basic situation tend to react in widely disparate fashions.

Weaknesses of the Experimental Theories

Apart from the relevance of their substantive content, the experimental theories discussed in this chapter share some weaknesses stemming from their form. To begin with, experimental findings constitute theory fragments. Thus one experimenter finds that a particular manipulation of the payoff structure has an important impact on the outcome and another finds sex or certain psychological characteristics to be important predictors of the outcome, but no overall framework is provided through which these two predictors can be placed along with others to form a coherent picture. Rather, relations between any given predictor and a host of known additional predictors remain an unchartered area, and the specification of the processes lying behind observed relations between predictors and a criterion vary widely across studies. This lack of parsimony and coherence stands in stark contrast to the process theories discussed in the preceding chapter. For bargaining analysts accustomed to the elegantly thorough mechanisms expressed in most economic theories of bargaining, the scattered pieces of the bargaining puzzle as approached through experimental research are a distressing sight; nowhere are predictor hierarchies or other ordering tools to be found. However, the lack of parsimony and coherence in this general style of theory does not preclude either insight or application to bargaining in international conflicts. George, Hall, and Simons (1971) and George and Smoke (1974) represent productive efforts to derive insight from cases of international conflict by comparing several instances through a series of standard questions. George works with isolated chunks of theory inasmuch as his questions do not form a neat package, as the models in the previous chapter do, and in this respect his efforts are similar in theoretical form to bargaining experiments.

Another problem is the relevance of experimental bargaining research for international conflicts. This concern is only one aspect of a larger issue of the general external validity of this research (Orwant and Orwant, 1970). Consider the matter of the effects of threats. Jervis (1976: 100–1) cites a list of experimental works that reach conflicting conclusions on the effects of threats. Jervis concludes, first, that experimental research using student subjects is of questionable validity for assessing the effects of threats on statesmen who are far more familiar and presumably adroit with threats than most undergraduates. Raser (1966) and Terhune (1970) also raise doubts as to whether conclusions about the effects of threats derived from undergraduate subjects can be glibly generalized to statesmen. And Knox and Douglas (1971) concur with the general principle that actions of students in trivial games offer poor indicators of the actions of the other persons in important conflicts. Second, Jervis feels that the results of the various experiments are highly dependent on peculiarities of the experimental situation that are not necessarily intended to be predictor variables. And again, others concur. Both Kelley (1965) and Vinacke

(1969) agree that experimenters have failed to pay adequate heed to the possibility that experimental subjects have their own ways of interpreting experimental situations and that these interpretations may differ from those of the experimenter. Pilisuk, Brandes, and van der Hove (1976) offer an example of an experimental situation in which the subjects may have developed an avenue of communication that was not initially part of the experimental design recognized by the researchers.

Strengths of the Experimental Theories

In spite of the fragmented character of experimental bargaining theory and limitations on generalizations from experiments to international conflicts, the focus of these theories fills a void in the study of bargaining in actual conflicts. If the process models of the preceding chapter are to be applied to actual bargaining situations, values for situational characteristics crucial to the relevance of one as opposed to another bargaining process must be determined. For instance, before an analyst can judge the relative importance of the conflict between distributive and integrative bargaining in the Walton and McKersie framework for a particular stituation, he must have a rough idea of the payoff structure for the situation at hand. If the situation is inalterably one of Prisoner's Dilemma, severe distributive-integrative contradictions are inherent. The integrative possibilities in Deadlock are virtually nonexistent, however. So the focus on specifics in the experimental theories provides a necessary complement to the focus of the process theories. The process theories provide frameworks that order and thus make sense of the myriad aspects of bargaining situations. The experimental theories through their focus on specific situational characteristics offer clues as to which aspects of the process models will be crucial for the specific situation at hand. In short, the experimental theories complete the frameworks of the process models by showing how general processes lead to particular outcomes under specific circumstances.

PART 2

BARGAINING IN SEVERE INTERNATIONAL CONFLICTS:

Processes & Situational Characteristics

The framework advanced here draws on both forms of theory presented in part 1. These two bodies of theory are complementary in their form. The process models direct attention to activities that are central in that they constitute the essence of bargaining in a particular milieu. The theory fragments of experimental research deal with more specific characteristics of individual bargaining situations. They provide clues as to why the general processes follow different courses in specific bargaining episodes. The foci of both these forms of theory are modified below in order to accommodate the peculiarities of severe international conflicts.

Process theories usually provide logical frameworks that encompass the entire bargaining problem as conceived by the theory. That is, a process model offers a coherent picture of all major aspects of the bargaining problem in relation to one another. So choosing the bargaining processes to be included in a theory sets some limits on what researchers look at when they investigate bargaining. And the choice of bargaining processes determines the questions asked about bargaining situations. One purpose of part II of this book is to delineate a subset of bargaining processes that are central to severe international conflicts. This selection of processes constitutes a definition of the bargaining problem. And this definition places limits both on the conception of bargaining offered here and on the questions asked about bargaining.

Three processes lie at the center of this conceptualization of bargaining. The first is information interpretation through which statesmen attempt to discover the nature of the situation confronting them. This process is viewed both as an intellectual activity undertaken by individual statesmen and as an organizational activity. This latter view is particularly important in the area of intelligence gathering, where, as Allison (1971) and Halperin and Kanter (1973) have shown, organizational standard operating procedures and bureaucratic interests partially determine the nature of the intelligence product. The second process is decision making. Here the statesman deals with the impact that the situation he confronts is apt to have on his political unit. The decision process is discussed in terms of the nature of choices and the nature of the decision body or unit. The final process is search for a strategy that will manage the situation. The strategy search process has a domestic political phase, an international phase, and some complex interaction between the two. Defining the bargaining problem in this fashion is surely arbitrary. This conception leaves on the sideline processes that others have considered important in other substantive areas—mediation and arbitration in labor-management negotiations, for example. It also virtually ignores factors that others have felt to be important in bargaining in international politics (Baldwin, 1971a). But an increasing volume of recent research on organization activity and the conduct of foreign policy suggests the central importance of these processes for bargaining in severe international conflicts. So while the conception is arbitrary, it is hardly a blind choice. Similar conceptualizations have been offered recently by Winham (1977) and Snyder and Diesing (1977)

These three processes provide the stable core of bargaining in severe international conflicts. That is, the analyst can understand such bargaining by focusing his attention on information interpretation, group choices among independent and conflicting constraints, and the dynamics of strategy search. But, as the discussion in part 1 implied, central processes follow different paths in different conflict instances. The presence of certain situational characteristics or the particular value of other contextual attributes leads to differences in the manner in which these processes are worked out. A second purpose of part 2 of this book is to discuss important characteristics of bargaining situations and the impact of their variation on bargaining outcomes. Specifically, the orientation here will be on how nations marshal their resources to support their objectives. One relevant factor is the nature of bargaining resources and a second involves issues related to their appropriate use. The conceptualization offered here does not, unfortunately, allow precise settlement predictions, but an examination of several important situational characteristics will offer clues as to the direction bargaining can take under specific situational configurations. Another way of relating the two subjects of this part of the book is to use Zartman's (1974) distinction between power and process. Chapter 3 examines processes that lie at the heart of bargaining in international conflicts. Chapter 4 examines the sources of power (resources) that drive these processes.

3.

Bargaining Processes in Severe International Conflicts

Information Interpretation

Information selected for attention by statesmen caught up in episodes of severe international conflict and the interpretation placed on this selected information are both highly subjective and yet crucial to the course of a conflict. Indeed, selective attention and interpretation separate severe conflict situations from more casual forms of international interaction. For instance, in 1962 United States statesmen interpreted the Soviet deployment of strategic nuclear weapons in Cuba as a threat grave enough to justify a severe conflict. Yet the subsequent Soviet force buildup in the Mediterranean was not perceived by many of the same statesmen as a challenge sufficient to warrant any conflict activity. The contextual nature of selective attention and interpretation becomes evident when one considers how United States statesmen might have reacted to recent Soviet activities in the Mediterranean if they had occurred fifteen years earlier.

Bargainers react to the situations they perceive to be confronting them. If the various national decision units that are party to international disputes generally agreed on and held accurate perceptions of important aspects of the bargaining situations, there would be no need to treat misperception as anything other than an occasional deviation from this norm. Formal models and even most gaming experiments shunt the problems raised by selective attention and interpretation to the side. In these theories such processes exist, but they are not the crux of the bargaining problem. They are in fact deviations from a standard of complete and accurate information, mild annoyances similar to air resistance on a pendulum or the mass of the pendulum cord. They cause actual results to shift from theoretical predictions, but they do not, and indeed they should not, require alteration of the theory.

However, statesmen differ in their perceptions of conflict situations across and even within nations, and these disparities in outlook require attention. When the statesmen from different nations hold systematically different views of international conflicts—including the issues raised by conflict episodes and the intentions, preferences, and objectives of the parties involved—and when such differences occur regularly in international conflicts, then it is no longer useful to maintain an analytical perspective presupposing a norm of similar and accurate perceptions. Since each party to a conflict reacts not to the situation as perceived by the other but rather to the situation as seen from its own perspective, the nations are not reacting directly to each other. Under these conditions it is necessary to understand the perspectives guiding each national unit's activity, and thus how these perspectives differ, in order to grasp the actual flow of strategic interaction. So selective attention and interpretation are crucial to bargaining in international conflicts. Rather than creating occasional deviations from a norm, they contribute to regular and pervasive discrepancies in perception among the parties to international conflicts. In 1914, for example, the German leaders could not be persuaded, in spite of the efforts of their ambassador to London, that the British would probably participate actively in a continental struggle on the side of France and Russia (Gooch, 1938: 100–1, 125–26, 274–86). Edward Grey, the British foreign secretary, did not realize the degree to which his message had failed to penetrate German perceptions. A single instance hardly demonstrates regular and pervasive differences, but other examples are not difficult to find.[1]

Overcoming mutual misperception, and/or managing and resolving in-

[1] For other examples of misperception in international politics see Jervis (1976, 1970, 1968), Diesing (1975), Stoessinger (1975), May (1973), O. R. Holsti (1972), White (1970).

ternational conflicts in spite of mutual misperception, is a central aspect of bargaining in many international conflicts and constitutes one of several foci in this analysis. This focus on misperception holds implications for works like that of Baldwin (1971a), who argues that more precise algorithms similar to those used in economics must be developed to analyze the activity and predict the outcomes of international conflicts. The suggestion of this book is that statesmen need at least as much help in determining what situation they face as they do in dealing with the situation once its outlines are accurately perceived (de Rivera, 1968).

In part, the importance of the processes identified as lying at the heart of bargaining here stems from the impact these processes have on bargaining solutions. Widespread misperception in international conflicts means that a statesman is often less fortunate than a man who knows he is lost. The statesman is sometimes convinced he knows the way. Parties to a conflict are often pretty thoroughly out of touch with each other and engage, sometimes unwittingly, in acts that others perceive as serious challenges (Knorr, 1964). In some instances misperception declines as a conflict progresses; in a few cases it may virtually disappear. Fortunately, a settlement of the immediate conflict episode normally does not hinge on misperception disappearing. The Eisenhower administration, for example, was satisfied with the outcome of the Lebanese crisis of 1958, although it held to the end of this affair a conception of the issues at stake that differed greatly from those of other participants.

But discrepancies in perception definitely have an impact on what is settled and thus on the durability and the meaning of the settlement. For instance, in the Agadir crisis of 1911 the central issue for the German government was Germany's position in European decisions (Lockhart, 1973). The specific problem that prompted the crisis was France's effort to control Morocco. A succession of French cabinets had obtained a free hand in Morocco by granting reciprocal concessions elsewhere to the Italians, the British, and the Spanish. The German government was affronted by its exclusion from this group and demanded compensation too. Although the Germans eventually worked out a modest compensation agreement with the French, the lengths to which the Germans had to press their case and the risks they had to take to achieve this end only underscored the original disparity between the treatment France granted other nations and the treatment that Germany received. In addition,

German tactics during the crisis brought Britain to the active aid of the French, and this British action renewed German fears of encirclement. Thus the Germans were deeply dissatisfied with the settlement, which, while granting compensation, raised more troubling issues than it resolved. The French, for their part, perceived the episode to consist of an entirely unwarranted German intervention in a matter of no concern to Germany. French leaders perceived Germany to be increasing the existing humiliation of France (German possession of Alsace-Lorraine) by carving up the French empire as well. And for the French it rankled to compromise with such villainy. Although the two governments reached a formal settlement to the Agadir affair, the conflicts of interest that remained unresolved festered and contributed to subsequent struggles between these nations.

On the other hand, the Anglo-French Fashoda crisis of 1898, which was characterized more by domestic political struggles within the French government than by misperception between the British and French leadership, led to a lasting settlement. The issue—which power was to control Northeast Africa—was resolved successfully. The British won, the French knew it, and resolving the dispute cleared the way for an Anglo-French rapprochement. Certainly labeling the settlements to conflicts in which the participants suffer from grave misperception as unstable across a span of years and labeling those for which misperception levels are low as stable would be an oversimplification, since other factors contribute to unstable solutions (Lockhart, 1977b). But while it is possible to resolve a conflict episode in spite of important misperception about the nature of the issues, it is extremely difficult to resolve the underlying conflict of interest without commonly accepted notions of what the conflicting interests are. The unresolved conflict of interest may give rise to additional conflict episodes in the future.

There are many ways to organize factors bearing on selective attention and selective interpretation. The material here is presented in the following manner: first, selective attention and interpretation will be discussed as inevitable consequences of limitations on human perceptual capabilities. Then three bases for selective attention and interpretation will be examined: personal ideology, domestic role, and national perspective. The structuring used here is similar to the conceptualization used in operational code studies (George, 1969).

Limits to Human Perceptual Capabilities

Life confronts all individuals with a far wider range of stimuli than the limited set on which any given individual or group of individuals can focus. For instance, an ambassador summoned to an urgent meeting with his host nation's foreign minister focuses his attention on the foreign minister's message, a threat. The ambassador "sees" the magnificent sunshine, the newly redecorated passages of the foreign office, the new painting on the minister's wall, the trace of a cigar burn on the arm of the chair in which the ambassador sits, the bubbles racing to the top of the foreign minister's seltzer, the slight nick on the minister's chin, and his immaculate suit. Yet the ambassador focuses on essentials. He does his best to get the foreign minister's message; his mind churns with implications, possible responses, fears, hopes; and the rest of what he has experienced slips away.

People—statesmen among them—focus their attention on aspects of their environments that experience has demonstrated to be of particular importance or use to them. Statesmen, who deal with the anarchical environment of international affairs, are often preoccupied with security. Their concern for their nations' security leads them to select for attention those aspects of the international environment that offer potential threats to the nation. A preoccupation of this nature led Nicolson and Crowe of the British Foreign Office to select for attention from the many German diplomatic maneuvers in the decade or so preceding the First World War those actions that *could* fit German efforts to form a continental league rather than those German actions designed to improve relations with Britain. In addition, they interpreted the former actions as threatening and sometimes formed no coherent interpretation for the latter actions, or twisted those actions to fit their security concerns. More recently, United States Department of Defense officials have focused on Soviet actions that might be consistent with Soviet efforts to develop a first strike capability and largely ignored other Soviet actions consistent with détente.[2]

[2] See the front page of the *Washington Post*, February 27, 1976, and of the *New York Times*, March 22, 1969. This interpretation of the actions of Department of Defense officials is admittedly incomplete. These actions will be discussed more fully below as an aspect of statesmen's roles.

Several aspects of actual conflict situations exacerbate this selective attention and interpretation that plague the perceptions of participants in international conflict episodes. One way of organizing these aspects is to contrast actual international conflicts with simple formal models. Two general distinctions arise from this comparison. First, the range of alternative courses of action is fixed and relatively small in simple formal models. In international conflicts the alternative set is open and undefined; the statesman's imagination provides the only limit. Second, in simple formal models the relation between means and ends is clear. To achieve a particular outcome a player adopts a specific alternative from a fixed and limited set. In international conflicts, generally the relationship between alternative courses of action (means) and outcomes (ends) is far from clear. Actual conflicts offer virtually unlimited aspects that are apt to be vague and that may well change as the conflict develops.[3] Confronted with this complexity, bargainers use clues arising from their experiences. That is, they select as the focus for their attention those aspects of situations that have been useful to them in the past. Personality differences and variations in previous experience impact on perception so that various individuals perceive given situations differently. Yet as a result of using previous experience as a guide, it is not unusual to find military men focusing on the military aspects of a situation or economists focusing on the economic aspects (Hartmann, 1975). The tendency for the United States to respond to foreign policy problems during the cold war period with military means is widely attributed to the increased influence military men had in the foreign policy process and the tendency of these men to focus on the military aspects of these problems.

Churchill (1923: 47–48) offers a fine example of selective attention and interpretation from an earlier era. The British were drawn into the Franco-German crisis over Morocco in 1911 through a public speech made by David Lloyd George, the chancellor of the exchequer. In an era in which

---

[3] Indeed, the complexity of general options—the blockade of Cuba in 1962—increases on closer inspection. The implementation of an abstract choice such as the blockade brings out this complexity and often involves aspects that are recognized only as they arise. The blockade could have been constituted through a vast number of combinations. The list of the quarantined articles, the tone of the blockade announcement, the speed of implementation, the degree of allied support sought, the treatment of Soviet ships, and placement of the blockade line, and many other considerations could have been—and some were—altered as the blockade was implemented.

diplomats chose their phrases carefully and communicated them privately, Lloyd George's public statement that the British would stand up to challenges from foreign powers, even if doing so meant war, made quite a splash in the press—both British and continental. Two stern exchanges between Grey, the British foreign secretary, and Metternich, the German ambassador to London, took place as a result of the German government's reaction to this press coverage. Grey was upset by these meetings and warned other British officials that a dangerous situation existed. In this atmosphere Churchill, home secretary but perhaps at heart first lord of the admiralty, was struck by, of all things, the vulnerability of the British naval powder stores. The powder reserve for the British navy was kept under minimal guard in a storehouse near the coast. Churchill set off immediately to personally secure this vital resource. Without doubt the leaders of other British ministries focused their attention on other matters.

The limited perceptual capabilities of bargainers in actual conflicts also confront immense complexity of consequence sets. The consequences of simple formal models form a fixed and limited set of homogeneous utilities that can be rank ordered and that remain constant over time. The consequences of actions in actual conflicts are far more complex. The long-term as opposed to the immediate consequences of actions are particularly vague. Surely the leaders of neither the United States nor the Soviet Union during the Cuban crisis of 1962 realized that this event would mark the beginning of an era of détente and the end of a crisis-laden cold war period. And the statesmen of 1914 certainly failed to visualize a conflict enormous in dimension and protracted in time that would drastically change the face of Europe.

Even the relatively immediate consequences of action are disturbingly unclear. Goals comprised of independent, even conflicting, constraints as opposed to homogeneous utilities cause some of the difficulties. An advisory group of seven will have little difficulty choosing between twelve utility units and twenty units. But choosing among independent and conflicting constraints is a more demanding task. If three members of the decision unit are adamantly opposed to the dangers inherent in escalating an ongoing conflict, two are desperately concerned with the domestic costs of not pressing the adversary further, one is convinced that the adversary is bluffing and that further escalation will call his bluff, and another is fearful that further escalation will leave the nation unable to respond to impending danger in another, more important region, the consequences and therefore the decision for an ultimate decision maker are more difficult to assess. In addition, consequences may change as a conflict unfolds. If the adversary in the example above delivers a particularly humiliating threat, two of the decision makers may shift their paramount concern from the dangers of escalation to the domestic costs of accepting this humiliation passively. An alternative mechanism that changes evaluations of consequences over time is the cost already incurred in a conflict. The United States, for instance, continued an active military involvement in Southeast Asia for roughly five years in an effort to gain a settlement that might be used to justify some of the costs already incurred by the spring of 1968.

Bases for Selective Attention and Interpretation

Capabilities of bargainers are severely taxed by the complexity of everyday life. The countless aspects—the limitless alternatives and the fuzzy, endless chains of possible consequences—force statesmen to focus on a limited selection of aspects that their experience indicates as crucial. One possible reaction of the statesman to his reliance on such a judgmental sample would be healthy skepticism. That is, if he were to shift his focus of attention slightly, he might see something else entirely; so he ought to be a bit circumspect about his limited vision. Unfortunately, statesmen (or for that matter people in general facing everyday decisions) do not adopt this posture with great frequency. They are generally sure that they know what is happening. Their experience directs their attention to important factors and provides clues to help them interpret what they see. Statesmen's personal ideologies, their domestic roles, and finally their national perspectives all contribute to selective attention and interpretation.

RELATIVE INFLUENCE OF PERSONAL IDEOLOGY
AND DOMESTIC ROLE

Recently the relative contribution of personality and role to individual perspectives has arisen as an issue in the study of foreign policy. The issue is a difficult one to study. One problem is that many roles are acquired by self-selection, and it is hard to distinguish men who hold perceptions typical of their roles because they hold a particular role from men who hold a role because the perspective it requires is similar to their own personal outlook. One way of dealing with this issue is to trace particular individuals across several roles. This method is far from foolproof, since personality changes with experience and maturation—although initial experiences or particularly traumatic subsequent events, such as Acheson's bout with McCarthyism, may fix some aspects of perspectives. Barnet (1968), for instance, argues that the latter process occurred for many Western statesmen during the Second World War. The hostility expressed by the United States statesmen toward any attempt to disrupt the established order or Eden's perception of Nasser as the reincarnation of Hitler in 1956 are explained in part for Barnet by a fixation on the traumatic formative and indelible experiences of these men during the Second World War.

In spite of these difficulties, tracing the careers of particular statesmen offers some insight on the issue of role and personality. Winston Churchill, for instance, occupied a variety of important positions in the British government dealing with both foreign and domestic policy over a period of roughly forty years. Churchill's attitude toward those who would violently disrupt the status quo—either across or within national boundaries—was held with remarkable consistency across his changing roles, various issues, and time. Churchill's suspicious attitude toward German intentions during most of this period offers an example of his general proclivity. Churchill has been given great credit for recognizing Hitler as a man with nearly unlimited expansionist objectives at a time when others were deceived. While this characterization is certainly correct and Churchill ought to be recognized for this feat, the characterization hardly gives the full story. This perception was Churchill's usual perception of German leaders whenever those leaders offered any threat to the status quo. It was Churchill's perception of Bethmann-Hollweg and the Kaiser prior to the First World War, when his perception was incorrect. For some years after the First World War Churchill's attitudes toward Germany softened. This shift in attitude arose in part from the weak and harmless democratic nature of the Weimar Republic and in part from the rise of a more ominous threat to the status quo—the Soviet Union—which created additional incentives for Anglo-German rapprochement.

But Churchill returned to his usual perceptions of German intentions as a new German leadership arose before the Second World War. Under Hitler Germany was clearly more dangerous than in the days of the Weimar Republic, and this change in leadership brought out Churchill's suspicions. But Churchill was as "lucky" during the late 1930s as he was insightful. The accuracy of his perceptions was due in part to the development of conditions in Germany that were coincidentally similar to images that Churchill was particularly prone to adopt. His fears of German intentions prior to the First World War had been exaggerations, and his fears of Hitlerian Germany were stronger than the ambiguous evidence about German intentions warranted for several years.[4]

More generally, the clearly defined images of men such as Churchill, Dulles, Chamberlain, or Adenauer provide material for the argument that individuals bring to their roles well-developed perspectives that are only marginally affected by their roles. It is difficult to imagine that Dulles would have offered anything resembling Stevenson's arguments for roughly reciprocal concessions in the Cuban crisis had he been the United States ambassador to the United Nations in 1962. O. R. Holsti's (1967) study examines in some detail how Dulles could fit widely disparate Soviet actions into his narrow and rigid image of Soviet leaders. In fact, all four of the men mentioned above are noted for, among other things, strong beliefs for which their roles merely provided vehicles. These selected statesmen do stand out in this regard, however, and it is fair to ask how the personalities of other statesmen interact with role. Was Kennedy preoccupied with being tough as a person, or was this preoccupation a result of his taking on the role of the presidency? There are many possibilities that are difficult to sort out. For instance, Dulles may be differentiated from a more modest secretary of state such as Rodgers by the breadth or even by the controversial nature of his preconceptions rather than by the depth of his convictions. Rodgers may have had equally unshakable beliefs, which his role did not develop but only gave voice to; but these beliefs may have been less controversial and thus have passed relatively unnoticed. Or they may have been narrower in scope—how to handle concessions rather than how to deal with adversaries—and have escaped the attention that Dulles's beliefs evoked.

[4] I am grateful to Bob Jervis for pointing out a greater range to Churchill's perceptions of German intentions than I had initially realized existed. Also Iklé (1971: 117) offers Eden as an example of a statesman whose images remained fixed across role and time.

Rosenau (1968) and Stassen (1972) have worked on the relative influence of personality and role and have reached different conclusions. The issue of the relative impact of personal ideology and role will not be decided in this book, but assumptions will be made, and these assumptions ought to be made explicitly. Therefore, following Snyder and Diesing (1977), personal ideology is accepted here as having greater impact than role on selective attention and interpretation among statesmen. This assumption runs counter to the postulate of much of the recent work on bureaucratic politics that role dominates personal predispositions generally. Role is accepted as more important than personal ideology for some criteria other than sources of selective attention and interpretation, and this impact of role will be discussed below in the section on decision characteristics. The dominance of personality in selective attention and interpretation is accepted more wholeheartedly for senior statesmen, who have considerable experience and success on their ledgers for whom any particular role may be viewed as but a portion of a total career. For men such as these—who can normally be expected to have the greatest impact on conflict decisions—several personality characteristics are important for selective attention and interpretation. The discussion here will focus on the content of the statesman's images and strategy preferences and the statesman's tendency to cling to these images and preferences.

PERSONAL IDEOLOGY

One factor of interest here is the statesman's view of international affairs. [5] That is, what sorts of threats does the international arena present, and what sorts of opportunities does it afford? Some statesmen—Wilson and Chamberlain, for instance—have been criticized for paying inadequate heed to the anarchical nature of international affairs. Other statesmen hold an awareness of the anarchical milieu and the problems for coordinating action that anarchy entails. Focusing on anarchy is apt to raise a concern for the security of the statesman's nation. Characteristically, statesmen will be suspicious of the capabilities, intentions, preferences, and objectives of other nations. They may use the capabilities of some nations as indices of their intentions. In addition, statesmen may be

[5] Studies on the operational codes of statesmen categorize this factor as a part of the philosophical aspect of personal ideologies. For a more detailed discussion see George (1969).

reluctant to conclude agreements that give an appearance of having backed away from a challenge. They recognize that in an anarchical environment occasionally there are no safeguards but a nation's ability to fight and its willingness to do so. Thus it is imperative to avoid setting a precedent in one conflict that could be interpreted by others as indicating the absence of a willingness to fight.

Beyond thoughts about the enduring and pervasive features of international interaction, however, statesmen are apt to differ widely in their conceptions of international conflict. In the contemporary West, for instance, cold war ideological blinders create visions of a free world staving off the repeated challenges of totalitarian communist nations. In contrast, statesmen in the East tend to see themselves in conflict with an anachronistic system that lashes out desperately and violently in periodic death throes. And there is a growing perspective among Third World statesmen that their nations face grave threats posed by the extractive and otherwise exploitative practices of the industrial nations. These views of the three worlds provide statesmen with a basis for interpreting specific actions in different ways. For the West threats against West Berlin have meant efforts on the part of totalitarian imperialism to snuff out an island of freedom. To the East these same efforts have been aimed at eliminating a source of decadent subversion undertaken from an obviously artificial and abnormal base of operations. For the industrial nations the collaborative efforts of the oil exporting nations have sometimes been perceived as a dagger thrust viciously at the heart of civilization, while the oil producers, although they differ in their objectives, undoubtedly have a common interest in redistributing the vast wealth of the industrial West.

A statesman's images of others, particularly adversaries, are another important part of the philosophical aspect of personal ideologies. The definition of a conflict in the sense of the values threatened and/or the opportunities afforded often hinges on the images of the adversary. For example, some British leaders in the 1930s perceived Hitler as a conservative nationalist interested in redressing obvious grievances suffered by the German people. For these leaders Hitler threatened no important values, and as a result of his conservatism and interest in settling several volatile issues Hitler appeared to some as a source of stability.

A statesman's ability to place himself in his adversary's shoes is a crucial determinant of his images of others. An empathetic statesman can cut through uncertainty and misperception to some degree. For example, in the Cuban crisis President Kennedy had an intuitive feeling that the Soviet Union would not sit idly by as the United States destroyed Soviet installations in Cuba. "They no more than we," said the President, drawing an analogy to the strategic deployment itself, "can let these things go by without doing something. They can't, after all their statements permit us to take out their missiles, kill a lot of Russians, and then do nothing" (Kennedy, 1971: 14). Empathy provides the statesman with guidelines for reciprocity and justice. On the other hand, a statesman who tries to put himself in the other fellow's shoes runs a couple of risks. First, he may exaggerate the other's position and thus not drive as hard a bargain as possible. This was one criticism Acheson (1969a) made of Kennedy in the Cuban crisis. Even worse, the empathetic statesman may be facing an adversary quite different from (and perhaps more hostile than) himself. The Chamberlain cabinet faced this situation in the late 1930s, and Chamberlain's efforts to put himself in Hitler's shoes foundered repeatedly on differences between Hitler and many other statesmen, including Chamberlain. But the dangers of failing to see the other fellow's point of view are surely impressive as well. If the Israelis had held any clear feeling for the helpless frustration and the injured sense of justice and pride on the part of the Egyptian leadership in 1973, they would have been less apt to be caught unprepared by the Yom Kippur War.[6]

German actions toward the French during the Agadir crisis of 1911 offer another useful example here. The German foreign minister, Kiderlen-Waechter, was trying to draw compensation from the French. The French were obviously in the final stages of consolidating their control over Morocco, and the Germans desired compensation similar to that given other nations by the French. Kiderlen proposed, among other things, that the Germans send gunboats to the southern Moroccan harbors of Mogador and Agadir, as the French would be reluctant to press their territorial control of southern Morocco with German warships sitting in these harbors (Lepsius, Bartholdy, and Thimme, 1925: 101–8).

[6] Etheredge (1975) makes a related point here. He suggests that statesmen project their own personalities onto their adversaries. Thus hard-liners will tend to see more disturbing adversaries than soft-liners (Snyder and Diesing, 1977). Projection might help to explain Chamberlain's problems with Hitler, but it does not help to explain the Israeli surprise in 1973. The hard-line Israelis, on the basis of projection, should have been more concerned about the preparations of the Arab nations.

But Kiderlen's argument went beyond blocking control of Morocco. He and his colleagues argued that holding the ports would ease the French government's burden of providing compensation to Germany. The German foreign ministry realized that French public opinion would make German compensation a difficult step for any French government, but Kiderlen's advisors felt that if the necessity for compensation could be demonstrated (that is, if there were German warships in Moroccan ports), then the problem for the French government would be eased (Pick, 1937: 326–28). Of course, the German warships only incensed the French—the public as well as the government—and made any compromise more difficult. Later in the crisis, when Kiderlen received what he perceived to be a public threat from the British, he became livid and bellicose. But he was unable to gauge the impact of similar German actions on the French. It is of interest that Barlow's (1940: 209) characterization of Kiderlen runs: "brusque, cynical, tactless, often truculent, with a certain strain of brutality and coarseness in his humor." A greater contrast to an empathetic statesman is hard to imagine.

In addition to philosophical content such as images of international affairs and of other parties, statesmen's personal ideologies include instrumental beliefs such as strategy preferences. That is, statesmen hold preferences on the responses they find appropriate for given situations. These instrumental beliefs interact with the philosophical beliefs. Images of adversaries provide bases for defining the nature of the conflict situation. They provide clues as to the nature of the adversary's general intentions and preferences and specific objectives. So these images offer an indication as to the severity of the conflict of interest. The statesman's strategy preference will depend in some measure on his assessment of the situation. But statesmen and scholars as well disagree as to how given situations are most appropriately handled. A basic distinction here is the dichotomy between coercive and accommodative preferences. Schoen, the German ambassador to Paris, despaired in his foreign minister's choice of strategies in 1911 (Schoen, 1922: 146–47). Schoen agreed generally with Kiderlen's assessment of the situation. The difference between them came on the point of appropriate German action. Schoen felt an accommodative approach would be preferable for obtaining German ends. Kiderlen favored a coercive policy. Academicians have similar disagreements. Iklé and Leites (1962) favor firmness—essentially threats—in order to push the adversary back along the bargaining line. Pruitt (1968), using a similar model, opts for mutual concessions as a preferred strategy.

Many factors contribute to the overall inclination toward coercion or accommodation. One prominent aspect would be confidence in the efficacy of military force or threats in general. During the 1960s the United States government was characterized by a reasonably heavy reliance on and a strong faith in the efficacy of military force. The Rostow brothers are examples of men with these attitudes, and few military men think of national security in terms of weapons limitation rather than arms acquisition. But, Kurt Schumacher and a number of other postwar German politicians were extremely leery about the efficacy of military force. Another characteristic that varies across statesmen and leads to differences in strategy preference is trust. Statesmen who generally trust others are better able to initiate accommodative compromise proposals than are their colleagues who carry an abiding distrust for others. Rouvier, the French prime minister during the Algeciras or first Moroccan crisis of 1905–6, was initially willing to trust the statements of the German adversary a good deal more than was Delcassé, his foreign minister. Unfortunately, Rouvier's trust in this instance turned out to be misplaced, and he eventually shifted his strategy accordingly (Etheredge, 1975). A third factor relevant here is the orientation of the statesman (Walton and McKersie, 1965). A problem solving orientation directs itself toward creating a mutually acceptable solution. A competitive orientation stresses winning the conflict. While a problem solving orientation by no means excludes the use of coercive tactics, a competitive orientation would be apt to place greater emphasis on a coercive approach. For example, Salisbury, the British prime minister in the Fashoda conflict of 1898, held a problem solving orientation and, while adopting a coercive strategy, did so in a low-key manner designed to minimize French humiliation and to help the French on matters such as communicating with their forces at Fashoda. In contrast, Aehrenthal, the Austrian foreign minister during the Bosnian crisis of 1908–9, held a highly competitive orientation. Not only did he follow a coercive strategy, but he appears to have actually gone out of his way to create difficulties for other statesmen.[7]

[7] These three factors are admittedly an arbitrary selection. A longer and more complete but equally arbitrary (in the sense of lacking an organizing theory) list is presented in de Rivera (1968: 166–67).

IMAGES AND STRATEGY PREFERENCES OVER TIME

The images and strategy preferences through which statesmen relate to the world are the result of experience, personality characteristics, and interaction between the two (O. R. Holsti, 1967). Images and preferences develop gradually over time. And, although the development is gradual, it is normally not regular. Irregularly spaced traumatic or otherwise gripping experiences contribute disproportionately to images and preferences, and little change is prompted by tranquil periods. In addition, the changes induced even by traumatic experiences probably have greater impact on the relatively blank slate of young impressionable minds than on the vast accumulated familiarity of experienced statesmen. Finally, experiences, even traumatic ones, often produce changes only after some period of reflection. A statesman has to have time to absorb the "lesson" he has just picked up. He has to reach conclusions as to the precise nature of the lesson and to integrate this new material with his previous experience.

These characteristics of image and preference development carry important implications for statesmen's perceptions of the conflicts that confront them. Each new conflict is viewed largely in terms of a fixed perspective (fixed in the short term, that is) that has developed in the past. If a statesman's initial views of important aspects of an emerging conflict, such as the adversary's intentions or the range of issues involved, are correct, coincidence is as realistic an explanation for this accuracy as insight. Of course, to the degree that a statesman faces similar instances of conflict, images and preferences arising from experience will be relevant across conflicts. Yet the differences among international conflicts, however subtle, are often important (May, 1973; George, Hall, and Simons, 1971). If there is a tendency to err here, it is in statesmen's tendency to overlook these differences, draw glib analogies, and see Hitlerian policies in Strauss or Nasser.[8] And the chances of a statesman's initially perceiving the situation with which he is actually confronted are slim. So the following statement can serve as a benchmark: statesmen generally enter international conflicts with images that include important errors about the situations confronting them. Mutual possession of erroneous images

[8] Jervis (1976: 217–87) provides an excellent discussion of various ways in which statesmen learn from history.

provides the first of two major dilutions of—or deviations from direct—strategic interaction among international adversaries. Because of their misperception statesmen bargain with shadow figures that arise as much from their own biases as from the actual activities of their adversaries.

Now, what happens to these perceptions during the course of a conflict? The answer to this question hinges on how closely the statesman clings to his beliefs. Some decision makers cling to their initial perceptions throughout conflicts—even long conflicts. The Rostow brothers did not noticeably alter their basic attitudes toward the conflict in Southeast Asia. Dulles and Adenauer are famous (or notorious) for their fixed visions, particularly of the cold-war adversary in Europe (Adenauer, 1968; O. R. Holsti, 1967). Aside from the question of accuracy, these views can be characterized as examples of premature closure. In each case the viewpoint adopted at the outset of a struggle was held stubbornly over a period of years in spite of evidence such as the conciliatory Soviet gestures toward Austria, the ability of the Vietnamese to mobilize their nation for a nationalist struggle, and the narrow political base and oppressive practices of some "free world" regimes. The point here is not that these men were wrong—although this seems likely on some issues. The point is that they either ignored evidence that was difficult to fit into their preexisting images or interpreted this evidence as consistent with their images. Through one or both of these processes their views remained unchanged.

Clinging to images is certainly not a characteristic peculiar to hard-line statesmen. Chamberlain managed to ignore obvious implications of Hitler's activities or to twist these activities to fit his predilections—whatever his faults, Chamberlain felt, Hitler was a bulwark against the Bolshevists. Yet the activity of one hard-line statesman provides an excellent example of premature closure. During the Cuban crisis of 1962 Acheson (1969a) argued that the Soviet Union would surely have acquiesced if the United States had destroyed the Soviet strategic installations in Cuba. Labeling this argument an instance of premature closure and thus as intolerant of ambiguity (White, 1970) does not exclude claims to veracity. It is possible that Acheson's "gut" feelings were coincidentally correct. But the label does criticize how Acheson arrived at his opinion. He did not do so empirically. There are no sufficiently similar historical instances that could be used to safely predict that the Soviet leaders would sit idly by as their

installations were destroyed. Nor did Acheson use empathy or even projection, for surely he would have urged a strong United States response to
any Soviet attack on United States installations. He used the prejudices of
his image—clearly stated elsewhere (Acheson, 1969b)—of an ambitious
yet cowardly, consciously evil Soviet elite. Acheson (1969a) criticizes
Kennedy's incremental approach to the Cuban affair and concludes that
Kennedy was merely trying to avoid difficult decisions. While there may
be some truth to Acheson's assertion, because of Acheson's own preferences Kennedy might reasonably have held doubts about what Acheson
"knew." Acheson, disregarding Roberta Wohlstetter's (1962) advice, uncritically accepted the interpretation of the unfolding conflict that was
compatible with his predilections. Certain in his "knowledge" of the situation, Acheson, in contrast to some of his colleagues who had not yet
reached the point at which they were willing to suspend judgment, was
willing to forge calmly ahead.

So far dependence on initial images has been discussed as a manifesta-
tion of premature closure. While manifesting itself in this way, clinging
to images may arise from various sources. One source is the statesman's
personality. A tendency to cling to initial images arising from this source
might be expected to remain fairly constant over long periods. For instance, Barber (1977) outlines some character or personality types which
differ in their psychological commitment to their perceptions. Actions
consistent with one of these types characterize presidents across several
decades of varying activity. But a tendency to cling to initial images may
also arise as a result of situationally specific factors. Thus in a situation
marked by time pressure, unclear alternatives, potentially disastrous consequences, and possibly other anxiety-creating characteristics, clinging to
images may offer statesmen relief in the form of reduced cognitive disso-
nance which these statesmen might not seek under less disturbing circumstances.[9]

Other statesmen offer an alternative to the clinging to images model by
demonstrating a tolerance for ambiguity. Tolerance for ambiguity within
the short time span of many international conflicts needs to be carefully
distinguished from the process of image development introduced above.
It is difficult to imagine a statesman whose image is forever fixed in every

[9] Alexander L. George's comments helped me sort out different factors that may create
the similar surface phenomenon of clinging to initial images.

detail, although some statesmen may approximate this condition for long periods; White (1970) uses the term "dogmatism" to distinguish this long-term stability of images from clinging to images within conflict episodes. Many statesmen change their images over time. Nixon, for example, shifted from implacable hostility toward communists to tête à têtes with Chou and to virtually an "old boy" relationship with Brezhnev. This change occurred over a period of years. And while Nixon was certainly not idle during much of this time, neither was he intimately involved with statecraft; so he had ample opportunity for disengaged reflection. Tolerance for ambiguity within the confines of a given conflict displays itself quite differently than these gradual shifts of certainty over time.

Tolerance for ambiguity entails both the ability of a statesman to recognize that a developing situation is not fulfilling his image, or at least that it may be fulfilling alternative images, and a willingness to suspend judgment pending further, clearer information. McNamara provides an example of a statesman with these characteristics. During the early years of the Vietnam conflict McNamara had clear-cut impressions of the situation in Southeast Asia. But he reached a point at which he was unable, in contrast to the Rostows or the Joint Chiefs of Staff, to twist feedback from the conflict into the mold of his original image. The crux of the distinction here is not the substance of McNamara's views. For McNamara is to be clearly distinguished from Senator Wayne Morse, who remained skeptical throughout the United States Southeast Asian war effort. The aspect of McNamara that creates interest here is his inability to fit the feedback he received into his preconceptions. While McNamara probably had neither the time nor, more importantly, the reflective interval to structure a new image, he did recognize that his existing image was inappropriate for the circumstances. Generally, statesmen who recognize discrepancies between their images and the events of a particular conflict episode do not have an opportunity to construct new images within the span of the conflict episode. Instead they develop expectations about this particular episode that are distinct from their images (Snyder and Diesing, 1977).

Kennedy's actions in the Cuban crisis represent another example of tolerance for ambiguity. In this instance the impetus for tolerance for ambiguity arose from situational as well as personal characteristics. Kennedy and his advisors all seemed certain in their initial images and action preferences. Yet the relatively small advisory group produced a broad range of advice, and several prominent advisors changed their opinions across conflicting options in the span of a week. Given this background of conflicting, shifting certainty Kennedy quickly grew reluctant to proceed as if he personally had no doubts. This influence of disparate group advice impacting on an initially certain individual is another way of achieving tolerance for ambiguity. Tolerance for ambiguity appears irregularly enough among statesmen to make this second variety important. An advantage of either informal (Janis, 1972) or institutionalized (George, 1972) multiple advocacy is that access to conflicting and perhaps even shifting viewpoints may induce a skeptical attitude in a statesman who would otherwise have been confident of his image.

Earlier examples of similar tolerance for ambiguity include Secretary of State Hull, who in 1941 was sensitive both to the danger of provoking Japan with United States firmness and to the need for United States firmness with respect to Japanese actions. For Hull Japan was expansionist and aggressively so, but he was for a while uncertain about the limits of Japanese objectives and felt that compromise might be possible (Hosoya, 1968: 103–9). In the negotiations surrounding the Munich crisis Halifax, the British foreign secretary, was partial to both the appeasement views of Chamberlain and the more hard-line position represented within his ministry by Cadogen, the head of the Foreign Office. Halifax was receptive to the views of both men and wavered between their positions (Colvin, 1971: 164).[10]

The hallmark, then, of tolerance for ambiguity is a willingness to suspend judgment. This willingness may be a characteristic of the individual, may be virtually forced on the individual by an advisory situation, or

[10] As the Halifax case suggests, tolerance for ambiguity can be carried to an extreme at which it becomes counterproductive. Bülow's shifting strategy in the Algeciras crisis of 1905–6 is a case in point (Snyder, 1971b). Bülow shifted back and forth between a soft-line strategy favored by the Kaiser and a hard-line strategy pressed by Holstein, a high-level Wilhelmstrasse official. When he followed the Kaiser's strategy Morocco represented a concession that Germany could give to France in return for French cooperation in a realignment of the continental powers. When he followed Holstein's strategy Morocco represented a prize to be wrested from France. According to the latter line of reasoning, when the French found the British would not support them in crucial struggles, they would form an alliance with Germany instead and the encirclement of Germany would be broken. Bülow's indecisiveness contributed to an ineffective policy and a French victory at the Algeciras conference.

may arise from a combination of the two. In any case, neither the substance of the views nor change of viewpoint over time is a key to the presence of tolerance for ambiguity. The key is a more subtle factor: the recognition within the span of particular conflict episodes that alternative perspectives also provide explanations for the course of events. In contrast to his certain colleague, the statesman with a tolerance for ambiguity is less apt to act precipitously or to burn his bridges. In these respects he stands closer to the diplomat as portrayed by Morgenthau (1973) than by Schelling (1966). And, as was Kennedy in 1962, he will be criticized for inaction by those more certain of the "truth." As popular accounts of the diplomacy surrounding Second World War suggest, delaying action until a situation is clearly defined carries practical problems. The adversary may take advantage of the delay. Yet jumping to conclusions also carries dangers, particularly if the conclusions turn out to be unfounded. And the statesman who demonstrates some patience in ascertaining the nature of the conflict before him is not necessarily outdistanced by his colleague who "recognizes" the situation instantly.

DOMESTIC ROLE

In addition to the aspects of a statesman's personal ideology discussed above, the statesman's role within the domestic system contributes to the way in which he selects and interprets information. Role impacts on the statesman's perspective in two independent ways. First, roles regularly carry what might be termed organizational responsibility. The secretary of defense, the chairman of the Senate Foreign Relations Committee, the ambassador to Japan all serve as leaders of organizations, and holders of these positions bear a responsibility toward the members of their organizations. An organization chief who is indifferent to the plight of the members of his operation is not apt to be particularly effective if he needs to rely on his organization for effectiveness. Men such as Henry Kissinger and John Foster Dulles have derived their influence from their relationship with the President rather than from their department. But if the organization's performance is important, then the leader will probably have to take note of and make compromises with his staff.

Secretary Laird's testimony before Congress provides an example of this aspect of role. In March 1969, Laird testified that the Soviet Union was striving to achieve a first strike capability (see the *New York Times*, March 22, 1969). Unless the secretary was using information held secret to this day, he had no firm basis for this judgment of Soviet intentions. What he did have was a problem within his organization. The Joint Chiefs of Staff were pressing hard for further ABM development. And the Senate Foreign Relations Committee was a prominent source of skepticism about the necessity for deployment of an ABM system. In part Laird's statement represents an effort to support the people in his department. Had he not pressed his case forcefully before this hostile audience, he would certainly have been poorly supported by prominent members of his organization; and Laird was dependent on harmonious relations with these people in order to perform other aspects of his job. The role of agency head regularly requires that the incumbent view issues from the standpoint of his organization's needs.

But most prominent public roles carry an entirely different responsibility as well. This other aspect is some form of national service. The secretary of defense or more generally defense ministers hold the highest positions specializing in national security. If the defense minister does not serve as a watchdog for national security, who will? The minister of agriculture has his day filled with other matters. The role carries a responsibility that reinforces the incentives inherent in the international system to be wary and suspicious of international conditions that could be threatening. This tendency is heightened for men whose careers are comprised of successive roles within one area of specialization. Career diplomats and particularly soldiers are examples of such men, in contrast to ministers, who are less often career specialists. The man whose career constitutes a series of positions within one specialty may, over time, gradually define the national interest in terms of this specialty (Steinbruner, 1974). Thus career soldiers or treasury officials may think of the national interest as encapsulated in a particular defense or trade policy.

So the earlier example of Secretary Laird has another side. In addition to looking out for his own people, Laird was charged with the responsibility for assuring the security of the United States. From this standpoint a strong warning about the nature of Soviet capabilities is reasonable, even required. It is even possible that Laird's close association with the career military men in his department and with their preoccupation with defense created an honest conviction that the Soviet Union was attempting a first strike capability. If neither this argument nor the previous one based on Laird's position as an organization chief is compelling alone, it may be because the separation of the two themes is artificial. While the themes are independent and in some senses contradictory, they are also concurrent and may have both been part of Laird's consciousness. Any explanation of his statement that ignored one of these aspects would be incomplete.

NATIONAL PERSPECTIVE

A third and probably the least important of the sources of selective attention and interpretation discussed here is national perspective. Similar personal ideologies and domestic roles may be shared by statesmen of varying nationalities, but national perspectives are, by definition, limited to a nation. Technically this would have been less true during the dynastic period of Europe (the eighteenth century, for instance), when diplomacy fell within the province of an international aristocracy. During that era a particularly able diplomat might serve different nations, and service for a nation other than the one in which an aristocrat had been reared was not unusual at all. Today, however, defining national perspective as limited to the citizenry of a single nation is a reasonably safe procedure. It does not follow that all citizens or even statesmen of one nationality will agree on policy. Each of the other two sources—personal ideology and domestic role—interacts with the perspective arising from national experience. This interaction is so strong that any coherent national point of view may be lost in specific instances. For example, in the Cuban crisis of 1962 Stevenson, the ambassador to the United Nations, suggested mutual withdrawal from Cuba—the Soviet Union withdrawing its forces and the United States removing its Guantanamo Bay facility. At the other end of the spectrum was LeMay, the air force chief of staff, who wanted to bomb the Soviet installations and invade Cuba. There is certainly little common "national" ground in these two perspectives.

Yet if other examples are used—the raid on Pearl Harbor—or if statesmen are viewed over a longer period of time, a national contribution to a statesman's overall perspective often emerges. For instance, K. J. Holsti

(1970) has been able to isolate a number of national roles that nations follow with respect to regional and/or global relations. On a more informal level, many successive British statesmen were conscious of the peculiar position Britain's insular status afforded them. The British role of balancer and concomitant policy of shifting friends progressively in order to deter the single most powerful continental nation was an integral part of the outlook of many British statesmen. Until 1945 certainly the statesmen of no other nation shared this perspective for their own nation. During the last decade of the nineteenth century and until 1945 the Germans were often preoccupied with quite a different problem—the danger of encirclement. Individual German leaders during this period may have ignored encirclement—even the British had exceptions such as Chamberlain to the balance notion—but it is fair to say that encirclement is a recurrent, enduring theme or fear characteristic of many German statesmen during this era. And by the end of the 1940s there was a broad consensus among the United States foreign policy elite that a new and active foreign policy of containment was both a challenge and an obligation for the nation. Even at the height of the cold war this sense of national obligation did not wash out the other two sources of perspective completely. For instance, Dulles differed from Eisenhower at times on the nature of United States intervention in Indochina. But there was undeniably a common view of a need for containment, open to varying interpretations in specific instances, that characterized United States statesmen and differentiated them from statesmen of other nations.

In addition to national roles or more informal foreign policy interests that characterize specific nations, national cultural characteristics may have an impact on patterns of information selection and interpretation. For instance, Wedge and Muromcew (1963) argue that the Russian language does not allow some ideas to be expressed in exactly the same way that they are expressed in English. And some common concepts may carry different affective connotations in the two languages. In English "compromising" carries no inherent negative connotations, whereas the Russian affective equivalent is "barter" (which can be a different process), since compromising carries inherent negative connotations. Nicolson (1964) discusses other, often tantilizingly abstract, national cultural characteristics that may systematically bias the selection and interpretation of information across different nations.

Decision Making

Decision processes common in international conflicts differ in a variety of ways from those found in gaming situations and most economic models of bargaining. Two differences are of particular importance for bargaining in international conflicts. First is the nature of objectives. Objectives composed of independent and conflicting constraints were introduced in chapter 1, and the discussion here will build on that introduction. A second difference is that the decisions of most modern nations are group decisions.

Decision Characteristics

INDEPENDENT AND CONFLICTING CONSTRAINTS

Actual political decisions—including those entailed in international conflicts—are inherently more difficult than decisions represented by theories that assume homogeneous utility. The various aspects of actual decisions form a set of constraints that define the boundaries of a satisfactory solution. These constraints are minimally independent in that achieving one does not necessarily mean achieving another, and are sometimes conflicting in that achieving one endangers the acquisition of other aspects of a satisfactory solution to a bargaining problem. For example, one United States constraint in the Cuban crisis of 1962 was avoiding war. Another constraint was bringing allies—primarily the OAS and NATO nations—aboard the coalition. Achieving either of these objectives could occur independently of the other (Ball, 1962).

In the Agadir conflict of 1911 the British held similar constraints—avoiding war and maintaining the entente with France. Avoiding war was conceptualized by the British as presenting a stern front to Germany and offering something less than an unconditional guarantee of support to the French. The stern position toward Germany and the flexibility exhibited toward the French were designed to restrain these powers respectively. However, the aspect of the constraint of avoiding war which entailed refusing France a clear guarantee conflicted with the British constraint of maintaining the Entente Cordiale. A firm British guarantee of support to France insured the entente. Anything less endangered the entente to some degree. The British tried to reduce the contradiction by increasing their pressure on Germany, but they simply reversed it. By provoking the Germans they endangered their constraint of avoiding war at the expense of the constraint of maintaining their alliance with France. The British had to tread a narrow pathway among these and other constraints.

GROUP DECISIONS

The independent or conflicting nature of constraints on a satisfactory solution is reinforced by another characteristic, namely the group nature of most decisions in international conflicts. Decisions are not normally made by a single individual. In some instances decisions may not even be the product of a dominant leader who casually checks with advisors, although the titles of various members of a decision unit may give this impression. Although one member of a decision unit may be a prime minister, a president, or a general secretary, other members are likely to be more than mere advisors. Some will represent segments of opinion different from the one represented by the chief executive; some will represent organizations that will implement the decisions reached by the decision unit. Associations of this nature serve as independent sources of power. A man who represents a minority opinion can leak information to a sympathetic public about a chief executive's majority stance during deliberation of a decision in order to create increased pressure for his point of view. Or if his advice is virtually ignored, he can turn his backers against the chief executive once the decision is made. This is a particularly potent threat in the case of a strategy that does not handle the international problem as expected. And an organization chief who disagrees with a decision that his organization must implement can drag his feet or otherwise alter the spirit of the decision through implementation. Lowenthal (1973) describes how the spirit of the Alliance for Progress was systematically violated through implementation by men with interests different from the interests of those who planned the alliance. In the 1906 Algeciras conference the Kaiser's desire to win concessions from the French through conciliation foundered repeatedly on the shoals of hard-line implementation. The hard-line negotiators at the conference violated the spirit of the Kaiser's conciliatory gestures. These possibilities for undermining the intentions of a chief executive create a requirement that most foreign policy decisions be backed by a broad segment of the decision makers who are involved in foreign policy.

"Group decision," as used in this book, is a complex concept that deserves some discussion. Two independent criteria are involved. The more obvious one relates to the number of persons making the choices. A group decision requires more than a single participant. And in practice the group character—different group or coalition members stressing different objectives—appears with three or more participants. Two-person decision units—Eisenhower-Dulles, Stalin-Molotov—tend to act like unitary actors (Snyder and Diesing, 1977), so that three is the threshold at which group characteristics begin to appear. A more subtle criterion relates to the nature of interests represented. As used here, "group decision" stands for the representation of parochial or organizational rather than societal or national interests by the decision participants. As a simple example, the joint chiefs represent the interests of their respective services, the secretary of commerce represents the interests of United States corporations with overseas investment, and the President represents his political party's domestic interests. This parochial representation need not be a conscious substitution of parochial for national interest. Most of the participants will honestly perceive the national interest through parochial lenses (Steinbruner, 1974). The parochial character of the interests expressed in group decisions characterizes one and two-person decision units as well as larger units. Americans, for instance, recognized that Stalin did not represent the broader interests of Soviet society, just as Soviet citizens saw that Eisenhower and Dulles did not represent the interests of all the American people. But within the nation making a decision, the parochial nature of the interests represented is often relatively unnoticed in the absence of differences of opinion *within* the decision unit, which tend to appear at the threshold of three participants.

Group decisions require the concurrence of the representatives of various domestic factions. The group nature of foreign policy decisions is clearly displayed in memoirs describing recent United States conflict decisions. The concern with getting everyone, or virtually everyone, on board for contemporary United States presidents is well documented

(Halperin, 1972; Hilsman, 1971). The group character of decisions in less pluralistic contemporary nations and the states of the nineteenth century is not so obvious. It is probably safe to say that the group character of important foreign policy decisions is most pronounced in modern, pluralistic society, although not all foreign policy decisions in pluralistic society are made by groups. For example, Eisenhower and Dulles dominated United States foreign policy decisions during the 1950s. Group decisions are found in the Soviet Union today and were even practiced by the powers of nineteenth-century Europe. The SALT talks have clearly demonstrated the collective nature of the current Soviet government and the necessity for General Secretary Brezhnev to consult with his colleagues. During the Stalin era consultation about major foreign policy issues was, at a minimum, less prominent than it is today in the Soviet Union. It is conceivable—if the most frightening Western accounts are true—that Stalin cared little for consultation with others and few dared to press this matter. If this is true, the Soviet Union during the Stalin era may have had few or no group decisions on foreign policy issues. Certainly the states of nineteenth-century Europe were generally less pluralistic than the contemporary great powers. Yet less pluralistic does not mean group decisions were entirely absent. Few heads of state among nineteenth-century powers directed foreign policy by their sovereign whim alone. But certainly the variety and strength of domestic constraints faced by the statesmen at the Congress of Vienna were muted in comparison to those found among the great powers today.

A related factor certainly constrained the freedom of action of nineteenth-century statesmen. In some limited respects the alliance rather than the individual nation is a more appropriate unit for comparison of nineteenth-century European and contemporary great power diplomacy. As Waltz (1967) points out, the superpowers have been relatively free from consultations with allies. And the allies' great displeasure with the relative absence of consultation, while hardly advantageous to the diplomatic and economic relations of either of the superpowers, has not threatened the overall balance of high politics. In contrast, the statesmen of nineteenth-century Europe generally had to consult with allies over major foreign policy decisions in a fashion similar to the advisory process which goes on within the superpowers today. After 1870, for instance, the French could make no major decision with respect to Germany independently.

INDEPENDENT AND CONFLICTING CONSTRAINTS
IN GROUP DECISIONS

Group character reinforces the independent constraint aspect of actual political decisions through the different preferences of various group members. Typically, different domestic factions will focus on one or perhaps two constraints as the essence of a satisfactory solution. Across some pairs of factions these points of focus will be identical or at least overlap, as is generally the case for two-person decision units. But if the group has several members, there are apt to be several different constraints, and several members may have no common focus of concern. Lindblom (1965) describes a similar situation in his concept of mutual adjustment. In domestic politics various interests, each striving to protect the values of greatest concern to its clientele, informally work out an agreement that is superior for the entire range of groups to any solution apt to emanate from a single central decision maker. The point here is not the inherent superiority of a group character but its inevitable impact on objectives. Invariably the various members of a decision unit will press for different goals. For example, in 1908 Izvolsky, the Russian foreign minister, focused his attention on improving Russia's access to the Turkish Straits. In September 1908 he and Aehrenthal, the Austrian foreign minister, reached a secret agreement by which the Austrians would support freedom of passage for Russian naval vessels through the Turkish Straits and the Russians would support the Austrian annexation of Bosnia and Herzegovina, Slav territories already under the administration of Austria but technically belonging to Turkey. Aehrenthal's surprise annexation of Bosnia-Herzegovina a few weeks later raised several problems for Izvolsky. The problem of greatest interest here is that the bulk of the Russian leadership chose to focus not on how to get Austrian help with the Turkish Straits but rather on maintaining Russian influence in the Balkans by supporting both Turkey and Serbia in resisting the Austrian annexation. Thus the concerns of other Russian leaders turned Russian policy toward resisting rather than supporting the Austrian annexation (Schmitt, 1937).

To the degree that the objectives pursued by various members of a decision unit are merely independent, it is often possible to devise a plan of action that offers a reasonable promise of procuring these independent objectives. In this case, creating a policy coalition is largely a matter of ingenuity. But if the objectives sought by various members conflict, then more difficult problems arise. In this instance, some potential members will have to be excluded from a policy coalition or at least relegated to a modest position through the low priority assigned to their objectives by the collective. In a group decision setting people are dropped from a coalition rather than objectives from a strategy (Snyder and Diesing, 1977). Whereas the latter instance would presumably entail dropping the objectives least consonant with the strategy as a whole, the former often entails dropping the coalition members least able to defend themselves and maintaining those members best able to create trouble for the coalition if they were to be discarded. There is no necessary correlation between domestic political strength and the pursuit of prudent or even consistent objectives in international conflicts. So the strategies developed for use in particular international conflicts are not necessarily designed specifically to meet the needs of the international situation; instead some aspects may be included to meet the demands of powerful domestic interests regardless of their impact on the international situation.

Hayes's (1972) analysis of recent United States foreign policy toward Southeast Asia offers a good example of this possibility. The escalation policy followed by the Johnson administration was essentially a compromise between the objectives of the doves and the increasing demands of the hawks, particularly the military. It met the objectives of extreme proponents of neither viewpoint but kept a broad range of proponents of each faction in the administration coalition. The compromise strategy that emerged was virtually irrelevant to the situation in Southeast Asia. But the foreign situation was a less potent threat to the Johnson administration than the breakup of the domestic coalition, and maintaining the domestic coalition required a policy ineffective in the foreign arena. While generalization of this conception of decision making will remain— in this book at least—speculative, some recent materials (Newhouse,

1973) on Soviet policy making indicate that Soviet SALT and perhaps other decisions may be similarly characterized. The civilian members of the SALT delegations often agree that the two nations share the problem of controlling their respective military bureaucracies, for instance.

Impact of Group Weights on Bargaining Positions

As the previous section illustrates, the two characteristics of independent, even conflicting, objectives and group decisions impart a domestic political aspect to the decisions that build the bargaining strategies of nations in international conflicts. These aspects are alien to most conceptions of bargaining in economics and the theories elicited from gaming situations. [11] Yet focusing on these factors as integral characteristics of the bargaining problem in international conflicts clarifies some aspects of bargaining procedures and settlements in these situations. For one, even if an optimal *national* strategy for dealing with an international conflict could be identified, use of it might be blocked by parochial interests that found the domestic impact of the strategy less than optimal for themselves. Thus a second problem—in addition to misperception—that regularly and importantly dilutes the purity of strategic interaction among international adversaries is disparity between the demands of the international situation as they confront the nation as a whole and the requirements of powerful domestic factions. So one nation may react to another with a strategy designed more to meet domestic than international objectives.

When changes in strategy occur under this conception of the bargaining problem, they may entail changing the coalition (Snyder and Diesing, 1977). It is not always necessary to change the coalition. Rouvier, the French premier during the 1905–6 Algeciras crisis, began his bargaining with the Germans by offering compromises in a spirit of reconciliation. The progressive failure of this policy gradually altered the Rouvier cabinet's approach, and the cabinet finally adopted a hard-line stance

---

[11] Behavioral theories of organization decisions (Tversky, 1972; Simon, 1969; Cyert and March, 1963) are exceptions to this statement.

(Anderson, 1966). But changes of this sort are unusual.[12] Often a given group of foreign policy leaders will hold fast to their initial strategy, and if a strategy change is necessary, the membership of the coalition sustaining the existing strategy will have to be changed. Renegotiating a policy coalition is not always difficult either. In the short-lived Cuban crisis of 1962 Dean Acheson simply left the decision unit when a coalition began to form around a strategy that he viewed with grave misgivings. But this too is unusual. Coalition members regularly struggle to maintain their positions and their influence. These two tendencies—for individuals to hold to their initial strategy choices and for them to struggle to maintain their positions within a coalition—mean that strategies are relatively inflexible. Changes in the intensity of fundamentally coercive or fundamentally accommodative strategies are far more likely than dramatic shifts from one approach to the other. The shifts that do occur between coercive and accommodative modes of interaction require coaxing and are normally both gradual and modest.

So this discussion of the nature of actual political decisions is not an idle or an academic exercise. The characteristics introduced in the preceding section hold some important implications for decision substance. First is that each domestic faction holds a narrow and often self-serving view of the nature of the satisfactory solution. For instance, in 1941 Matsuoka, the Japanese foreign minister, wanted to break out of the encirclement of the Western imperial powers; the Japanese army wanted to win the land war in China and then live in peace; the Japanese navy wanted United States guarantees for Japanese access to raw materials and wished to avoid war with the United States. As another example, repeatedly during the last decade United States military leaders have focused their attention on obtaining a military victory. This viewpoint has at times excluded consideration of factors such as avoiding war (Cuba) or avoiding broader war (Southeast Asia). During the Cuban conflict the United States Ambassador to the United Nations, Stevenson, suggested the United States withdraw its base on Cuba if the Soviets withdrew their strategic installations. This suggestion focused narrowly on avoiding war

[12] There was an important change in the personnel of the French side during this conflict. Delcassé, the architect of French Moroccan policy, was removed from his position as foreign minister in an attempt to placate the Germans. The policy shift in the Rouvier cabinet occurred after Delcassé's dismissal.

and ignored safeguards considered desirable by others from the standpoint of avoiding a dangerous precedent. That is, if the United States uncritically withdrew an established installation within a recognized sphere of influence, the Soviet Union might reasonably be emboldened to engage in future adventures that might be even more provoking from the United States standpoint.

Another implication is that whether or not the solution that a particular faction perceives to be satisfactory is accepted as *the* satisfactory solution or as a part of the satisfactory solution is largely a matter of the political power of its supporting faction. A variety of constraints may have considerable theoretical merit—not allowing the adversary to impinge on the nation's crucial values, avoiding war, avoiding alienation of allies. Yet one of these may differ from the others in the domestic political support it enjoys. Thus the definition of the satisfactory solution essentially hinges on the political power behind the various constraints raised, and a constraint is included in the definition of a satisfactory solution if it is supported by sufficient political strength. Since the larger the number of constraints, the more difficult it will be to find a suitable course of action, constraints will probably be ignored if they are not pressed by an important faction; and if a faction has a strong domestic position, excluding entirely the constraints it supports will be extremely difficult. For instance, Democratic presidents in particular have been reluctant to challenge conservatives on the constraint of "don't give up more territory to communism."

A third and related implication revives an issue discussed at an earlier point in this chapter: the relative impact of personal ideology and role. In the earlier discussion, personal ideology was labeled a more fundamental source of selective attention and interpretation than role. The discussion of the last few paragraphs points out an area of major impact for role. Role is a major determinant of the weight of an individual's preferences. If the strategy under consideration is a naval blockade, the chief of naval operations—the man who will actually oversee the blockade—carries a lot of weight. In essence, he will probably implement the blockade as he chooses (Allison, 1971). Kohl (1975) isolates six different styles of group decision that vary in the degree to which they foster or attenuate the role parochialism of the considerations on which decisions are based. And both Leacacos (1971–72) and George (1972) have examined how policy analysis can be used as a tool to reduce the impact of role or organizational parochialism on decisions. Both McNamara in the Department of Defense and Kissinger in directing the National Security Council attempted to use rigorous procedures of policy analysis for managing organizational parochialism. Both McNamara and Kissinger experienced some success in reducing the impact of organizational parochialism on decisions. But in each case the struggle was difficult, and parochial factions were able to reassert themselves as McNamara and Kissinger began to turn their attention to other problems.

A further implication is that, apart from the influence the various elements of a coalition exert on the initial definition of a satisfactory solution and thus on the strategy chosen to achieve this solution, the relative influence of coalition members determines what if any compromises can be made in the initial position. A compromise means not only a reduction in the importance of a theoretical possibility; it means a reduction in the importance of a political faction or interest as well. In a situation in which all coalition members agree on a single constraint—not allowing the adversary to hold a portion of the homeland, for instance—compromise is virtually impossible. If, on the other hand, a decision unit is split among several constraints, compromise is more readily achieved. A shift of even a single member of the decision unit might allow the relaxation of a constraint owing to the reduction of political support for it.

Sometimes compromises indicate shifting positions on issues rather than shifting power positions. The recent United States shift in seeking a limitation on MIRV's in the SALT talks is a case in point. The military opposed this limitation for several years on the basis that MIRV's could not be detected through national or satellite surveillance procedures. The military finally accepted that monitoring the testing of Soviet weapons systems would provide an adequate safeguard and began to bargain with its former objection to MIRV limitations.

Finally, the necessity for the concurrence of a range of domestic factions on alterations of bargaining positions vis-à-vis international adversaries means that compromises or other strategy shifts do not occur among international adversaries through the same mechanism as they do in gaming experiments or formal models in which the bargainers are considered as unitary actors. May (1973) makes a similar point and supports it with a fine example of the Italian government during the closing days of Italian participation in the Second World War. May's point is that, while from the standpoint of a disinterested outside observer Italy as a nation might have been better off surrendering quickly to Allied forces than continuing to struggle against them in a lost cause, some factions within the Italian government required the struggle to continue their existence and thus perpetuated the conflict. The general point here is that nations, as opposed to individuals, do not react directly to the pains or pleasures of adversary strategies (Iklé, 1971). Domestic factions with strong interests in a specific position or factions that are insulated from attempts at influence by adversary nations may hold a nation to a policy line in spite of severe manipulative efforts on the part of foreign adversaries (Randle, 1970). So it is hard to be certain that bombing North Vietnam in a virtually unrestricted fashion would have had the impact on the policy of its political leadership that United States leaders desired.

Strategy Search

Nations, or the men who govern them, develop strategies that are designed to achieve solutions deemed satisfactory. The two preceding sections of this chapter have outlined the processes statesmen follow in determining the nature of the situations that confront them and the threats these situations pose or the opportunities they afford. This section deals with the process through which a satisfactory solution to impending or existing problems is created. The analysis of this section closely follows that of Snyder and Diesing (1977).

The process of creating a satisfactory solution to foreign policy problems is a search process. The concept of problem oriented search developed in the writing of Simon (1955) and has been picked up and amplified by a variety of scholars in different areas since (Tversky, 1972; Gore, 1964; Cyert and March, 1963). Roughly, statesmen use a procedure of gradually closing in on a satisfactory solution through repeated efforts. Yet for a variety of reasons—primarily the dilution of strategic interaction created by misperception and the group nature of decisions—the foreign policy search process is not the flexible tool that trial and error normally brings to mind. The search process has two phases that are distinct in time, arena, and purpose. First these two phases will be described as independent activities, and then the interaction between them will be discussed.

Internal Search

The first phase of the search process has an internal or domestic political orientation. The basis for this phase has been laid in the previous discussion. A particular foreign policy challenge will be perceived in highly subjective ways by different factions of the target nation. McNamara, who was essentially a management specialist, initially perceived no problem in the Soviet deployment of strategic weapons in Cuba. Acheson, a cold warrior, perceived a Soviet probe of United States resolve. The Joint Chiefs of Staff focused on the facts that this deployment circumvented the United States early warning and air defense systems and that the reduced distance traveled by missiles coming from Cuba reduced the attack warning time below that for which the SAC was trained. While the deployment probably raised some vague aspects of challenge as well, these were the concrete problems the deployment raised from a military standpoint. The President, a politician, was obviously concerned with the domestic political consequences of the deployment. An election was just around the corner; Cuba was a particularly weak point for Kennedy, and being "soft on communism" was a weak point for the President's party. On the other hand, presidents who lead their nations to national destruction bear political liabilities too, and Kennedy was anxious to use caution in removing the Soviet installations.

So one nation's action creates problems that vary in kind and severity among varying factions in the target nation. What this target nation defines as *the* problem and thus what it searches for a solution to is a function of who has the domestic position to make the problem he sees count. In the Cuban case the military focused on a narrow definition of the problem in the constraint, "do not allow the Soviets to create and maintain strategic installations in Cuba." Given this definition of the problem, the military focused on a solution that met this single constraint: destroying the installations before they become operational. The difficulty for the joint chiefs was that they did not have the domestic political influence to bring about this solution. The President, torn by the conflicting constraints of "do not allow the Soviets to create and maintain strategic installations in Cuba" and "avoid actions apt to provoke a holocaust," opted for a more indirect method of meeting the first constraint. The differences here between the joint chiefs and the President include moral priorities, practical sensibilities, and—the key to who won—domestic political strength.

The Cuban case is a particularly well documented search for a coalition that can sustain and is willing to sustain a particular course of action. Sometimes certain members of a foreign policy elite will have a particular strategy in mind and search for—ask, persuade through careful analysis, pressure—others who can help them to make this strategy feasible. That is, they develop a group that can implement and sustain the strategy they desire. In other instances the course of action is gradually defined by the various demands of a more or less fixed group whose support is essential for foreign policy initiatives in general. The first of these options is more common for cases in which advance warning of a problem exists. For instance, in 1914 Grey, the British foreign minister, coordinated his persuasion carefully with the development of events on the continent so as to build support in a reluctant cabinet for a policy to which he was personally committed. Unexpected crises may elicit the second form of coalition formation. The activity of Kennedy's advisors in developing a response to the Soviet deployment of nuclear weapons in Cuba offers an example of this approach. In either case the problem that is accepted as the national problem is the one that acquires broad enough support to make it defensible against domestic critics. How broad this support has to be varies considerably. In the Soviet Union under Stalin, Stalin's support was apparently sufficient in some instances to sustain a policy. Contemporary United States presidents usually have to have more on board than the White House staff—although Halperin (1972) argues that on certain decisions the President is not just quantitatively different from other participants, but qualitatively different. The crucial question to ask when considering the sufficiency of a coalition is whether it can sustain or survive the policy it favors or whether the elements excluded from participation in defining the national problem will be able to destroy the coalition.

This question raises the topic of the sources of coalition strength. One of the most obvious sources of power is policy implementation. If a policy requires military operations, the influence of the military will probably be great. A politician may reasonably feel that conducting military operations against the advice of military professionals is irresponsible. Also, faced with intricate operations with which it disagreed, the military might well implement them half-heartedly or clumsily, thereby altering the intended policy. Other sources of influence within a coalition include a collection of factors which offer influence within the domestic structure of politics. Retribution through these means—impeachment or losing an election—may be slower than retribution from those responsible for implementation. But the costs are just as high if not higher. Chief executives are probably more willing to run a risk of foreign than of domestic disaster. Thus President Nixon pressed hard against Pentagon intransigence on the issue of Israeli resupply during the October 1973 war when the Israeli ambassador threatened to go public and bring down the wrath of Zionist pressures on the already besieged Nixon White House (Kalb and Kalb, 1974: 474–75).[13] A criterion useful for gauging who or what is necessary from the standpoint of domestic political strength is: what sort of damage can this fellow or organization do if he or it speaks out against the policy of the coalition? If the damage is dangerously high, it is prudent to bring the dissenter on board. And this is accomplished by including in the definition of the national problem the dissenter's point of view—including his notion of the solution. By this criterion groups impotent in domestic politics in general—blacks, migrant workers—are excluded from foreign policy coalitions as well.

So the crucial question raised by the internal search process is: what policy vis-à-vis the adversary can win domestic support? And gradually the strategy desires of the groups that cannot be excluded from a policy coalition are aggregated. In some instances competing groups may vie for dominance, and a choice among clearly distinct alternatives arises. The first West German election in 1949 offers an example of this situation. Adenauer (CDU) and Schumacher (SPD) stood for irreconcilable foreign

[13] Sheehan (1976) suggests that the Kalb and Kalb account exaggerates struggles within the United States government during this conflict episode. So this intriguing example ought to be considered along with others. President Johnson was clearly less concerned with the inadequacies of his policies in Southeast Asia than he was with keeping his domestic policy coalition together. And Kennedy risked nuclear war in 1962 for a collection of reasons that included domestic political considerations as extremely prominent concerns.

policy stances. Each was searching for a coalition—in this case a parliamentary majority—that would serve to support his policy. A decision point between two irreconcilable or even distinct alternatives is unusual. In the example mentioned, the Federal Republic was choosing a starting point—an unusual act. More generally an effort is made to develop a compromise policy that does not leave a viable opposition that may win the coalition struggle another day.

Several examples of building compromise coalitions appear in recent United States responses to conflict episodes. The public records of the Cuban and Southeast Asian cases allow a particularly close look at this process. Instead of choosing between a blockade and an air strike, for instance, Kennedy put the two together as stages of a single policy. He also granted the joint chiefs a special, last-minute session. This final exchange of views was a courtesy paid in an effort to keep the military in the coalition. Johnson gave neither the doves nor the hawks what they desired in the Southeast Asian conflict (Ellsberg, 1972; Hayes, 1972; Gelb, 1971). The military succeeded in raising the level of United States involvement between 1964 and 1968. This escalation kept the military from an open break with Johnson. Yet the military repeatedly failed to get as much as it asked for, and the difference between what the military wanted and what it got was the payoff for the doves. The discrepancy offered hope which kept moderate doves on board. The resulting policy was tragic. It was designed more to maintain an administration against domestic critics than to meet the needs of the foreign situation it ostensibly addressed. United States policy in the long conflict over Berlin (1958–62) was essentially a compromise between two extremes within the alliance—Adenauer and Macmillan. The hard-liners won a firm stand on essential, nonnegotiable points—a NATO presence in West Berlin, military access to West Berlin, and the economic viability of West Berlin—although the essentials chosen represented Acheson's essentials more than Adenauer's. The soft-liners won a problem solving orientation toward the Soviets on other matters involved in the Berlin conflict. Other examples of compromise coalitions appear in the policy deliberations of other nations. In 1940–41 Japanese factions worked out several different positions in internal bargaining, but none of these positions were acceptable to the United States. British warnings to Hitler during the Munich crisis were designed to placate the isolated but vociferous British hard-liners. These warnings were watered down so as not to upset the appeasers, and the mild signals were ignored by Hitler.

External Search

If the initial strategy works pretty much as anticipated, the search process ends with the internal phase. Statesmen do not always enjoy such success, however. Sometimes initial strategies run into difficulties, as the Soviets found with their blockade of Berlin or as the United States found in the recent conflict in Southeast Asia. In these instances an external search for alternative strategies more acceptable to the adversary nation was necessary.

When an initial strategy runs into trouble, a strategy change may be necessary, and this is no easy task. Several hurdles stand in the way. First, some individuals will simply fail to recognize that strategy change is necessary. In the recent debacle in Southeast Asia some prominent United States officials claimed to the bitter end—and some are still claiming—that what was needed was more of the same. Second, even if some officials begin to see the need for policy change, they may be reluctant to rock the boat. Janis (1972) provides a tantalizing description of the incentives for conformity. And Thomson (1968) and Halberstam (1972) offer indications that several senior officials in the Johnson administration acted so as to nip internal criticism in the bud. Third, even if advisors notice the need for policy change and are willing to raise the issue, there is no certainty that they will have the political power to effect change. Changing a policy, as we have seen, may mean changing the coalition that sustains the policy. And changing the coalition can be, and often is, a desperate political struggle. This process of coalition change or renegotiation will be discussed in the section on interaction between internal and external search. For the moment strategy change will be considered possible.

FINDING LIMITS

External search is often a reciprocal process. While one party is performing certain acts with respect to a second, the second may be acting in a similar fashion relative to the first. Statesmen often enter conflicts striving for what amounts retrospectively to an ideal. Given the initial aspirations, the ideal may well be a minimally acceptable state of affairs, but initial aspirations are often unrealistically high. Initial positions can often be reduced. That is, they contain both essential goals and what retrospectively turn out to be less important side issues. Sometimes positions are consciously stripped down nearly to their essentials prior to conflict. Kennedy turned away efforts to include removal of the Castro government—an essential for some—from the initial United States position in the Cuban crisis. Kennedy could live with Castro; he could not live with Soviet strategic nuclear installations in the Caribbean. And he expressed the attitude: "I am not going to push the Russians an inch beyond what is necessary" (Kennedy, 1971: 105). Kennedy was fortunate: his initial strategy worked, and his minimal goals stayed roughly intact. [14] Possibly paring down his initial goals to a minimum added to his chances for success (George, Hall, and Simons, 1971). But initial goals are often reduced.

External search amounts to a search for information about the nature of a bargaining strategy which will gain the acceptance of the foreign adversary. Essentially what is required here are coercive initiatives that divulge information about what the adversary will accept, as opposed to information about what powerful domestic factions will accept. That is, a decision unit resorts to external search because the initial strategy—a strategy based on the preferences of powerful domestic groups—has failed in some fashion. Normally, failure arises through the initial strategy's being unacceptable to the adversary; so information about what aspects are unacceptable and how unacceptable they are becomes the focus of the external search process. The first activity of external search is normally goal decomposition. Here the bargainer tries to determine what portions of the adversary's position are flexible and by how much.

For instance, the initial French position in the crisis over the Moroccan question in 1911 was to deny compensation to Germany. This had been the usual French stance for a decade, although the French had

[14] The removal of the Soviet installations was achieved through a combination of President Kennedy's formal personal pledge of noninvasion and Robert Kennedy's informal ultimatum that the United States would remove the missiles with military means if the Soviets did not remove them and his informal suggestion that United States missiles in Turkey would probably be removed (Gromyko, 1971; Kennedy, 1971). Khrushchev (1970: 498; 1974: 512) emphasizes the importance of the pledge rather than the ultimatum or the missiles in Turkey.

made modest concessions in 1906 at the Algeciras conference and again in 1909. These concessions were—from the French standpoint—gestures of goodwill designed to erase any lingering bad feelings the Germans harbored about the Moroccan question. In 1911, however, German pressure—in conjunction with less than enthusiastic support from France's allies—demonstrated that the French were actually willing to provide the Germans with some sort of compensation—other than Moroccan territory—in order to resolve the Moroccan question. Persistent German pressure on the French position decomposed the initial French stance (which, although it seemed to the French at the beginning of the conflict to express a minimal position, turned out to be an ideal) into crucial goals that had to be achieved (the territorial integrity of French Morocco) and negotiable issues (the principle of compensation).

A considerably different example of goal decomposition occurred during the Fashoda crisis of 1898. In this conflict the French government was by no means united. In fact, French policy in this episode offers as tortuous an example of bureaucratic politics as any imaginable. Some elements of the French cabinet were surprised when the British-French contact was made along the upper Nile. The contact jolted their memories of a French force that had been sent out two years earlier by the Ministry of Colonies and that was now raising a claim on the Sudan (Fuchs, 1971; Brown, 1970). This initial position of the French in the Fashoda crisis hardly represents a stable coalition defending its minimal goals, and the French position collapsed progressively under British pressure. The French held a series of positions starting with a portion of the Sudan becoming French and ending with acceptance of British-French discussions that would hear French complaints about British dominance in Northeast Africa. Diplomatic representatives met and listened, and the British proceeded in their activity in Northeast Africa quite unmoved. External search for the French in this case amounted to reducing their position to a point acceptable to the British—the status quo ante.

The Berlin crisis of 1948–49 offers another clear example of goal decomposition. The initial Soviet strategy was to use pressure against a vulnerable point—Berlin—in order to gain greater Western cooperation in a common policy toward Germany. The issue was never really perceived in this fashion in the West. It was perceived immediately as a struggle over West Berlin and more diffusely as a test of will between the Soviets and the Western allies. Thus the Western response was first harsher than the Soviets anticipated and, through the fortuitous airlift, more successful than either side originally foresaw. Eventually the Soviets decided that their blockade was apt to gain neither Western cooperation over Germany nor West Berlin—the initial minimum. So while Berlin was to remain a severe irritant for over a decade, the Soviets set about looking for other solutions to the German problem. These efforts to resolve Soviet and other Eastern European fears about Germany created difficulties repeatedly throughout the next fifteen years. [15]

Insight into the strength of the adversary's preferences can be obtained in two independent ways. It can be actively sought by coercive actions that test the adversary's position. In this case the adversary reveals preferences—perhaps obscure until this moment even to himself—inadvertently in his response to the testing. Or statesmen may rely on the willful signals of others (obtained through diplomatic inquiry) to reveal their preferences. Jervis (1970) calls these indices and signals, respectively. The problem with signals is that they can be manipulated for purposes of deceit. Information can be withheld altogether or actual positions can be misrepresented. Nations are generally—but not always—reluctant to specify limits to their aspirations. For instance, on their own initiative the Germans in 1911 did not relinquish a claim to Moroccan territory. In response to specific French queries the Germans replied that compensation elsewhere would be acceptable. However, on their own initiative the German statesmen would not have issued a statement that Moroccan territory was superfluous. Hitler was infamous not only for withholding information but for misrepresenting his tolerances as well.

These problems with signals point up the advantages of indices. Carefully selected coercive measures can actually test whether a particular objective is worth a struggle to the adversary. Kiderlen sent ships to a southern Moroccan harbor in 1911. The French Ministry of Colonies sent a small force to the Sudan in the 1890s. In a more recent period Ulbricht closed the Autobahns, raised rates on the barge canals, and tried to inspect military traffic to Berlin. General Clay countered with helicopter flights across East German territory to enclaves such as Steinstucken. The Soviets began their arms buildup in Cuba in 1962 with

---

[15] Perhaps the slickest goal decomposition activity on record is that of Ulbricht during the 1958–62 Berlin conflict. See Snyder and Diesing (1977).

modest conventional weapons and escalated the nature of the equipment introduced into Cuba. The United States initially responded with a blockade or a modest—in comparison to an air strike–invasion—infringement on Soviet activity. The Soviet response to the United States blockade provided an indication as to whether further efforts to gain a peaceful solution would be worth trying. And this illustrates how probing the adversary's tolerances is a useful external search device. The adversary's position is tested in a modest way. If he backs down, this portion of the problem is open to compromise and may even be resolved. If the adversary stands fast, this portion of the problem is going to be difficult, and it may pay to search elsewhere for limits on the adversary's tolerances.

The essence of goal decomposition is discriminating among the various aspects of the adversary's initial position those that are in fact minimal requirements from those that are desirable but superfluous to a minimally acceptable solution. This decomposition of original goals is an important process in itself, but perhaps even more important is a perceptual shift that can accompany the discrimination process. The adversary's initial position is often perceived as a challenge with virtually unlimited implications. The Germans viewed a French triumph in Morocco unaccompanied by compensation to Germany as tantamount to destroying Germany's voice in European decisions and thus Germany's European position. The British in the Fashoda case felt a French presence in the Sudan would jeopardize their position in Egypt. The French had publicly discussed damming the Nile and destroying the Egyptian economy, and the threat to Egypt in turn threatened communication with India and the British empire generally. The Soviet blockade of Berlin stood as a symbol of Soviet intransigence and expansionist desires for many Western statesmen. This Soviet action and the Western reaction to it were then viewed as crucial actions in a struggle for dominance in Europe.

So learning that reductions are possible is often more important than gaining specific reductions in the adversary's position. That is, a broader purpose that external search serves is altering perceptions of what the conflict is about. If external search is successful in discovering and/or imposing specific limitations on the adversary's position, it may also alter the decision maker's perception of the conflict. Thus perceptions may shift from a fear of virtually unlimited conflict of principle to a notion of conflict over clearly delimited, concrete issues. In this fashion goal decomposition prepares the ground for the second external search activity.

DEVELOPING SOLUTIONS

Reconciliation of differences is the theme of the second activity of the external search process. The action here centers around compromise rather than the coercive activities. Several factors are critical to the success of compromise activity. The effort to reconcile differences is apt to be more fruitful if it follows adequate goal decomposition activity. Goal decomposition activity has served its purpose when both some limitations on aspirations have appeared *and* a perceptual shift from conflict of principle to conflict over specific issues has occurred. This shift lays the optimal background for compromise. It is possible to reach compromise agreements without complete success in the goal decomposition phase. But the process is often more difficult, subject to subsequent disappointment, and unstable.

A classic case of moving prematurely from the goal decomposition phase of search to the reconciliation of differences phase appears in the 1911 crisis over the Moroccan question. Kiderlen, the German foreign minister, and Jules Cambon, the French ambassador to Berlin, held a series of meetings prior to the coercive moves of the Germans and the British. At this time—late June—the French were willing to grant Germany compensation in order to obtain a free hand in Morocco, but they were still clinging to the hope that compensation would take the form of German economic privileges throughout French controlled regions of the world rather than territorial concessions. Nevertheless, the subject of territorial compensation in the area of the French Congo—a French concession—was discussed during the June meetings. In response to this French position Kiderlen offered to trade a smaller amount of German colonial territory so that the French cabinet could sell the deal to the Senate as a territorial exchange—a German concession. In each case these offers met the adversary's basic needs. In fact, while no specific boundaries were discussed, the outlines of the concessions of late June formed the basis of the agreement reached the following November. However, a crisis—in terms of a high risk of war—began early in July and reached a peak in late August and early September. More than two months of severe pressure were necessary to return to the proposals of late June and another two months were required to work out the details of these proposals. In part these risks and delays were undertaken because neither side knew enough about the other's tolerances in late June to view the proposals of this time period as a reasonable agreement.

Several solution characteristics that foster or discourage a settlement are also relevant to the success of compromise initiatives. These considerations fit more appropriately into the discussion of the next chapter and will only be introduced here. The first of these is whether the solutions proposed give the conflict a constant or variable-sum character. Creating a bigger pie by upgrading the interests of *both* parties—a variable-sum situation—may offer more opportunities for successful resolution than does arguing over shares of a fixed pie—a constant-sum situation.

For instance, one characteristic that eased the settlement of the Fashoda conflict was that Delcassé, the French foreign minister, saw more at stake in the conflict than just the division of territory in Northeast Africa. This issue offered no substantive reward to the French, inasmuch as the British refused to give up any aspect of their influence over the Nile basin.[16] But Delcassé saw another issue: future Anglo-French relations. Delcassé was anxious to remove rivalry over the Nile basin from the concerns of France and Britain so as to clear the way for improved relations between the two nations. Delcassé saw Germany as an increasingly important French adversary and wanted to be able to rely on British help in future struggles with Germany. While some other French leaders did not share his perspective, for Delcassé granting the British control of the Nile basin was not a French loss in a constant-sum situation. The French received a clear path for improved relations with Britain and for Delcassé, this solution upgraded both British and French interests. In contrast, Aehrenthal, the Austrian foreign minister during the Bosnian crisis of 1908–9, first constructed a potential agreement that upgraded the interests of both Austria and Russia by trading Russian support on Austrian control of Bosnia-Herzegovina for Austrian support for increased

---

[16] Salisbury, the British prime minister, did make *procedural* compromises. He announced the French withdrawal from Fashoda as an aside in a speech on other topics. And he changed the name to "Kodok" so that the location would not appear as a continual embarrassment to the French.

Russian access to the Turkish Straits. This agreement would have been paid for by Turkey and Serbia. But after creating this tool for upgrading the interests of both of the major powers in the Balkans, Aehrenthal annexed Bosnia-Herzegovina in a fait accompli and left the Russians no payoff. The Russians both opposed the Austrian annexation in the short run and became increasingly reluctant to compromise with the Austrians in the long run, as the events of the summer of 1914 indicate.

The proportion of the spoils going to each party is a second characteristic of interest here. The impact of this factor is often hard to separate from the impact of constant as opposed to variable-sum solutions. A third characteristic, the degree to which a solution appears salient to the parties involved, may also undercut the importance of the second characteristic. Often nations will have particularly salient objectives, and their crucial considerations are achieving these objectives rather than comparing these objectives with those of other parties to the conflict. A fourth characteristic is the degree to which a resolution to conflict activity resolves the underlying issue. The repeated crises over Berlin, for instance, arose largely from Soviet concern about the capabilities and intentions of Germans allied with the West. Resolving the conflict activity focused on Berlin did not resolve the underlying issue for the Soviets.

Interaction

Up to now the internal and external search processes have been discussed as if they were independent of one another. The convenient simplicity of this arrangement can be maintained no longer. Each process feeds into the other. First, the search for a domestic coalition is not completely separated from the nature of the foreign policy problem. It is unlikely that the United States would respond to a new crisis in the Middle East with an intervention in Latin America simply because support for a Latin American intervention could be found. The nature of the foreign problem provides a focus for the initial search process (Cyert and March, 1963), and internal search can be expected to loosely follow this guideline. The modifier "loosely" is necessary because the foreign policy problem will be perceived differently by different groups and will probably be vague enough so that no single obvious problem and strategy emerge from this guideline alone. The composition of the policy coalition determines the exact nature of the foreign problem. In the early 1960s United States leaders were aware of a growing problem in South Vietnam. The problem guided attention toward South Vietnam and provided the general issues as to whether South Vietnam should receive United States assistance and, if so, what kind and degree of assistance it should receive. But a wide range of options remained as possible United States responses to this external stimulus and an internal search process determined how the United States would deal with this situation.

Specific forms of interaction vary, and several different contingencies are possible. The initial coalition may be able to accept changes in the existing strategy if some coalition members are willing to relax constraints that they have previously considered inviolable. Another possibility is that specific changes desired by the adversary will not be acceptable within the decision unit and will have to be rejected. Perhaps the most interesting possibility occurs when efforts to renegotiate the domestic coalition take place in an effort to obtain a domestic coalition that will meet the demands of the international situation. Examples of all three instances and the problems specific to them follow.

The Agadir crisis is a good example of compromises being accepted by the coalition sponsoring the initial strategy. During the conflict no major coalition member of either side was absolutely intransigent over time or was replaced in order to gain a compromise solution. Yet even in this example of the easiest relationship between the requirements of internal and external search, there was considerable conflict within decision units. The German foreign minister tendered his resignation twice in July because he felt he was not getting adequate support from the Kaiser and the chancellor. The German minister of colonies, Lindequist, was so upset by the territorial exchange agreement that he attempted to resign in protest. He was kept on until the agreement was finalized and then allowed to resign. On the French side a lower level of domestic disagreement was visible during the crisis itself. But when the Senate began ratification procedures in early 1912, a number of internal conflicts surfaced. Caillaux, the French prime minister during much of the crisis period, had directed Jules Cambon, the French ambassador to Berlin, to report some aspects of the negotiations directly to him rather than to de Selves, the foreign minister, at the Quai d'Orsay. Caillaux desired this arrangement so that elements of the French foreign office which were implacably hostile to Germany would not be able to destroy a Franco-German agreement through internal bargaining or press leaks (both occurred). This conflict between de Selves and Caillaux emerged in the Senate hearings. Caillaux was accused of humiliating the French foreign minister before the German adversary. The Caillaux cabinet fell in January 1912, and Caillaux was even imprisoned as a traitor a few years later when anti-German feeling was running particularly high in France. So the contradictions between external and internal search are important even when agreements are reached without the appearance of major upheaval.

Britain's side of the Fashoda conflict offers an example of internal coalition demands' overwhelming the adversary's desires for certain concessions. The British preferences were clear. Diplomacy should be used to dislodge the French from the Nile basin. But if diplomacy failed, then stronger coercive measures would be used. The British did not seriously consider allowing even the most modest French intrusion in this area. In this instance domestic coalition constraints foreclosed compromise with the international adversary, and external search was limited to finding a strategy that would win the initial terms. The British succeeded in pressuring the French to accept their initial terms, but external search within such narrow limitations is not always this productive. In 1941 the Japanese were unable to offer withdrawal from China as a concession. While some members of the Japanese cabinet were willing to consider this option, which might have triggered United States compromises, the Japanese army would not accept withdrawal from China; so external search leading to Pearl Harbor was pressed forward, and in this case external search ran into severe difficulties.

Western—particularly British—negotiations with Hitler in the late 1930s and the United States conflict in Southeast Asia in the 1960s provide illustrations of external search overwhelming the domestic coalition behind the initial strategy. This pattern is roughly the reverse of the one discussed in the preceding paragraph. For the British in the late 1930s the problem was the resurgence of German power in Central Europe. While suspicious of this expansion, the Chamberlain cabinet was struck by several other factors that mitigated the British response to German expansion. First, Chamberlain and others felt that Germany and the Germans had been dealt an injustice by the Treaty of Versailles. Second, there was a feeling that a strong Germany provided Western Europe with some protection from the socialist East. Third, Chamberlain was relatively unfamiliar with international politics and judged international actions from a legalistic point of view stemming from his domestic orientation. Fourth, as a former finance minister Chamberlain was acutely sensitive to the costs of rearmament or, even worse, war. After the German invasion of Poland in the autumn of 1939 the policy of allowing Hitler a series of seemingly legitimate increments was thoroughly discredited. Chamberlain was swept out and the Churchill war cabinet began a new policy.

For the United States in the late 1960s the problem was a military struggle in Southeast Asia that was increasingly questioned both domestically and abroad on legal, moral, and practical political grounds. Repeated promises by administration officials that the "end of the tunnel" was in sight were quashed by adversary actions. The most obvious discrepancy between administration claims and conditions in Southeast Asia came in the Tet offensive of February 1968. This debacle was followed closely by a poor administration showing in some early Democratic primaries and by increased opposition to the current direction of the war within the administration (Clark Clifford, for instance). By the end of March, Johnson had decided that remaining in office was no longer worth the price. His successor was elected on a ticket that included ending the conflict in Southeast Asia as a high priority. In both the British and United States cases an external strategy that had failed over a period of years simply became impractical domestically. In each case the government in power had become so thoroughly identified with the existing strategy that it was necessary to change the personnel of government in order to change the strategy.

Summary

The crux of bargaining in international conflicts as depicted by this chapter is a series of three processes: information interpretation, decisions among independent constraints in a group setting, and search for a satisfactory strategy. These processes address the following sequence of questions. What situation does the statesman face? What does this situation mean in terms of interests threatened or opportunities afforded? What general actions must be undertaken to meet the demands of the situation? The answers to these questions are subjective. The different national units party to specific international conflicts will answer these questions differently, and generally the members of each national decision unit will disagree among themselves about the answers to these questions. It is in fact this pervasive disagreement that makes these questions—and thus the processes that they prompt—so central to bargaining in international conflicts. Two mathematicians who apply these questions to a two-by-two Prisoner's Dilemma matrix are apt to reach similar and deductively reasonable answers. Two students running through experimental trials with the same matrix may practice different strategies from those deduced by the mathematicians, but nevertheless intuitively reach a roughly similar understanding of the situation. In the areas of formal modeling and experimental gaming, bargaining theory may reasonably focus on other questions more advanced than those which currently lie at the crux of bargaining in severe international conflicts. But the disparity of views, the complexity of goals, and the difficulties of accurately perceiving the consequences of actions make the questions of this paragraph central to bargaining in international conflicts.

For bargaining in contemporary international conflicts, then, these topics form the most fruitful focus of attention. This choice inevitably places limits on what will be studied and on the nature of the theoretical results. The three processes are all vague, for instance, with respect to the location of settlements in specific cases; in fact, they do not explicitly address the location of settlements. They do address other matters of interest. They help to explain why the parties hold such disparate views of the conflicting interests, why some settlements are inherently unstable, why strategies are often less than optimal from the standpoint of international strategic interactions, why strategies are relatively inflexible, why clear-cut choices among strategic options rarely arise, why certain compromises are possible and others are not. Answers to these questions are important, but so are answers to other questions. With these other questions in mind, the discussion of the next chapter introduces a class of variables termed bargaining resources.

4.

Important Situational Characteristics

While the essential processes of bargaining in international conflicts presented in the last chapter raise important questions about bargaining in these episodes and answer some of these questions, the factors considered in the preceding chapter leave numerous gaps in desirable knowledge about bargaining in international conflicts. This chapter is designed to fill some of these gaps.

Bargaining Resources

The thesis of this section is that in a rough way the outcomes of bargaining episodes reflect the resources that each party brings to the support of its objectives. At least two problems cut away at this argument. First, the thesis is potentially tautological, or at least could beg the question. That is, the answer as to why France (or any nation) got the better of Britain (or any other nation) in any given conflict could be reduced to a glib "France brought more resources to bear on the conflict." This unsatisfying approach has appeared before in the study of international politics. For instance, the criticism that raged around Morgenthau's concept of power said that the concept was weak. In a vague sense power meant or could be used to explain everything. In more specific senses the effect of power was difficult to pin down. Each time a concrete index emerged, the explanatory power of the vague concept seemed to disappear.

A second problem is that focusing on resources should not lead to ignoring the manner in which those resources are used. Theoretically, if two nations bring equal resources to bear on a problem, advantage might go to the party that utilized its resources more effectively. Each of these problems will be confronted in this chapter. While the concept of bargaining resources will retain a hopefully healthy openness of meaning, several efforts to provide some concrete amplification will be discussed. The second half of this chapter will deal with a variety of problems related to the application of resources to bargaining in severe international conflicts.

Problems with Traditional Indices of National Power

In a limited sense indices used to gauge the overall power of nations can provide useful information for determining the bargaining resources available to a nation. The United States would presumably have better luck bargaining with a series of adversaries than Sri Lanka would have with the same set of adversaries. Yet indices such as gross national product, quantity and quality of military armaments, and population are at best rough and often misleading sources of inference about bargaining resources. A discussion of conventional indices of national power is unnecessary. Detailed discussions of these indices can be found in many international relations texts (Morgenthau, 1973; K. J. Holsti, 1972). Instead the discussion here will focus on some problems and limitations characteristic of these indices. One problem with using conventional indices of national power is that they may not make fine enough distinctions. Consider the following two examples.

In 1898 Great Britain and France were both great powers. It would have been difficult to compare their respective power for bargaining purposes in the abstract, however, since they funneled their power into different enterprises. France was primarily a land power. The traditional threats to its security came from continental attack, and the French, although they had a fleet, responded primarily in terms of an army. The British tradition was quite different. In modern times Britain had little fear of continental attack and some early disenchanting experiences with a large standing army. Britain as the first industrial power and as an island nation had acquired a large navy. The upshot of all this was that Britain was *the* primary naval power during the period of the Fashoda crisis. France could not hope to carry on a struggle against the British in Northeast Africa unless France's continental allies could be persuaded to put pressure on the British empire at other locations. (There was little hope for such pressure, and the French made no effort to develop it.) Even in the Mediterranean British seapower was or could be made supreme. So France's national power was inappropriate for the Fashoda context and was of little use as a bargaining resource.

In 1962 the United States and the Soviet Union were dominant in terms of military, economic, and diplomatic power. The United States had numerical superiority in strategic or nuclear arms. However, the full dimension of the United States superiority was not clear at the time, and it is debatable whether the numerical superiority the United States possessed was sufficient for a first strike capability. So there was uncertainty as to whether a strategic balance existed. The Soviet Union unquestionably had superior conventional forces. These forces were considerably superior in number and at a minimum enjoyed equipment of equal quality. Yet the nuclear stalemate and the conventional superiority of Soviet forces—which might be decisive in Europe or the Middle East—were of relatively little use in the Cuban crisis of 1962. In this affair the Soviet Union introduced limited strategic and conventional forces to a region in which the United States enjoyed unquestioned military supremacy.[1] If the United States adopted a violent military response to the Soviet military presence in the Caribbean, the Soviet Union would have had to face either a military defeat in the Caribbean or a much broader conventional conflict in which the Soviet Union's military advantages elsewhere could be utilized. Naturally this expanded conflict would have carried grave

[1] It is curious that the tripwire aspect of these Soviet forces in the Caribbean was not mentioned by United States military officials who had spent over a decade extolling the tripwire function of United States forces in Western Europe and Berlin in particular.

dangers for the survival of both the United States and the Soviet Union, and there is no evidence that Soviet leaders were interested in such a conflict.

All four of the nations in these two examples had extensive human and material resources which provided a basis for great power status. In addition, each of the powers had transformed these resources into impressive capabilities for influencing the actions of other nations. However, in each conflict episode one of the powers, Great Britain and the United States respectively, had developed capabilities that offered usable options for influencing its adversary of the moment, whereas the capabilities held by the adversaries, France and the Soviet Union respectively, did not support options that were of much practical use in influencing Britain and the United States in the context of these particular conflict episodes. In order to have any significant influence in bargaining, national resources must create options that are useful within the context of the specific encounters a nation faces.[2]

Another problem with conventional indices of national power is that items relevant to bargaining influence may not be included among these indices. Vietnam is certainly less powerful in terms of conventional indices than the United States. Yet the Vietnamese were able to draw a hard bargain in gaining United States withdrawal from the conflict in Southeast Asia. The Vietnamese had a variety of bargaining chips that others have already discussed (Mack, 1975). Nevertheless, some resources on which they were able to draw will be mentioned here. First, the Vietnamese, if not possessed of allies, at least knew that if the United States broadened the war beyond South Vietnam and the border areas of Cambodia and Laos, other major powers would grow gravely concerned about United States intentions. So in order to avoid the risk of a conflict with other great powers, the United States was forced to limit its military activity largely to a level at which the Vietnamese could compete. In essence, Soviet and Chinese interest in the conflict in Southeast Asia limited the usable options of the United States to a fraction of those available from the standpoint of United States national power.

Second, the Vietnamese government was fighting for a reasonably important goal—a homeland. As the conflict progressed one reason after

[2]I am grateful to Alexander George for suggesting this breakdown of the bargaining resource concept to me.

another for the United States government's involvement fell by the wayside. And increasingly United States involvement seemed to have the purely negative constraint of avoiding a defeat that would be embarrassing—at least domestically—for the party and president in power (Gelb, 1971). Certainly one factor that affects the rank ordering of outcomes such as war, compromise, and capitulation is a nation's power. If a nation is quite powerful in comparison to its rivals, war will be less fearsome and capitulation all the more disturbing. But another factor that affects the same rank ordering is the valuation of the stakes. If a government is fighting for a core value—its home territory—it may fight long and hard against overwhelming odds. And an asymmetry in the evaluation of the stakes may offset an asymmetry in the national power of the participants in a struggle. Sometimes stalemate arises not because the more powerful nation cannot impose its will but because the price of enforcing its will is not considered worth the effort.[3]

Third, while status quo is normally thought of as a static state, it can also be viewed as a phase of dynamic process (Murdock, 1971). From the standpoint of the Vietnamese nationalist forces a military stalemate favored them. They were on their home ground; stalemate allowed them to continue their local political efforts to develop their nationalist movement; and stalemate offered an opportunity to win more international recognition for their struggle against foreign imperialism. For the United States a military stalemate carried concomitant disadvantages. A stalemate left the United States military as a foreign occupation army. At best this situation was difficult. At worst it raised for relevant audiences the continual image of a white civilization fighting the yellow man in Asia— and using black soldiers to do so, no less. A military stalemate could be and was used for the purpose of building up local military forces which had some of the same adversaries as the United States forces. Theoretically, the stalemate could have been used to develop a more responsive government in South Vietnam. But military stalemate also fueled increasing domestic and international pressure on the United States government to withdraw from active military engagement in Southeast Asia. In short, the United States in Vietnam, like the British in the American revolution, had to win outright in order to be successful.

[3]George, Hall, and Simons (1971) stress a similar concept, a favorable "asymmetry of motivation," as an important prerequisite for coercive diplomacy.

In summary, then, while conventional sources of national power should not be ignored in estimating the bargaining influence available to specific nations in specific contexts, these indices have two important drawbacks. First, they may fail to discriminate adequately whether recognized forms of national power can create usable options for influencing the adversary in the specific conflict at hand. The French continental army was helpless with respect to a conflict in Northeast Africa, since the British controlled the sea separating Europe from Africa. Soviet conventional supremacy on the Eurasian continent was of little use for a confrontation in the Caribbean. Second, these indices may fail to recognize some situational asymmetries that are crucial to the outcomes of particular conflict episodes. Factors such as the relative centralness of the conflict to the goals of the respective adversaries, alliance relationships, or other less formal considerations that tie third parties to the conflict and the relative advantage at different levels of success all constitute important sources of bargaining influence. But these factors are often too intangible or subtle to be included among conventional indices of national power. So other possibilities will have to be developed in the search for clues as to the ability of nations to bring their resources to bear in specific conflict situations.

The Strengths of Weakness[4]

To reinforce the contentions of the preceding section, this one will take a brief look at examples of weak nations that have been able to take strong bargaining positions in specific conflicts. For years Taiwan and South Korea exerted considerable pressure on the United States. The United States and the Vatican, for instance, are the only two Western nations that still maintain the fiction—formally at least—that Taiwan represents the Chinese people. The United States is gradually shifting from this position, but its major allies in Western Europe have long since adopted a more realistic position, and the question naturally arises as to why the United States is lagging behind these reasonable examples. To

[4]This concept comes from Schelling (1960).

what does the Chinese government on Taiwan owe its ability to hold United States allegiance? In part, the United States may be reluctant to drop an ally because of its position as the major Western nation, particularly when such an action would probably be followed closely by stronger relations with the former ally's most serious adversary. An action of this nature might be viewed with suspicion by other regional powers (India, Pakistan, Israel, Japan) and thus set a dangerous precedent. The precedent might be particularly disturbing to others for, as Keohane (1971) points out, Taiwan played the role of a superloyal ally with respect to the United States policy of containment. Park (1975) indicates that South Korea was able to use moral suasion against the desertion of a government that was fighting communists to draw the United States to its support in the early 1950s. But at least as important for United States leaders are the domestic dangers of dropping such an ally. While these existed for many years for all postwar United States statesmen, they were particularly severe for Democrats. The Democrats were or have felt themselves to be vulnerable on this issue. They felt that a small but well-financed and vociferous Taiwan lobby had an ability to mobilize mass public and important elite opinion in the United States if government officials took actions that threatened Taiwan. The same two factors—probably less strong in each case—explain in large measure why the United States' active military participation in Southeast Asia ended in January 1973 rather than in October 1972 when Kissinger explained that peace was at hand (Kalb and Kalb, 1974). The South Vietnamese could use roughly the same resources the Chinese leadership on Taiwan has used in order to delay the signing of an agreement.[5]

Certainly the bargaining resources of the Arab oil producers have surprised the Western world in the last few years. Saudi Arabia, Kuwait, and Libya are hardly "powers" in the conventional sense. Yet their ability to use the distribution of their raw materials as a source of bargaining influence has been remarkable. They forced significant changes in the foreign policies of the Western powers and Japan in a short period of time. Indeed, they may have begun a change in the way of life of some Western

[5] Keohane (1971) points out that, in addition to the ability of nations such as South Korea and Taiwan to draw United States support as a result of the United States interest in containment, these nations have had allies in the form of United States military services which have vested interests of their own in extensive United States support of these nations.

nations. In contrast to Taiwan and South Korea, whose ultimate hold over the United States government has been the destruction that they would experience if they were not supported, the Arab nations are not strong because of their weakness. Rather they are strong in spite of their weakness on most conventional indicators. Their small populations, modest economies, and limited military strength mean they are vulnerable to foreign attack. Yet they have valuable mineral resources that they can use to influence the actions of others. And so far they have relied successfully on the fact that neither the United States nor the Soviet Union is anxious to confront the other by intervening in an area of considerable interest to both.

In earlier eras too, small states were able to exert considerable influence in specific situations. During the decade or so of European conflict over Morocco, France had to win approval of its desire for a Moroccan protectorate. One of the nations interested in Morocco was Spain, hardly a great power in the early twentieth century. Spain was interested in the Mediterranean coast of Morocco directly across the sea from Spain. And here Spain was able to draw on an unexpected source of influence. Great Britain was concerned that the Mediterranean coast of Morocco stay out of the hands of another great power and that the coastline remain unfortified. A fortified position held by a major power would have threatened British colonial communications and perhaps even the British base at Gibraltar. So the British were also concerned that France not control the Mediterranean coast of Morocco. And the French were not able to drive a hard bargain on the division of Morocco. The Spanish, relying on support from the British, were able to gain a sphere of influence in Morocco larger than anything the French had originally anticipated. The strength of the Spanish position here was Spanish weakness. The British did not feel threatened with the Moroccan Mediterranean coast in Spanish hands.

Creating Usable Options

One implication of the two preceding sections is that bargaining influence is highly contextual. For example, it is difficult to imagine that the ability to airlift the supplies for a large city—Berlin 1948-49—would be crucial on a regular basis in international conflicts. And as the previous paragraphs have shown, conventional indices of national power do not reflect this contextual character adequately. They are too inflexible or too narrowly focused. An enterprise directed toward listing the sources of bargaining influence crucial to specific past and probable future conflicts would be misdirected. It would fail to be useful minimally on grounds of parsimony. The disparate factors—actual and speculative—that have been or might be influential in bargaining situations over the period of, say, 1890-1990 would be numerous, and simply listing them would probably confuse more than clarify. What is needed instead is a core or essence common to the variety of factors that have been important sources of bargaining influence. Unfortunately, the various factors— geographic position, control of the sea, strong allied support, to name just a few—do not appear to have a common thread. However, there do appear to be some common threads in their application. What makes these factors sources of bargaining influence is resourcefulness that sees and develops a connection between a source of influence and a problem and applies the one to the other.

"Resourcefulness" as used in the preceding paragraph is a vague term and must be specified more carefully. In part, the term refers to ingenuity or even problem-oriented brainstorming. In retrospect tactics such as the airlift, occupying the Rhineland, the Berlin wall, and an international conference in 1912 seem obvious responses to the problems faced by Truman, Hitler, Ulbricht, and Grey, respectively. But these tactics were not obvious before their actual use. In contrast to the options in a game matrix, these tactics were not preconceived and thus existing options that could simply be picked up and used. Rather, someone had to develop them as ideas and link them to the ongoing conflict. This may sound like a simple, even pedantic, task. Yet developing a solution to a severe foreign policy problem is a legitimate creative effort. Success in this endeavor is all the more impressive in that, as O. R. Holsti (1972) and others (Wiegele, 1973) show, creative thinking is attenuated under the traumatic conditions that severe conflicts produce. Creative ingenuity under these circumstances is particularly impressive.

But more than creative ingenuity is required in order to use tactics like the airlift. Ideas must be politically acceptable to the coalition necessary to support a policy. A partial mobilization of Russian forces in 1914 or a British-French invasion of the Rhineland are examples of ideas which, if they had been implemented, might have altered history considerably. They were not implemented because they could not be accepted by important coalition elements. So resourcefulness includes a practical political component that in some instances reduces to salesmanship. With these characteristics of resourcefulness in mind the conditions in the decision unit that are supportive of resourcefulness should be examined. Then some principles that guide creative policy efforts will be discussed.

Janis (1972), George (1972), and Cline (1974–75) all emphasize the utility of something similar to George's institutionalized multiple advocacy as a prerequisite for sweeping and penetrating policy analysis. Allowing the expression of multiple viewpoints may not guarantee sweeping and penetrating policy analysis, but the presence of multiple viewpoints favors such analysis. Policies that meet the changing needs of dynamic conflict situations are apt to arise with greater difficulty in the absence of some procedure similar to multiple advocacy. Several characteristics of the environment in which a decision unit operates are relevant from the standpoint of eliciting resourcefulness. To the degree that the views of a number of advisors are solicited, a chief executive opens the way for a reasonable spectrum of opinion and thus a variety of ideas. If the views of only a few individuals close to the chief executive are considered, then the range and variety of ideas will probably be narrower. For instance, Presidents Nixon and Ford were unquestionably served by an extraordinarily capable senior foreign policy advisor. Yet the system of severely limited access to important decisions and White House directed debate placed the burden for the bulk of policy creativity on a small group whose members were limited in the range of matters on which they could focus. It is conceivable that more open access and debate would have gotten important problems that Kissinger chose to put on the back burner—food, population, economic relations with Western Europe and Japan—more attention and might have elicited different perspectives of problems that he granted considerable attention.

Simply soliciting the views of a number of advisors does not assure that novel viewpoints will be broached, however. if the chief executive and/or unit heads below him are known for impatience with novel viewpoints or with any viewpoint that differs from the known or suspected position of superiors, novel suggestions will disappear over time. Even if superiors throughout the executive system are known for their openness to new and different ideas, it is probably a good idea to seek opinions at different levels of authority independently rather than in groups that cross levels of authority. International conflict episodes come and go, yet life within the bureaucracy goes on, and few bureaucrats desire an open difference of viewpoint with their superiors. During the Vietnam years the Johnson administration became notorious for its impatience with views that differed from those of administration kingpins or that expressed novel approaches to problems. It is conceivable that Johnson could have managed, as the Nixon administration did, to survive a very carefully orchestrated declaration of victory and have pulled out to let the South Vietnamese carry on. But, a suggestion of "Let's declare a victory and go home" would probably (and may actually) have earned a stern frown and reduced future access to policy making in the Johnson administration.

Soliciting a variety of views and rewarding novel suggestions facilitate the decision unit's search for means that apply the nation's resources to its bargaining problems in an efficient manner. As George (1972) and Hargrove (1973) point out, however, even these characteristics are no guarantee that sweeping and penetrating analysis will arise from the decision unit's deliberations. One problem may be that all the members of the decision unit share a common set of ideological blinders, so that each of them sees the situation pretty much as the others do. While the Cuban missile crisis was, by the standards of other United States cold war conflicts, a reasonably open situation with respect to novel viewpoints, the range of alternatives considered was limited. When Stevenson suggested an option a bit beyond the range of those being tossed around by the regular advisory group, he was bitterly criticized. Yet mutual withdrawal from bases in Cuba was certainly as reasonable as an attack on the Soviet installations, and withdrawal from Guantanamo would seem a modest price to pay to avoid the destruction of modern civilization.

So the cards are stacked against innovation and spectacular ideas. Most conflict decisions apply existing and recognized—thus highly conventional—sources of national power in highly conventional ways. Often the tactics used in bargaining arise from common parlance or government contingency plans. In 1914 Grey called for an international conference that he had tried without effect in 1911 over Morocco and successfully in

1912 over the Balkans (Snyder and Diesing, 1977). The air strike–invasion option became the immediate focus for attention in 1962 because the military actually had contingency plans for action of this nature. The blockade option surfaced quickly because the idea had already been suggested in the press and other public forums. In other words, the blockade had had an opportunity to become prominent in the minds of Kennedy's advisors. In 1911 Kiderlen-Waechter suggested sending German warships to southern Moroccan ports in order to impress the French with German determination. The initial ship to anchor at Agadir, the *Panther*, had grown notorious from other similar episodes of gunboat diplomacy (Vagts, 1956: 236). Ingenuity is the exception, not the rule. The "Trollope ploy" [6] of the 1962 missile crisis or the Berlin airlift (which was successful beyond the wildest expectations of those who introduced it) are unusual instances.

Sometimes applying a nation's conventional forms of power in conventional ways is sufficient. Whether or not this is true will depend on the appropriateness of these means for the specific context and on the relative power of and interests at stake for the contestants. Even if conventional approaches are not sufficient, they may be the best a decision unit can be reasonably expected to produce. But two major problems hamper conventional approaches. First, they will not be of much help to the nation if the conventionally recognized resources do not create options usable in the specific situation at hand—the French at Fashoda. Second, conventional forms of power are easily anticipated and thus relatively easy to balance. The French, fearful of standing alone in the West against Germany prior to the First World War, relied increasingly on a conventional source of influence—an alliance with Britain—in order to balance German power. Under these conditions strategies without flair or imagination (that is, with limited resourcefulness) are apt to cancel one another. The Agadir crisis is an excellent example of nations engaging in considerable effort and generating a great deal of risk for little benefit.

[6] This label was apparently coined retroactively by the participants to describe Robert Kennedy's suggestion that the United States ignore the Soviet Union's second, more demanding compromise proposal and accept the first. The term refers to the novels of Anthony Trollope through which runs a theme of acceptance of an offer never clearly made.

PRINCIPLES OF RESOURCEFULNESS

A better handle on the linkage between resources and usable options can be found by taking a look at some principles that guide resourcefulness. One of these principles is *blocking* the adversary's progress toward his goal. This particular objective has two aspects that recommend it. First, an action that blocks the adversary's progress has obvious value as a coercive probe that tests the adversary's tolerances. It forces the adversary to decide whether he really needs this particular goal and whether he is willing to struggle further for it. Second, blocking has communicative or signaling value, from the blocker's standpoint as well. Often a nation's statesmen do not understand that their actions constitute important challenges to others. Blocking their progress toward their goals is about as clear as possible a means of signaling them that they are challenging the blocking nation's crucial values. Two prominent examples of blocking actions are the Cuban blockade and the German move to anchor naval vessels at the southern Moroccan harbor of Agadir. The Cuban blockade caught the Soviet Union in the middle of its strategic deployment. It signaled to the Soviets that they were challenging important United States values and required the Soviets to reassess their own goals in light of this new information. The German warships at Agadir effectively blocked further French efforts to unilaterally solve the Moroccan question by occupying Morocco. The French were reluctant to push their control into southern Morocco for fear of precipitating a war with Germany—a war from which British support might well have been absent.

A second guideline for resourcefulness is *circumventing* the adversary's position. The purpose here is primarily coercive rather than communicative, and these actions often take the form of faits accomplis. If the adversary has a strong position, so that blocking it would be ineffective—or perhaps the adversary has himself undertaken a blocking action—this principle suggests looking for ways to circumvent his strong position so that the statesman's own objectives may still be achieved. Circumventing actions have had mixed success over the last century of international conflict. This alone is not particularly unusual, but circumventing activities, when successful, seem to have an intuitive, spur-of-the-moment quality as opposed to the conscious, strategic character of blocking actions. The Berlin airlift began as a temporary stalling measure. Only after several weeks of experience with the airlift did its potential for circumventing the Soviet commitment become realized. The Kaiser's visit and challenging speech at Tangier in 1905 that precipitated the first Moroccan or Algeciras crisis had mixed value. The Kaiser momentarily circumvented the French effort for a Moroccan protectorate by declaring that his government would carry on relations with the independent sultanate of Morocco. This step was successful in gaining several French concessions, including an international conference at Algeciras to determine the fate of Morocco. However, the Germans had little success at the conference. This circumventing action was not really part of a planned strategy; the Kaiser got carried away with a festive mood at Tangier and said more than he had intended. Another example of a circumventing ploy would be the Berlin wall. A wall is more easily depicted as a blocking action than as a circumventing action, so this categorization may seem strange. From the perspective of an individual who wished to leave the East for the West through Berlin, the wall was definitely a blocking activity. But from the standpoint of the East-West struggle the wall was a circumventing action. It circumvented issues for which the United States was willing to fight—military access to and preservation of West Berlin—and preserved the minimal Eastern demand—the economic viability of East Germany. The circumventing principle encompasses a range of activity, as not only the fait accompli but also the stall comes under this label. Characteristically, stalling is adopted when a situation looks bleak. The idea behind stalling is that things cannot get worse and sooner or later something better will turn up (Snyder and Diesing, 1977). Stalling can entail action—the airlift—or virtual inaction—Stalin's response to the airlift for several months.

Statesmen sometimes follow a principle of *detouring* in order to bring their resources to bear on a problem. In contrast to blocking and circumventing actions, which both relate to the crux of the existing conflict, detouring activity tries to shift the conflict into an arena in which the detouring party has a better chance to compete. The detouring party picks a related issue, a new forum for contesting the issue, or a different mode of competition that favors its position. In one respect the fact that crises occurred over Berlin at all was due to Soviet efforts to solve a larger German question. The central issue for the Soviet Union in 1948–49 and 1958–62 was a common policy toward Germany prompted by varying economic policies and by the introduction of tactical nuclear weapons to western Germany, respectively (Diesing, 1970). The Soviets turned to Berlin in each case because in Berlin the Soviets were in a position both to get the attention of the Western allies and to exert some coercive pressure. During the Cuban missile crisis, United States leaders feared that the Soviets would use Berlin to counter United States pressure in the Caribbean. Apparently these issues were not linked from the Soviet standpoint, or the linkage was perceived as unproductive. The Soviets did with some success link the Turkish situation with Cuba. The interest in conferences on issues—the Germans over Morocco in 1905–6 and the Russians over Bosnia in 1908–9—is sometimes a detouring action. In both of these cases the nation most interested in the conference was in a weak position and hoped the merits of its case in the formal multilateral setting of an international conference would offer a better settlement than the influence it could generate in informal, bilateral bargaining.

The United States involvement in a military struggle in Vietnam and adjacent areas offers another example of a detour. The central problem in the Indochina peninsula for the United States during the decade after the Geneva agreements of 1954 was that the government the United States chose to back in South Vietnam became increasingly unable to command the loyalty of the population. While the problem had military and, by some semantics, even international military aspects, it was in essence a political problem. A popular regime in South Vietnam could have managed local military difficulties. Yet the United States—perhaps unconsciously—chose increasingly to define the problem as a military one. In part the cold war ideology of the day with its emphasis on "communist aggression and insurgency" and America's world police role was responsible for this definition of the problem. Drawing on misleading analogies (Greece, Malaysia, the Philippines) contributed as well. But an important aspect of how this definition arose involved a series of practical questions such as: what could the United States do on its own to solve the problem; what sorts of activity would provide the greatest public image of ongoing progress; in what ways could the United States influence the South Vietnamese government to help itself? The most persuasive answers to questions such as these (at least from the perspectives of the United States leaders of the early and mid-1960s) were repeatedly military. It was by focusing on the military at the expense of the political situation that the

United States leaders felt their influence over events in Southeast Asia would be increased. So they detoured the problem into a military struggle.

In the summer of 1914 all three entente powers, but particularly the British, tried detouring through an international conference. The British had enjoyed some success with an international conference in the instance of the Balkan wars (1912–13), and they were hopeful once again to detour the most immediate contestants in the Balkan problems of 1914— Austria, Serbia, and Russia—from a path of struggling in the Balkans to the alternative of talking around a conference table. This British effort, in conjunction with several of the examples in preceding paragraphs, suggests that detouring attempts are usually ineffective. This conclusion is consistent with the origins of these efforts. Detouring is often the resort of disadvantaged parties that are seeking—sometimes desperately—any means of avoiding disaster.

Blocking, circumventing, and sometimes even detouring share a characteristic of shifting the burden of further action and risk to the adversary. That is, if the adversary wishes to avoid a setback, he has to escalate. The advantages of shifting this burden have been analyzed by Schelling (1966; 1960) and others (Young, 1968), and these advantages make blocking and circumventing frequent methods of linking a nation's sources of bargaining influence to policy. But these three principles of resourcefulness are not the only guidelines followed by statesmen. Two others, *"compellence"* and *force* (violence), find their way into bargaining in severe international conflicts as well. Both of these principles lack the characteristic shared by the three discussed above—shifting the burden of further action and risk to the adversary. Through compellence a party generally acquires for itself the burden of escalation.[7] Contrasting examples of the use of compellence are offered by the Fashoda and 1914 conflicts. The British use in the Fashoda case was relatively subtle, considering what they were doing. Without issuing an explicit threat the British managed to get the French to realize that if the French did not withdraw their small force from the Nile basin relatively quickly, the British would destroy the French force, and that additional repercussions might be felt in other

---

[7] Schelling (1966 and 1960) discusses compellence as a technique for transferring risk in the sense of the last clear chance to avoid violence. In practice it is difficult to use compellence as a device for transferring risk.

regions of the French colonial empire. The British coupled their stick in this instance with a carrot that consisted of a variety of procedural concessions that allowed the French to accept a substantive defeat gracefully.

In 1914 the Austrians initially used compellence with respect to Serbia. The Austrians drew up an ultimatum that essentially entailed Serbian loss of sovereignty for the foreseeable future. The Austrians stressed quick acceptance of the ultimatum as the only way for Serbia to avoid an Austrian invasion. For practical purposes the Serbs accepted the ultimatum, but the Austrians took advantage of Serbian questions on a few points to shift from compellence to the fifth principle of resourcefulness, force. The Austrians invaded Serbia and in the process touched off reactions throughout Europe that culminated in the First World War. While compellence may place the onus for initiating violence on the party using it (a British attack on the French force in the upper Nile region), successful use of compellence may enable a party to avoid violence altogether. The British did not have to attack the French force in the Nile basin; they persuaded the French through compellence to withdraw their small military unit. The use of force as in the case of Austria in 1914, however, virtually always necessarily involves violence.[8] And this characteristic makes force the most irrevocable and dangerous of the five principles of resourcefulness discussed here. A blocking action, a circumventing fait accompli, an attempt to detour a bilateral conflict into a broader, more formal international forum, and even compellence pressure can all be withdrawn after a period of time if they are successful or clearly inappropriate. But the use of force generally has irrevocable costs that are apt to exacerbate a conflict of interest even if the use of force resolves a conflict episode.

It is the salience these irrevocable costs have for statesmen, in fact, that reinforces the distinction between force and the other four principles discussed here. Blocking, circumventing, detouring, and compelling can all be coupled with the use of force, but this linkage is not necessary and is sometimes counterproductive. And the other four principles of resourcefulness are often used as techniques for achieving national objectives without crossing the threshold of violence. Blocking intercepts the adver-

---

[8] A modest Franco-German crisis over Morocco in 1909 contains examples of the use of force—French nationals forcing German nationals to act in certain ways at gunpoint—that did not cross the threshold of violence (Barlow, 1940).

sary's pursuit of goals the statesman finds objectionable. Circumventing helps the statesman achieve goals the adversary might contest or is contesting. Detouring shifts the conflict into a forum advantageous to the statesman. Compellence puts pressure on the adversary to relinquish objectives already obtained. While force can be a part of any of these of forts, force also merits discussion as an independent principle of resourcefulness. In this sense force may be used to destroy the resources the adversary has at his disposal. It is in this sense that the Austrians used force against Serbia in 1914. The existence of Serbia was considered a grave threat by the Austrian leaders and they wished to destroy this threat (Fischer, 1967; Albertini, 1966).

USABLE OPTIONS AND BARGAINING PROCESSES

If the general strength or weakness of a nation is a poor indicator of the bargaining influence that a party brings to specific conflict situations, it is nevertheless necessary for a party to have sources of influence that support its position. That is, a bargaining nation must have resources that create options usable for gaining influence over the adversary in the situation at hand if the nation is to expect a successful outcome. This necessity raises a question of interaction with the bargaining processes discussed in the preceding chapter. What impact does information interpretation, for instance, hold for the creation of usable options? Do decision makers perceive situations accurately enough to recognize the types of options that they need? Or do they instead misperceive these matters and flounder helplessly? They do both. But on the whole they do a better job of dredging up the resources they perceive they need than they do of perceiving their needs accurately. That is, resourcefulness is a more successful endeavor considered on its own than perception of the problem. But since perception of the problem is a more fundamental aspect of bargaining, resourcefulness is sometimes misplaced or even counterproductive.

Consider the example of the German warships at Agadir in 1911. Kiderlen perceived the need to block the French from consolidating their control over Morocco. If the French were allowed to do this they would have a fait accompli and the German position would be weaker. Kiderlen filed through some standard techniques of the diplomacy of the day and came up with warships to Agadir. If in fact the French had still been maintaining a stance of no compensation to Germany, this would have been a plausible move. But the French had altered their stance and were willing to accept the principle of compensation. And the interpretation many French leaders made of the *Panther* at Agadir was that the Germans found anything short of a partition of Morocco unacceptable. Even Schoen, the German ambassador to Paris, admitted that the timing of the *Panther* could not have been worse (1922: 146–47).

In a more recent example, the Soviet Union for a variety of reasons came up with the imaginative idea of a deployment of strategic nuclear weapons in Cuba. From the Soviet standpoint this deployment would give the socialist world a strong position from which to deter future United States efforts to invade Cuba; the deployment also provided a modest improvement with respect to the strategic weapons deficit the Soviet Union faced; and by stressing the principle of reciprocity between the United States and the Soviet Union—each superpower deploying forward-based strategic weapons—the Soviets hoped to obtain the status they felt they deserved as a great power both in the socialist world and on a global basis. All this once again seems plausible enough in the abstract. But the Soviet Union failed to consider that the United States would not perceive the introduction of adversary strategic nuclear weapons into its sphere of influence to be simply undesirable, as the Soviets had done when the positions were reversed.

Alternative Strategies and Their Use

What forms of strategy ought to be followed in severe international conflict situations? Several strategic options exist (George, Hall, and Simons, 1971: 15–21), and within each strategic category are myriad opportunities for resourcefulness. Three different strategies will be discussed here: adaptation and the manipulative strategies of coercion and accommodation. These distinct strategies may be appropriate for different situations or within conflict episodes at different points in time. Choices of which strategy to use when have a great deal to do with a bargainer's success in bringing his sources of bargaining influence to bear on the bargaining problem he faces. Several issues connected with the use of these three strategy options are discussed below.

Distinguishing Characteristics of Adaptive and Manipulative Action

An actor adapts to his environment by adjusting to it. Adaptation is appropriate when the actor feels that, while the environment may be predictable, it is in the short run inalterable, or at least the costs of altering it are too high. Savage's famous omelette example is a classic instance of adaptive activity. The dilemma here is whether to break the sixth egg of an omelette directly into a pan containing five other eggs that will all be lost if the sixth egg is bad or whether to break the sixth egg into a separate dish that must needlessly be washed if the egg is good. While the theoretical dilemma depends in part on the particular values assigned to each of the four outcomes—extra dish/pan only × good egg/bad egg—and on the precise nature of the decision rule, the practical solution is basically contingent on the probable nature of the egg. If bad eggs are common, people adapt by breaking eggs first into separate dishes. If bad eggs are exceedingly rare, people feel few qualms about breaking eggs into dishes containing other eggs. While it is true that individuals in our society attempt over the long haul to manipulate relevant aspects of the environment in terms of better poultry breeding, incubation, shipping, and wholesale and retail handling processes, the person with the dilemma in the example must adapt. The egg in his hand is either good or bad; there is nothing he can do to manipulate the character of this egg; so he adapts by acting in a reasonable fashion based on his prediction about the egg. Constraints imposed by the environment—including adversary nations— are accepted in adaptive activity, and the actor shifts his activity until it is consonant with these constraints.

The difference between adaptive and manipulative activity can be stated simply. Manipulative activity attempts to alter the environment. Here the environment is not the only source of constraints on activity. The actor's goals also provide constraints, and in at least some instances this latter source overrides some aspects of the existing environmental conditions. The environment's resistance to change is generally considered in determining when and at what point manipulation will be initiated. And the environment may overcome manipulation attempts. Manipulation is an inherent aspect of international conflicts. Each national unit attempts to manipulate, through both coercion and accommodation, resisting elements of the environment, such as its adversaries, to gain acceptance of its objectives.

Adaptation is clearly distinct conceptually from coercion. But the abstract distinction between adaptation and accommodation is sometimes cloudy. A discussion of tactics relevant to adaptation will help to clarify the distinction. Adaptation entails a passive approach toward the aspect of the external environment that is creating the problem. Although adaptation may require active policies of some sort, these policies are not directed toward manipulating the portion of the environment that is creating the problem. For instance, over the last decade, during which the Soviet Union has achieved parity in strategic weapons and superiority in conventional forces in Eurasia and in adjacent waters, the United States has made little effort to manipulate the Soviet Union in order to maintain its superiority in some armament categories. SALT and MBFR in some limited aspects are manipulative, and the Soviets may well be suspicious that many aspects of these two negotiations are so motivated. But the United States has essentially accepted the new power of the Soviet Union and has adapted to this changing situation by following a less ambitious foreign policy than the world policeman role envisioned little more than a decade ago. [9] The United States has taken some active measures—developing Iran's military power in order to assure the "stability" of the Persian Gulf—that are compatible with the increased Soviet power and the reduced United States role. In fact, these active measures may be viewed by United States policy makers as necessitated by the other two changes. But the tactics of adaptation itself are largely passive. Adaptation often involves a change in aspiration level, and unopposed

[9] To be sure, factors other than the growth of Soviet strategic and forward-based conventional military forces contribute to this "retreat from empire." More realistic attitudes toward the ability of United States intervention to affect the forces shaping developments, particularly in the Third World, as well as the obvious need to apply resources to a variety of pressing domestic problems are a pair of additional important contributors.

policies commensurate with either lowered or raised aspirations are relevant for adaptation. In this sense adaptive activity amounts essentially to realizing new capabilities that are uncontested—filling power vacuums—or withdrawing gracefully from overextended positions before these positions are explicitly assaulted. Adaptation may also be a means of buying time. That is, a nation may adapt to environmental factors in the short run in order to prepare for a demanding struggle or to wait for a particularly propitious opportunity to deal manipulatively with problems presented by the environment. Either way the tactics here are apt to be those of unopposed and perhaps even unconscious advance and retreat. Sometimes activity that is adaptive with respect to some groups is coercive or accommodative with respect to others. Increased postwar Soviet influence in the Balkans was adaptive activity with respect to the major powers, coercive with respect to some local political groups, and accommodative in terms of providing for some economic needs within the region. With the distinction between adaptive and manipulative activity in mind, the following paragraphs will examine the merits and drawbacks of each form of activity.

Adaptive activity is an absolute essential in a nation's list of strategic options. No nation can challenge all others on all fronts. The resources—particularly the leadership's attention—of even the most powerful nations are limited, and each nation must reserve the privilege to ignore certain potential conflicts. For instance, in contrast to the stiff resistance the United States offered to a Soviet military buildup in the Caribbean, the United States offered no resistance whatsoever to the Soviet naval buildup in the Mediterranean. Instead of manipulating the Soviet Union in the latter case, the United States adapted to this changing situation. The United States mobilized considerable resources for a conflict on the Indochina peninsula, but mobilized virtually no forces during the same time period for several conflicts in Africa; and the resources mobilized for conflicts in South Asia during this span of time were definitely modest by the standards of Southeast Asia. Britain during the latter half of the nineteenth century remained relatively aloof from the quarrels among the powers in Europe, but kept a close eye on developments in the colonial world. During the first decade of this century, British attention shifted. Britain's preoccupation with the colonial arena began to fade, and British governments began to view serious implications in a variety of continental developments. In a more specific example, the French accepted as inevitable and adapted to Italian, British, and Spanish claims on compensation for a French Moroccan protectorate. Yet they rejected similar German claims and struggled with the Germans several times over this issue.

The fact that adaptive activity is handy for keeping nations out of bitter conflict each time the existing situation changes does not explain why nations respond to some environmental changes by adapting and to others with manipulative efforts. Probably no exhaustive listing can be provided, but a number of recurring considerations can be discussed. Although the first possibility is growing increasingly rare with the growth of global politics, there are still examples of changes in international conditions that are not "seen." [10] Conflicts in Central Africa have had a low profile for United States leaders until recently. Neither border altercations among a variety of African nations (Uganda-Rwanda for example) nor severe domestic strife (Nigeria-Biafra) captured the attention of the United States policy makers. United States leaders were, of course, aware of these conflicts, but the conflicts were not cause for major concern or resource mobilization. In these instances the reason for indifference appears to be that these conflicts were not perceived to threaten United States interests in any important way. The conflicts were generally interpreted in the United States as isolated, and even men who saw the sinister arms of an international communist conspiracy elsewhere were hard pressed for a similar vision of most African conflicts. Further, these conflicts occurred in a region in which the United States has few important economic interests, and since the United States' major adversaries had not, until recently, appeared particularly interested in this region either, few concrete diplomatic or military interests arose for the United States from this region.

Another possibility through which a nation opts for adaptive as opposed to manipulative activity is the impossibility—or at least extreme difficulty—of the latter. For instance, with respect to removing Soviet strategic weapons from the Caribbean, the United States had the advantages of a long precedent of great power privilege in this area, overwhelming

---

[10] By "seen" reference is made to the distinction raised in chapter 3. The ambassador saw the bubbles in the seltzer, the frayed arm on the chair in the foreign minister's office, and numerous other things, but he focused on the foreign minister's threatening message.

military strength in the Caribbean, and the reasonably strong—seemingly even sincere—support of the other nations in the area. The United States enjoyed none of these advantages in the Mediterranean. It is not certain that the absence of these advantages made challenging the Soviet naval buildup in the Mediterranean futile. The United States could have challenged this buildup, and it is conceivable that the United States could have brought enough resources to bear to arrest the Soviet effort. But the price would have been immense—and the benefits highly disputed. At the very least, the costs would have included some risk of a military conflict with the Soviet Union and thus movement away from the détente atmosphere of the post-Cuba period. Resources would have been shunted away from other problems and used for this conflict. So while the United States could have reacted to the Soviet Mediterranean buildup with a manipulative policy, the large costs and modest benefits—even if the manipulative effort had been successful—argued against such a course. Instead prudence suggested that the United States simply accept this change to the status quo and adapt to the new situation by altering some aspects of its policies that were no longer feasible under the new conditions.

Still another reason for choosing to adapt to a particular situation arises neither from the lack of importance of nor from the difficulty of dealing with the situation but from circumstances of resources being stretched to the limit in order to handle a variety of other, existing problems (Howe, 1971). The perception that the United States was in such a predicament was widespread in Western Europe during the era of active United States involvement in Southeast Asia, and this perception contributed to problems within the Atlantic alliance. The Western European nations feared that the United States government had its hands full with the domestic and international problems arising from the conflict in Southeast Asia. Thus, if an important issue were raised in Europe or the Middle East, the Western European NATO members were fearful that the United States would not be able to free the attention and mobilize the additional resources this problem might reasonably demand. In the first decade of this century the British began to realize that if they continued to concentrate their attention and resources on the colonial arena, they might not be able to deal adequately with a variety of increasingly important continental problems. After 1890 the preoccupation of German leaders was the problem of a two-front war—an instance of having too many problems that are too important to overlook. The Soviet Union faces a similar dilemma today, and the prospect has prompted considerable Soviet effort toward détente on the Western front.

Adaptation is necessary for all the reasons advanced above, but adaptive activity is designed to deal with problems by avoiding them. Some problems are too important to be handled in this fashion, and it is for problems such as these that manipulative strategies are necessary. Members of national decision units are apt to disagree about whether particular issues merit manipulative as opposed to adaptive responses. Navy spokesmen—and some Zionists—were more concerned about the Soviet buildup in the Mediterranean than were other United States leaders, and the adaptive response the United States followed in this instance indicates, among other things, that these groups were unable to build a coalition around their position. In 1911 the Kaiser had just returned from a pleasant visit with the British King. He was optimistic about improved relations with Britain, and he was reluctant to press the Moroccan question—which he felt did not promise either French cooperation with German objectives or fulfillment of important German needs even if the French were willing to cooperate—and thus endanger what he perceived as growing Anglo-German rapprochement. Kiderlen and others in the Wilhelmstrasse saw the issues differently and were able to argue for modest measures that, once granted, put them in a reasonable position to bargain within the German government—Kiderlen's two resignation attempts in July—for further measures at a later date. These instances are examples of cases in which the importance of the issue, its relation to other issues, the possibility of resolving it, and the availability of usable options were subject to different views.

Other examples—the crises over Berlin—have been generally considered important throughout the decision units involved, and cases such as these are not initially relevant to adaptive strategy. These cases require manipulative action in order to achieve goals that the adversary contests. In circumstances such as these adaptive activity is limited in relevance to a later point in time. After a confrontation point has been reached, one party may determine that, owing to the other party's overwhelming strength or as a result of determining that an issue is too modest to merit further struggle, it will no longer contest the issue. In the case of the adversary's overwhelming strength, the decision probably represents lowering objectives so that the nation's goals no longer conflict with those of the environment—Fashoda (1898). In the case of issue clarification the nation may find that its earlier perceptions were simply erroneous and there is no need to manipulate the adversary in order to obtain the nation's objectives. According to Howe (1971), for instance, the United States knew by September of 1958 that the Chinese were not going to invade Quemoy, since the Chinese did not commit their air force to the conflict. So while adaptive activity is not irrelevant to serious conflicts, it is not appropriate as an initial strategy.

Manipulative activity's strengths counter the weaknesses of adaptive activity. Manipulation is designed to deal with an adversary whose goals conflict with those of the statesmen's own nation. But manipulation also has drawbacks. Coercive activity can exacerbate conflicts rather than deriving a favorable compromise solution. Exacerbating an existing conflict by engaging additional issues or by angering the adversary through bellicose moves is not a problem for adaptive activity. If adaptive activity exacerbates a conflict, it tends to do so over the long term by giving the adversary an impression of inadequate resolve. This is a problem shared with accommodative manipulation. Problems common to refusing to make an issue of a matter or offering the adversary a concession in order to resolve a conflict are that the lack of resistance may whet the adversary's appetite and lead him to raise his aspirations or that the adversary may underestimate the seriousness of this and perhaps other problems. But these issues are best discussed in the next section.

Distinguishing Characteristics of Coercive and Accommodative Action

Within the realm of manipulative activity there are two strategy options: coercive and accommodative. Coercion involves creating or threatening to create adverse conditions. For example Soviet leaders in the 1948–49 Berlin conflict wanted to gain Western cooperation in a common stance toward a nonthreatening Germany. So the Soviets blocked

Western ground access to West Berlin. This was a coercive action designed to induce changes in the actions of the Western powers. At best the Soviets hoped the costs of Soviet noncooperation over Berlin would alter the Western attitude toward cooperation on the overall question. At worst the Soviets thought they would force a Western exodus from Berlin. Manipulation need not be coercive, however. Manipulation can occur through promises as well as threats. Manipulation of this sort operates through the mechanism of creating or promising to create propitious conditions. Khrushchev was able to get a noninvasion pledge with respect to Cuba from the United States by stressing that this action would lead to a withdrawal of Soviet strategic nuclear weapons. Here one state attempted to alter the preferences of another by making the nature of the outcome it desired more attractive to the other.

COERCIVE AND ACCOMMODATIVE TACTICS

Coercive tactics have generally raised more interest than either accommodative or adaptative ones. Coercive tactics are typically discussed in terms of their use by the adversary (Hitler and, in the West, the Soviets), although the basic tools of coercion—commitments and threats—are available to and are used by most nations at one time or another. Both commitment and threat tactics have been discussed so thoroughly and admirably in recent literature (Snyder, 1972; George, Hall, and Simons, 1971; Schelling, 1966 and 1960) that going into this area in detail seems unwarranted. Instead only two areas will be broached here.

The first is the distinction between commitments and threats. As used here, "commitments" involve an irrevocable choice to act in a particular fashion. This choice is clear to the committed actor, and his problem tends to be communicating his choice credibly to his adversary. Threats are efforts to induce some change in the adversary's attitudes and/or actions through the application or contingent application of punishment. Conceptually these two actions are distinct, but distinctions between them are blurred in actual practice involving various national audiences. For example, an existing tacit commitment on the part of the United States government to defend the coast of Connecticut from foreign attack is probably not perceived as a threat by any other nation. But the commitment of the United States to support Chiang's government on Taiwan (particularly coupled with unofficial references about "unleashing" Chiang) represented both a commitment and a threat. For the United States there was a commitment to support a regime that by virtue of its existence represented a threat to the Chinese government on the mainland. United States strategic bases in East and Southeast Asia carried a similar dual meaning. For the United States they represented a commitment to contain the expansion of communist powers. To the Chinese they have unquestionably represented a threat. The two meanings can even coincide. The buildup of United States forces for the invasion of Cuba in 1962 was perceived as both a commitment and a threat by both the United States and the Soviet Union. The point here is that the target may perceive a different action (signal) than the initiator of coercion intends to send. And unless the initiator is aware of this possibility, he may well misinterpret the target's response.

A second and related point is that honestly communicating existing commitments to an adversary—warning the adversary of these commitments—is a more productive endeavor than using threats that develop commitments as a by-product (Snyder, 1969; Schelling, 1960: 123–24). Such threats have both communicative and committal value; communicating them develops or at least strengthens the commitment to act as the threat indicates, and these actions might be called committal threats. Warnings have only communicative value; they alert the adversary to a commitment that existed before its communication to the adversary. Warnings are better able to appeal to the target's sense of empathy and reciprocity than threats which develop new and larger commitments during the course of a conflict. So warnings are less prone to engage additional values or to drive the adversary from a deliberative perspective on the conflict. Yet warnings can be made as effective in attracting the adversary's attention as the more contrived committal threats. So extravagant claims and tactics have little to recommend them over more conservative warnings.

Explicit compromise bids or concessions are the basic tactic of accommodation. Concessions vary in terms of characteristics such as size, importance of substantive issues, mutualness, reversibility, enforceability, and clarity of offer. And these differences give concessions highly variable impact on the course of bargaining. For instance, a Soviet proposal in the mid-1950s to reduce inventories of strategic weapons and their delivery systems was quite a different sort of concession than the Soviet proposal to neutralize an independent Austria. Given the technology of the day and the mutual antagonism to on-site inspection—United States proposals for such inspection notwithstanding—concessions on strategic weapons were unenforceable and would have been easy to reverse in a clandestine fashion. Thus this concession was highly suspect to United States statesmen. The neutralization of Austria was less easily reversible owing to the visibility of potential violations, although the neutralization was not easily enforceable and represented a gamble and a goodwill gesture on the part of the Soviet leaders. Nitze (1974–75: 142–43) discusses a number of procedures that can be used in presenting concessions in order to gain a favorable bargain. In general, procedures such as a statesman's getting his adversary to accept his version of a draft agreement so that the issues are discussed in his terms or exploiting the nuance differences between the "same" word in different languages are appropriate for the negotiating table near the end of a conflict when a basic understanding has been reached. Other procedures, such as using intelligence tools to learn the internal debates and positions of the adversary, are not limited in relevance to accommodation but are useful in coercion as well.

USING COERCION PRODUCTIVELY

Coercion is unquestionably a crucial strategy for international conflicts. Through coercive actions some nations force other nations to relinquish values that would otherwise not be relinquished. Nevertheless, coercion carries concomitant dangers which place limitations on its effective use. One problem with coercive strategies is that they may engage additional values for the adversary and thus make concession all the more costly for him. The primary consideration here is the target's perception of the coercer's goals. If the target perceives the adversary as using *limited coercion* in order to achieve *limited goals* that are clearly of *central importance* to him, then dysfunctional resistance to coercive pressure by the target is minimized. Minimizing this resistance does not guarantee compliance. The coercer may be pressing the target on an issue of crucial importance to the target. But minimizing this resistance ought to maximize the likelihood of target compliance on any specific issue. To the degree that coercion exceeds appropriate levels and needlessly humiliates the adversary, resistance is apt to increase. To the degree that the adversary's position seems open to whatever can be achieved through coercive measures rather than being clearly limited to specific issues, the target's resistance is apt to increase. And to the degree that the objectives for which this coercion is undertaken are perceived by the target to be peripheral as opposed to central objectives of the coercing party, the target's resistance is apt to increase.

International anarchy and the concomitant sovereignty enjoyed by the various units of the international system create a sense of rough equality among nations. Often, through their own resources or through alliance arrangements, a rough equality actually prevails among nations. Yet threats and related coercive measures are inherently destructive of this equality, real or imagined. Through coercion one nation gives itself the right to tell another how to act, and this action violates proper relations among equals. The most dangerous aspect of the violation is that it occurs at the whim of the coercing party. Statesmen normally understand that nations occasionally have to get tough in order to protect themselves from conscious or even unconscious challenges to their crucial values. Statesmen find particularly disturbing, however, actions that appear to be taken in the hope of windfalls. That is, a statesman may try coercive activity for less than crucial values in the hope of cheap gains. Activity of this sort is virtually certain to engage additional values for the target. The concern here is the specter of acquiescence in one instance of whimsical coercion leading to ever more frequent and severe efforts at coercion. Thus one aspect about the Soviet deployment of strategic weapons in Cuba that bothered Kennedy's advisors was that if the Soviet Union was able to sustain this particular challenge to the United States values, it might be emboldened to engage in new challenges in Latin America and Europe. A norm of restraint in the sense of limiting actions to support of legitimate national interests is necessary and is often practiced by nations in their coercive relations with others. This norm of restraint carries along with it the possibility for abuse. Any one nation is better off not recognizing the norm followed by others, and in the anarchical international environment no supranational enforcers of this norm exist. The norm prevails to the degree that the various members of the international system refuse to tolerate coercive acts other than those of a most obviously central character.

Irritation may also enter as a counterproductive aspect of coercive activity in that particularly blatant coercive acts may drive the target from a strategic or deliberative attitude toward the conflict (a game) to a spasmodic or emotional attitude (a fight). This danger is less prominent than the previous one of value engagement. Probably few cases of an entire decision unit being driven from a deliberative perspective by provocation exist in modern times. Individual statesmen do lose a deliberative perspective, however. Late in the Agadir conflict in 1911 the Kaiser, who had originally been a restraining influence on the foreign minister, was greatly perturbed by a French ultimatum in conjunction with French press articles that characterized him as "Wilhelm the Timid." The articles, coming on the heels of the ultimatum, drove the Kaiser into a rage in which he urged strong action on Kiderlen.

Coercive acts that are perceived by the target to be capricious, whimsical, vicarious, or vindictive are particularly dangerous. As Milburn (1973) points out, a target's compliance with coercion is apt to be associated with the target's perception of contingency. That is, will the coercion cease if compliance is rendered? If the coercing party can convince the target that the efforts stem from his pressing, essential need for limited actions on the target's part, compliance is more likely than if neither the urgency of the demands nor their limited nature is emphasized. Demands that seem to the target to arise without warning carry an aura of capriciousness or even whimsy about them. Demands that are not clearly limited raise fears in the target that the coercer is acting vicariously—that is, the coercer does not value the issues in conflict so much as the target's pain—or vindictively. In each of these instances the target may legitimately begin to doubt that he can meet the coercing party's demands. If the demands are indeed capricious rather than crucial, new demands may be raised more or less at the coercer's whim. Demands that the target can meet with difficulty if at all are clues that what the adversary may really be after is to see the target squirm. Each of these perceptions couples compliance in the present instance more firmly to increasing frequency and severity of future demands.

For a nation undertaking coercive action, it is no easy task to remain within the limits of modest coercion for limited objectives that are central to the coercer's goal structure. What matters is not that the coercing party perceive the situation in this fashion but that the target perceive the activity this way. The earlier suggestions are all couched in terms of the target's perceptions. As the preceding chapter pointed out, these perceptions are apt to be inaccurate, and with specific reference to the problems of coercive strategy, targets' perceptions are apt to err by perceiving modest coercion designed to gain limited central goals as virtually unlimited, cavalier manipulation than to err by underestimating the significance of the adversaries' moves. So one problem a nation using coercion faces is that of developing a coercive strategy in such a manner that its impact on the target is not counterproductive. Targets of coercion cannot really be expected to and probably never perceive the coercive efforts as the initiator intends them to. There are almost certainly some dysfunctional aspects to all coercive actions stemming from the deleterious impact of coercion on the target. What is crucial to the success of coercive activity is that these dysfunctional aspects not grow so large that the target crosses the fine line separating compliance from resistance and conflict escalation. Since statesmen who engage in coercion also misperceive their adversaries, this point is of particular importance. It is not uncommon for statesmen to perceive the targets of their coercive measures as disinclined to resist in the face of the statesman's own show of force.

With these restrictions in mind, some guidelines for the use of coercive activity ought to be developed. The first of these relates to the constraint that coercion must be perceived by the target as being limited and appropriate to the situation rather than as a blatant attempt to humiliate him. From this standpoint an incremental signal series that begins with mild-mannered signals and gradually increases in coercive impact until the objectives of the signal series are achieved is an attractive option. Several factors may hamper such a signal series, however. The first of these is that while avoiding the dysfunctional aspects of coercion the statesman has to get the adversary's attention before a signal series can accomplish its goal. President Kennedy gave the Soviets a series of verbal signals that the United States would not accept Soviet strategic weapons in Cuba, but these messages were vague and designed primarily for domestic consumption, and the first message that got through was the blockade. The Soviet Union sent a series of messages about nuclear weapons in West Germany to the United States in the year before the conflict that began in late 1958. The United States never did understand the substantive issue and focused on the six-month time limit of a November 1958 message instead (Diesing, 1970). A second factor is that, particularly in crises, a need exists for an urgent signal to prevent an immediate disaster. A third problem with an incremental approach is that such a signal series can gain a domestic momentum apart from any purposes of communicating with the adversary. Domestic factions that benefit from the various signals—stages of limited war, for instance—may struggle to maintain these measures long after their signaling value has dissipated. Finally, a series of signals that gradually escalates may create in the target's mind the perception that the signaler is increasing his demands rather than the severity of his communications about stable demands. Given the nature of these problems, two specifications need to be made (Lockhart, 1975). First, a signal series should be designed to gain feedback quickly before the various signals become domestic institutions. And second, even the initial signals of the series should carry a sharpness that distinguishes them from background diplomacy and thus attracts the target's attention. In order to attract the adversary's attention, however, the public humiliation of a severe threat is not always necessary. Stern but secret diplomacy about Soviet strategic weapons in Cuba appears to have accomplished in 1970 what brought the world to the brink of nuclear war eight years earlier (Kalb and Kalb, 1974; Quester, 1971).[11] But, for instances in which the urgency of the situation demands that the adversary alter his activity immediately, a blocking action as low-key as possible is ideal.

The second constraint involves limiting the goals for which coercion is undertaken. If the coercive activity is prudently enough planned so that the adversary remains within a deliberative state of mind, the limitations on the goals for which coercion is undertaken are often crucial. While in particular instances importance may hinge on specific limitations—asking for X but not for Y—the importance of specific limitations is highly contextual. The central concern here is with the *existence* of limitations, so that the target can recognize the demands as limited. Once again, this endeavor must work under less than ideal conditions. The target's initial perceptions tend to exaggerate the implications of coercive measures, and verbal statements that demands are limited are apt to be unconvincing. Nonverbal indices—as opposed to signals—such as the disposition of

[11] But in 1970 Nixon had the advantage of being able to draw upon what Kennedy had done in 1962.

forces or the coercer's response to the target's own probing activity are generally of considerably more importance. For instance, the Soviets deployed troops in defensive configurations in the Berlin area in the middle of August 1961 The United States understood this deployment, which had been preceded by a message from the Soviets that possible forthcoming activities would be defensive (Diesing, 1970). The target will probably want to verify on indices he considers reliable the extent of his adversary's objectives. But this still places important burdens on the coercing decision unit. There is always the temptation to expand goals once a conflict is under way. Some of Kennedy's advisors thought the Soviet deployment of strategic weapons in Cuba provided an excellent excuse to change the nature of the government in Cuba. Some of Kiderlen's backers thought warships at Agadir would serve as a base for taking the southern Moroccan Sous Valley. So what the target sees when he picks an index he considers reliable is important. If the military is preparing for future contingencies that are not supported by the nation's political leaders, the target's perceptions of exaggerated implications will be confirmed. If the target probes a particular point and the response is slow and grudging because some members of the coercer's decision unit are pressing for an expansion of goals, the target will not receive an impression of limited objectives on his adversary's part.

The third constraint is that the goals for which coercion is undertaken be important or central rather than peripheral or whimsical. Some issues—the integrity of the homeland—appear at first glance to offer little difficulty. Yet claims in areas of shifting borders for what was the homeland a century or even a quarter of a century ago are not always viewed as sincere by targets but often as excuses for generally hostile attitudes. Perhaps the most important caveat here is that new demands should not be raised during the course of a conflict. There is no surer method for convincing the target that the challenger is striving for whatever he can get than to raise his demands during the course of the bargaining. Even the Chamberlain cabinet was exceedingly upset when Hitler raised his demands during the course of the Bad Godesberg conferences. Beyond this suggestion of stable positions, the position taken by the challenger is far better off in having some obvious aspect that appeals to the target's sense of justice. When this aspect is present, the target can empathize with the adversary's claims to some degree. At a minimum the target can see that such a claim could be made by reasonable men. Thus the claim cannot be preemptively dismissed as the rhetoric of madmen. Khrushchev's six-month ultimatum during the 1958–62 Berlin conflict violated both these principles from the standpoint of United States decision makers. The time limit was perceived as an increase in demands that was not justifiable from the Western standpoint. Another appeal with strong potential is reciprocity. This appeal seems to work better when the parties to a conflict perceive themselves as equals (Frei, 1974). The Soviets had some success when they compared their installations in Cuba to the United States installations in Turkey (Gromyko, 1971; Kennedy, 1971).

These paragraphs on coercion can be tied together through a brief discussion of bargaining norms. Statesmen are concerned about matters such as equality, justice, reciprocity, and honesty. Statesmen are concerned when they perceive themselves, as the German statesmen did over French Moroccan compensation diplomacy, to be less than equals in the eyes of their counterparts in other nations. Statesmen exhibit deep emotion over the justness of the status quo—the West over West Berlin—or of legitimate national interests which require altering existing conditions—the East over West Berlin. Statesmen usually feel that their counterparts in other nations need to be reminded to restrain their actions either to those justifiable by the status quo or to changes necessitated by legitimate national interest. Statesmen are easily upset, as the French were by German gunboat diplomacy in 1911, by offending acts of counterparts that they are certain the counterparts would not want to experience as recipients. And statesmen get upset—as Izvolsky, the Russian foreign minister, was at the Austrian annexation of Bosnia-Herzegovina—when they perceive they cannot trust their counterparts in other nations to communicate fully and accurately on important issues. Some coercive acts violate these norms; others do not. A few coercive acts actually foster or reestablish the norms. Values are engaged by actions that appear to others to violate these norms. When the opponent is violating norms, he is a brigand. And resistance is justified in the name of a collective need to restore the norms—the international counterpart of law and order. The seriousness of the violation depends in part on how widely the action is perceived to be a violation of a norm. Izvolsky stood virtually alone in his wrath at Aehrenthal's lack of candor over Bosnia. But Hitler's prevarications attracted a wider audience. The guidelines for coercion discussed in the paragraphs above are designed to keep coercive activity within accepted norms.

Walton and McKersie (1965) develop a distinction related to this discussion of norms. Conflicting parties may hold different orientations toward conflicts. One possibility is a problem-solving orientation. A party with such an orientation views the conflict of interest as a problem to be worked out in a fashion acceptable to all the parties involved. Or, if this is impossible, a statesman with a problem-solving orientation will at least be interested in reducing the deleterious aspects of a solution to a minimum. Another possible orientation is a competitive outlook. A party with this sort of orientation seeks to win the conflict of interest. National leaders with problem-solving orientations, such as Kennedy in the Cuban crisis of 1962, will have relatively few difficulties keeping their coercive actions within the limits suggested in this section. Competitive statesmen, such as Aehrenthal in the Bosnian conflict of 1908–9, will tend to have a more difficult time keeping their coercive actions within these same limits.

USING ACCOMMODATION PRODUCTIVELY

Accommodation is equally central to the conduct of international conflicts. Coercion for the purpose of resolving a conflict of interest is usually meaningless unless it elicits accommodation. Conflicts that are resolved normally include some form of accommodation. The problems that plague coercive action—engaging additional issues or driving the adversary from a deliberative perspective on the problem—do not plague accommodative strategies. Accommodation is not without drawbacks, however.

For one thing, a conciliatory approach stressing mutual compromise may be interpreted by the adversary as an indication that the issue at hand is not particularly important. Under these circumstances a well-intentioned effort to avoid increasing the stakes for the adversary may well fail to generate the pressure necessary to shake essential conncessions from the adversary. When decorous efforts are ignored, brushed aside, or otherwise repulsed, however, the party making the proposals may be moved to precipitous escalation through frustration and even anger. For instance, during the early years of this century German statesmen tried repeatedly to get the French to negotiate the future of Morocco with them as well as with the Italians, British, and Spanish (Barlow, 1940). Their initial mild-mannered requests were brushed aside by the French who thought that the issue was of little importance to the Germans. Between 1905 and 1911, however, a series of crises occurred between France and Germany because of German dissatisfaction over the Moroccan question.

Another important difficulty for accommodation lies in the potential for compromise to be misconstrued by the adversary as weakness, in which case compromise initiatives may only whet his appetite. This problem is particularly important in that, as shown earlier, there is often a bureaucratic momentum that urges increased goals during the course of a conflict. If a coercing party runs directly into a concession on the target's part, restraining this domestic pressure will be all the more difficult. The crux of the solution to this dilemma involves the timing of compromise initiatives. If a compromise is offered when the adversary's coercive momentum is still strong, the compromise will be of less value from the perspective of resolving the conflict than if it is offered once the adversary has come to accept a given limit on objectives. Thus the proficient use of compromise involves careful sequencing, and this problem will be discussed more thoroughly in the next section of this chapter.

A series of solution characteristics raises other issues about the success of accommodation or compromise offers. The first of these is whether the proposed compromise divides a fixed payoff or whether a method is found to upgrade the interests of both (or all if there are more than two) parties to the conflict. Haas's (1964) concept of mutually upgrading interests has attracted much attention among bargaining theorists. Iklé (1964) discusses a related concept, innovative bargaining, in his treatment of how nations negotiate, and Walton and McKersie (1965) use a different term, integrative bargaining, in their examination of a similar concept in labor-management negotiation. Zartman (1976), while picking up only a portion of Haas's concept, offers the sound principle that progress toward a mutually satisfactory solution is eased to the degree that the issues at stake can be divided into a series of mutual concessions each of which costs the granting party little but is highly valued by the recipient. The relative merits of different methods of dividing the issues in such a series of concessions are discussed in the psychological literature of bargaining experiments. Froman and Cohen (1970) argue that considering a group of issues simultaneously facilitates logrolling. But Fisher (1971) counters that taking up the individual issues sequentially allows for both resolutions based on the merit of individual issues and progress on one issue while another more difficult issue is being prepared for the negotiating table. As Winham (1977) points out, some contemporary examples of international bargaining such as the SALT and GATT negotiations involve a combination of these two suggestions.

A more immediately relevant point here is that even in conflict episodes in which the parties appear to have diametrically opposed goals, there is often some opportunity for upgrading the interests of both parties. These opportunities are an important yet often overlooked factor in the success of compromise initiatives. For instance, several conflict episodes (Fashoda, 1898; Berlin, 1948–49; Cuba, 1962) suggest that even when a statesman accepts defeat or at least a major shift of objectives, he does so conditionally with the understanding that his adversary will grant concessions—often of a procedural rather than a substantive nature—that upgrade the outcome for the party getting little or no satisfaction on the substantive issues. The French (Fashoda, 1898) and the Soviets (Berlin, 1948–49) both received procedural concessions in the form of conferences that discussed their grievances and were held after the substantive issues had been resolved with no benefit to them. And in 1962 the Soviets, in addition to receiving satisfaction with respect to a portion of their initial goals—protection of Cuba via the noninvasion pledge—received a promise about the removal of United States missiles from Turkey in the near future.

A second relevant solution characteristic involves the degree of mutualness of compromise. At first glance it would appear as though an agreement in which one party gives a lot and the other gives only the most modest concession would be less likely to lead to a quick or stable resolution of the issues than a situation involving roughly equal concessions. But a couple of problems plague this notion. First, the contrary examples are so obvious that the principle cannot be sustained. The Fashoda and Suez conflicts are instances in which one-sided or relatively one-sided concessions not only resolved the conflict but paved the way for improved relations among at least some of the immediate contestants and their allies. The Agadir conflict, a case of roughly equivalent concessions, was a difficult conflict episode to resolve and led only to further embitterment. The Algeciras, Munich, and Berlin (1948–49) cases are examples of one-sided concessions leading to future conflicts and thus not resolving the long-term issues. The Taiwan Straits, Lebanese, and Berlin (1958–62) crises simply withered away with roughly equal tacit concessions on each side. Clearly some principle other than equality of concessions is at work in these cases. Second, Carroll (1969: 305) notes that gauging the relative success of parties to conflict episodes may be more difficult than it initially appears. Victory may be characterized by the parties in different ways. One of these is the relationship among the parties, but another is the relationship between the conflict objectives and the conflict outcomes for each party. A party that achieves its own objectives may be uninterested in how its adversary does. Also, each party may look at a conflict in terms of whether its gains outweigh its losses rather than comparing either to the adversary's position.

At least two other solution characteristics impact on the effectiveness of concessions and thus help to explain the jumbled pattern. The first of these is whether the size of the concessions seems appropriate or salient to the parties involved in the conflict. As Schelling (1966 and 1960) has pointed out, a 50–50 break is only one possibility for a prominent solution. This principle seems to hold for the Germans in the Agadir conflict. Kiderlen felt that Germany ought to be compensated in a fashion roughly equivalent to the French windfall in Morocco. In terms of land area the final settlement was in this ballpark, but the reasonableness of the agreement was discounted for the Germans both by the fact that the land they received was of little value and by their need to struggle so desperately for what others—the Italians, British, and Spanish—had received as a matter of course. For the French too the reasonableness of the solution was discounted by the specific division of the Congo region, which cut the French area into two pieces separated by a strip of German territory, and by the need to compensate Germans at all over an issue that to the French mind precluded legitimate German interest.

But in the Fashoda episode the French accepted a one-sided settlement. The British position, that the French could plunder Northwest Africa if they chose so long as the British controlled the Nile area, was eventually accepted by both parties. Delcassé saw little opportunity for obtaining anything more than a clear pathway for improved future relations with Britain (a salient objective for him), and he accepted this outcome to the conflict. In the 1962 Cuban affair each side needed a crucial minimum. For the United States this was removal of the Soviet strategic weapons from Cuba. For the Soviet Union it seems to have been a noninvasion pledge and an avenue leading away from military confrontation paved with devices to disguise what could appear as a retreat as thoroughly as possible.

A fourth solution characteristic important to the success of mutual compromise is whether or not the compromises are relevant to the central issues of a dispute. What bothered the German leaders so in the Moroccan question was the highly arbitrary French exclusion of Germany from the principle of compensation to others for a free hand in Morocco. There were other issues from time to time, of course, but the crux of the problem was German status in the decision procedures of the great powers. The actual resolution of concrete issues created by the Algeciras and Agadir conflicts provided the Germans with little relief in this regard. In essence, Germany had to labor for benefits other nations received by virtue of their position in the council of Europe. And British intervention in the Agadir episode raised for the Germans the specter of encirclement. Yet for the French, compensating the nation that held Alsace-Lorraine, and particularly compensating this nation over a matter in which it was not legitimately involved, created frustration and rancor. So the final European crisis over the Moroccan question actually raised more important issues than it resolved. The Fashoda affair represents an interesting contrast to the Agadir conflict and the Moroccan question generally. On the one hand, colonial gains at British expense were enticing and popular among the French. But, particularly for Delcassé, Britain increasingly appeared as a potential ally of considerable value in light of growing German power. Fashoda forced the French to choose in their long-term relations with the British, and while the fruit of this choice, the Entente Cordiale, was still six years off, Delcassé made his decision and was satisfied with closing the issue of French influence on the upper Nile.

As Baldwin (1971b) suggests, promises may have more effect on the resolution of conflicts than either practitioners or theorists of statecraft generally realize. It is easy to think of contingent promises that have failed. President Johnson's offer to include Vietnam in a giant TVA-type project in the Mekong basin if the Vietnamese agreed to resolve their dispute with the South off the battlefield is one example. But the fact that the decade-long effort of the United States to coerce the Vietnamese failed as well should not be overlooked. It is also possible to think of examples of promises—even tacit or unwitting promises—that have succeeded. An admittedly stretched example would be the promise Delcassé saw in British help in the future with respect to Germany. This "promise" had an important influence on the French during the Fashoda crisis. The British did not make any explicit promise of aid, and in 1898 may, in contrast to the French, have been virtually unaware of the need for such Anglo-French cooperation. Yet Britain's presence coupled with its diplomatic tradition of "balancer" alerted the French to the promise on which Britain might deliver. The basic problem with promises is that they are difficult to collect. The promiser's interests may change so that his incentive to live up to his promise is diminished. For instance, if the promise was made contingent upon prior cooperation, the incentive to follow through may disappear entirely once the cooperation is granted. The 1907 British promise to help Russia on the Turkish Straits question in return for a settlement in the Persian region was valued more highly by the Russians than by the British, who lost interest in pressing for Russian privileges in the straits once the Persian settlement was achieved. Yet Quester (1970) suggests that mechanisms for enforcing promises are not absent even in the anarchical relations among nations.

Sequencing Strategy Choices

While adaptation, coercion, and accommodation all have particular advantages and drawbacks when considered abstractly, the various strategies are optimally used at different points as a conflict unfolds. At different points in time during a conflict statesmen face different problems that may be most appropriately handled by one of these three strategies. When a statesman faces a certain problem, he reaches for a particular tactic from one of these three options that seems to meet the needs of the context immediately at hand. The specific tactic used depends heavily on the context of the situation.

Adaptive tactics are means of avoiding conflict, perhaps with the idea of buying time for a manipulative response at a later date. There are generally two points in time during a conflict when tactics of this type are useful. One of these is prior to a potential conflict. Although, as Schelling says, if you are asked to play Chicken and decline, you have already played, nations can carefully fail to pick up invitations. Naturally this last option can be used to feign missing an invitation as well as in instances in which a potential challenge is actually not perceived. A second point at which adaptation becomes relevant is with respect to accepting an altered status quo. Sometimes an escalation process will make both parties leery of carrying a conflict further. Yet neither will be willing to engage in any form of compromise, either in granting additional concessions or in recognizing explicitly that previous changes amount to concessions. The Berlin conflict (1958–62) ended in this fashion. Neither side achieved an initially acceptable solution. Yet neither was willing to press further or to admit that, by failing to alter the existing situation, it was tacitly accepting a compromise. Instead what appeared to be an inconclusive stage of the conflict was gradually accepted by both East and West as a solution.

Some challenges to existing international conditions are simply too important to handle through adaptation. When one nation's leaders feel they must respond more actively to what appears to be the challenge of another nation, they often rely on coercive measures. This initial response point in a conflict is an appropriate one for the use of coercion. This does not mean that coercion must be used at this point, but if coercion is to be used, this is the time at which its use can be productive. Three characteristics of coercive activity make its use appropriate at this stage. First, coercive activity can be used to effectively signal the adversary that his actions constitute an intolerable infringement on the signaling nation's own values. Coercive action can focus adversary's attention on signals when more conventional diplomatic messages have failed. Blocking is relevant here. Second, coercive activity can alter the adversary's calculation of cost and benefit. Coercion can raise the costs of the adversary's continuing his current plan of action. In this regard coercion is the stick of the carrot-stick combination (George, Hall, and Simons, 1971). Coercion alone rarely increases the benefits the target incurs by shifting his plan of action. Any change in preference arising from coercion usually stems from the increased costs of failing to alter the course of current policy. And, as mentioned earlier, coercion carries dangers of increasing the target's resistance as well. So the argument here is not that coercive activity in general will give the adversary adequate incentives to alter his strategy; only carefully implemented, appropriately chosen coercive measures can contribute to this end. Third, coercive measures can be used to probe the adversary's position and to differentiate the adversary's crucial interests from side issues. In this fashion coercion can lay the groundwork for accommodation by uncovering areas that offer lucrative possibilities for compromise.

The timing of accommodation ranks with choosing an appropriate degree of coercion as a crucial problem. In some instances statesmen may be able to bargain effectively by using accommodation from the start of their negotiations (Winham, 1977). However, this approach is not generally appropriate for severe conflicts among adversary nations except on the most trivial issues. Usually accommodation in important conflicts among international adversaries requires an antecedent coercive stage for reasons related to the three bases of coercion presented above. Initial use of accommodation for these instances faces several difficulties. First, it may not provide a signal capable of penetrating the adversary's system of selective attention and interpretation with the message that a change in the adversary's current policy is essential. Second, even if this message gets through, accommodation may not provide an adequate incentive structure to accomplish a change in the adversary's strategy. While accommodation can—through the carrot—make other options increasingly attractive, the increased attractiveness of these other options may be insufficient to persuade the adversary to shift his policy from an ongoing strategy that he has already determined is attractive. The point here is not that the stick is more effective than the carrot—although in specific instances one may be more useful than the other—but that an effective bargaining strategy will include both and include them in a specific sequence (Snyder and Diesing, 1977; George, Hall, and Simons, 1971). Third, a statesman often needs better information about the adversary's preferences than the information he has at the beginning of a conflict in order to develop successful compromise proposals, and the necessary information is often available only through indices such as the adversary's reaction to coercive probes.

Experimental gaming offers some support for the sequencing of coercion and accommodation suggested here. The results of gaming experiments often vary considerably across minor experimental and unanticipated confounding characteristics specific to different experimental circumstances; so even ignoring other important factors, such as the relevance of trivial games for actual crucial conflicts, this evidence from experimental gaming should not weigh too heavily.[12] Komorita (1973) found concessions to be effective after a long stalemate among competitive players. Concessions were able to break down the stalemate by serving as signals of cooperative intent. Komorita and Esser (1975) found an initially tough but, to the target's perception, fair stance useful for reaching solutions. Benton, Kelley, and Liebling (1972) found a process of gradually making concessions from a firm initial position an effective means of deriving cooperation. The sequence suggested here is vague in terms of degree and duration. As George, Hall, and Simons (1971) point out, it is possible to press the adversary so hard with coercive measures that he is driven into a corner from which subsequent accommodative moves cannot lure him. An initially appropriate level of coercion can also be continued past productiveness and lead to a similar result. On the other hand, if accommodative activity is begun prematurely—that is, before coercion has accomplished the goals discussed above—the adversary may remain intransigent or even raise his aspirations in the face of accommodation. Or if the transition from coercion to accommodation occurs at an appropriate time but is too precipitous, the adversary may feel his opponent is exhausted by the previous coercion and may harden his stance. To large extent judgments about degree and duration are both contextual and subtle, but some limited guidelines will appear in the final chapter.

Summary

Bargaining resources for severe international conflicts are highly contextual. Capabilities crucial for one conflict may be virtually useless in another. Traditional conceptualizations of national power may miss

[12] Hamner (1974) provides a concise summary of experiments that support conflicting bargaining principles. Considerable experimental evidence supports the efficacy of both hard and soft-line approaches to conflict.

sources of influence critical in specific conflict episodes. Thus relatively weak nations are sometimes able to bargain with surprising success with great powers, and conflict episodes among great powers are sometimes one-sided affairs. In such a setting bargaining success is contingent on re-sourcefulness: that is, on recognizing options usable in the conflict epi-sode at hand and gaining acceptance for the use of these options within the decision unit. The need for resourcefulness in this sense is present throughout an entire conflict episode rather than being important only at the outset. This pervasive need arises because not all relevant options are perceived by bargaining parties at the outset of conflicts. Indeed, options may go unrecognized even at the conclusion of conflict episodes. But as information is gathered about a situation, initially unrecognized options may be uncovered. The Berlin wall was not an ever-present option for Ulbricht in the Berlin conflict of 1958–62. Rather, this option grew in Ulbricht's mind as a result of what he learned by probing the Western position. Western essentials all involved the military position in and eco-nomic viability of West Berlin, and a wall circumvented these essentials while providing for the minimal Eastern goal—the economic viability of East Germany (Snyder and Diesing, 1977). Statesmen do not face an utter void as they search for options relevant to their problems. Several principles serve as guidelines for resourcefulness. These principles in-clude blocking, circumventing, detouring, compellence and the use of force.

In addition to his struggles with these guidelines to create usable op-tions, the statesman faces several difficult decisions with respect to spe-cific strategy choices. Adaptation, coercion, and accommodation all have inherent advantages and drawbacks, as well as appropriate and inappro-priate times of use within conflict episodes. A coercive action which vio-lates the guidelines and international norms discussed in this chapter or an accommodative gesture that catches the adversary before he has come to accept specific limits on his objectives for the conflict episode at hand are both apt to be counterproductive. Options that are misused can be more damaging to the outcome for the party applying them than an ab-sence of options or options which go unrecognized. So an examination of how sources of influence are actually applied to bargaining situations is an integral part of analyzing how the core processes of bargaining (dis-cussed in chapter 3) follow different paths in different conflict episodes.

PART 3

BARGAINING
IN SEVERE
INTERNATIONAL
CONFLICT
EPISODES

This final portion of the book will develop an analytical chronology of bargaining activity in severe international conflict episodes that places the implications of the two preceding chapters in perspective. While conflict can arise from one party's conscious challenge of another, many international conflicts are not initially the conjunction of two consciously manipulative strategies, as they are so often depicted by journalists and even scholars. Conflicts often arise from efforts within nations to meet the demands of powerful domestic factions that only inadvertently damage the positions of foreign powers. And nations are sometimes slow to recognize that others perceive their actions as challenges. When one nation's action does create inadvertent difficulties for a second, the aggrieved nation's response is apt to be perceived as the conflict initiating activity by the first party. At this point of mutual hostility, regardless of how it is reached, a period follows in which both parties cling to their original perspectives and confront one another. This confrontation gradually provides the information and incentives necessary for one of a variety of forms of agreement, and the conflict episode gradually dissipates as a new relationship or condition is accepted by the parties to the conflict. The discussion here will draw on five specific categories of material developed in part 2: information interpretation, decision foci, strategy search, principles of resourcefulness, and strategy dilemmas. These five factors will be tied together in a chronology depicting four phases of conflict activity.

An Analytical Chronology of Bargaining in Severe International Conflict Episodes

The various topics of the chapters in part 2 would be more useful if they could be related to one another through association with a single conceptual framework. Toward this end, an analytical chronology of bargaining activity will be developed in this chapter, using phases as the central organizing mechanism. The phases depict characteristic patterns of information interpretation, decision foci, strategy search, resourcefulness, and strategy dilemmas and thus tie these five factors together.

A conflict episode or bargaining situation is conceived in terms of four phases: an intolerable violation, act of resistance, a confrontation, and an accommodation (cf. Gochman, 1976: 559; Barringer, 1972: 23). All these phases are present in severe international conflict episodes, but they may vary considerably in absolute and proportional length across cases. The Cuban crisis of 1962 lasted only a couple of weeks. The Berlin conflict (1958–62) lasted several years. The intolerable violation phase of the Agadir crisis lasted for over two months—about a third of the crisis. The intolerable violation phase of the Berlin (1948–49) crisis lasted only a few days—a minute proportion of the conflict. These differences in duration, absolute or proportional, are simply surface variations, however. The important differences are shifts that can be anticipated from phase to phase in the five factors—information interpretation, decision foci, strategy search, resourcefulness, and strategy dilemmas. Shifts across phases can be noticed empirically in many conflict instances in which statesmen intuitively alter their patterns of action to fit the changing demands of an unfolding situation. But some conflict episodes exhibit inappropriate, counterproductive, out-of-phase actions, and the chronology of conflict activity depicted by the phases offers prescriptive guidelines for avoiding counterproductive actions. [1]

Violation of Tolerances

The impact of conceptualizing bargaining in terms of interpreting information, decision foci, and strategy search pervades all phases of conflict episodes. The specific impact that most easily attracts attention at the outset of a conflict episode is raised by the varying perceptions of the different parties, which offer inconsistent answers to the question of how a conflict starts. How an international conflict starts has unfortunately often been linked in scholarly analysis as it has in practical statecraft to the issue of guilt or blame. The party whose action "starts" the conflict is the party who is "to blame" or the "guilty" party. If indeed one party actually started international conflicts, the task of analyzing them would be con-

---

[1] The analytical chronology developed here is applicable to severe conflicts among the great powers, including those in which two or more nations are allied and constitute one party to a conflict. It is also applicable to some conflicts among regional powers and to some conflicts between great powers and regional powers, such as the war in Southeast Asia. It is not as appropriate for some conflicts among regional powers in which third parties play crucial mitigating or mediating roles. United States pressure on Israel to halt the military action of the Yom Kippur War in 1973 would be an example of conflict activity on which this chronology does not focus adequately. For extensive analysis of such third party intervention, see Young (1967).

siderably eased. But for each side in a conflict, the other side started the dispute and thus is to blame. And each side will normally be able to find nations that will accept its interpretation of the conflict—including which actions started the conflict—as well as those, who, being in a position to view the situation more dispassionately, will find that each party bears some responsibility.

Yet scholars must be able to place some concrete limitations on the initiation of particular conflict episodes. While it may be possible to develop some persuasive arguments that the cold war that crystallized in the Berlin conflict of 1948–49 actually began with the Russian revolution (Seabury, 1967), it is nevertheless useful to be able to say something concrete about the Berlin episode, which, once under way, presumably had a dynamic of its own. From this standpoint a conflict episode begins when some change of existing circumstances creates a situation in which one nation must confront another. This change can be obvious—a nation expanding its territory by attacking a small formerly independent region—or it can be subtle—gradually rising aspirations among the leaders of a nation that finally pass a threshold at which a stable external situation becomes intolerable. It is common to speak of conflict initiating actions as aggressive. There may be instances in which the initiators of such actions perceive them in this fashion, but such instances are rare. Normally statesmen view the acts their adversaries call "aggression" as efforts to *defend* interests threatened by others.

Two points emerge here. First, any delineation of an act that starts a conflict is highly arbitrary. From the viewpoint of the party that commits the act, it is probably a defensive reaction to previous actions undertaken by others. So for simplicity, the beginning of a conflict episode is defined here in the following way. The confrontation of two consciously conflicting strategies is the common notion of a conflict episode. In order to reach this state one party must implement a policy that another finds intolerable, and the second must therefore choose to oppose this policy. So an arbitrary beginning of the episode can be derived by moving two steps back from the confrontation. It should be emphasized that this arbitrary beginning does not imply blame or guilt for the party who thus initiates the conflict. It is conceivable that this party is reacting defensively to earlier actions of others that would almost universally be considered provocative. Nevertheless, the party making the move twice removed from the confrontation initiates the conflict for the purposes of this book. Second, conflict initiation in this sense may be consciously volitional, conscious but seemingly obligatory in order to defend interests threatened by others, or entirely inadvertent. Nations drift into conflicts of interest inadvertently as well as consciously challenging one another, and the "initiation" of a conflict as the term is used here does not necessarily imply conscious manipulation. Through adaptation nations inadvertently violate the tolerance boundaries of other nations. And, while conscious manipulative actions certainly occur, they hold no monopoly on the initiation of international conflicts. [2]

Interpretation Patterns

Wide variations exist in the perception patterns that characterize the violation of tolerances phase. One possibility is for the statesmen of the conflict initiating nation to actually perceive themselves as initiating a conflict. That is, they are disturbing an otherwise peaceful status quo with a conscious challenge to its conditions. While this scenario represents a relevant theoretical possibility and is a common misperception of targets of coercive activity, it is not particularly common in modern statecraft. Few obvious instances come to mind. Generally one of two other conditions provides the initial step for a conflict episode. By one of these the initiator is acting in a consciously coercive fashion but perceives himself as reacting to the prior challenges of others. The Kaiser in Tangier in 1905 was reacting to what he (correctly) perceived as repeated French efforts to settle the Moroccan question without a German input. And even Hitler—the nearest approximation to the conscious challenger described above—can be viewed as reacting to the indignities placed on Germany by the Versailles peace. A second common way by which conflicts are initiated can be called drift. Nations drift into conflict not through conscious design but rather by failing to recognize the impact

[2] In fact, an earlier version of this book termed the phase "challenge." While this term avoids the clumsiness of the "intolerable violation" title, it is too narrow in focus and thus misleading. Some intolerable violations are challenges (conscious manipulative attempts); others are not.

their actions will have on others. United States leaders never perceived their deployment of tactical weapons to Western Europe as the precipitant of a long conflict over the German question (Diesing, 1970).

These two different scenarios for conflict initiation share at least one characteristic: faulty perceptions on the part of the initiator. The particular false estimate made about the target's tolerances changes with the violating party's intent. In the case of an inadvertent violation, the misperception problem centers on falsely judging or perhaps not even considering the other nation's interests. So an act the other finds intolerable is taken without realizing that the act has this character. In addition to the example of United States tactical nuclear weapons in Western Europe in the late 1950s, this scenario covers the first Moroccan or Algeciras conflict from the standpoint of French actions. The French did not perceive that the Moroccan question was a serious matter for the Germans, and once they realized this error in their perceptions, they initially made an effort at conciliation. Knorr (1964) argues that the Soviets drifted into the Cuban crisis of 1962 and had no idea that the United States would react as strongly as it did. In the case of conscious manipulation, the false estimate of the adversary centers on the adversary's ability and/or willingness to bring resources to bear on the issues in conflict. The target is perceived as lacking either the resources or the willingness to use them necessary to withstand the contemplated manipulation. The Southeast Asian and Berlin (1948–49) instances are examples of this error for the United States with respect to the Vietnamese and for the Soviets with respect to the United States. Conflicts arise through these mechanisms in part because the various parties are out of touch with one another on important matters. They do not adequately recognize one another's interests, or they misperceive that others are able and willing to support these interests.

Decision Focus

The focus of decision making in this phase lies in meeting the needs of powerful domestic factions for activity that has implications (albeit perhaps unrecognized) in foreign arenas. Policies with foreign implications emanate both from changes in the nation's own capabilities or intentions and as reactions to developments in the international environment. For example, while the changes in German foreign policy during the 1930s were affected by international developments such as the worldwide depression, a marked change in the goals and capabilities of changing German elites funneled German policy in the precise direction it followed. But statesmen react to new aspects in the international milieu only to the degree that they perceive these aspects and to the degree that they desire and are able to turn the limited resources of the nation away from other uses and into new international pursuits. The domestic focus of decisions in this phase does not imply that what goes on in the international environment is unimportant. International developments provide domestic factions with essential cues. But international developments offer few necessities for specific actions.[3] International developments must first gain the attention of domestic factions. Although they have to compete with a variety of other stimuli, this task is eased by the fact that specialized subsystems of nations—the foreign ministry, the military, international businesses, ethnic groups—closely monitor some aspects of international affairs. Once noticed, new problems or opportunities in the international environment must compete with a variety of other objectives, although foreign affairs rarely have difficulty acquiring significant amounts of nations' scarce resources. Finally, which problems receive resources and at what level are not matters decided abstractly. They are political matters for which the solution depends largely on the strength of the factions backing various objectives.

The size of the decision unit, as noted earlier, is an important determinant of the difficulty in reaching a decision as to the precise nature of the problem. One- and two-member decision units usually reach this decision with minimal difficulty, since internal disagreement is modest or nonexistent. Sometimes these units will reach a decision a bit cavalierly and will change it under pressure at a subsequent point. The French (Mollet and Pineau's) decision on the problem posed by Egyptian nation-

[3] Wolfers (1962: 13–14) uses the "house on fire" analogy to express this point. When extreme circumstances exist—the house is actually on fire—actors will follow identical courses of action (leave the house). Under less extreme conditions—the house is too warm—several different courses (ignoring the problem, turning down the heat, opening windows, donning lighter clothing) will be followed by different individuals.

alization of the Suez Canal is an example (Snyder and Diesing, 1977). A larger decision unit with three or more members is apt to have greater difficulty reaching a decision. In the 1905–6 conflict over Morocco, Bülow, the German chancellor, was torn between the Kaiser's notion of using a German compromise on French control over Morocco to lure the French from the entente with Britain and Holstein's notion of wresting control of Morocco from France and thus demonstrating the uselessness of the entente. Adenauer and Macmillan saw dramatically different problems in the Soviet pressure on Berlin (1958–62) and so placed markedly different demands on Kennedy. And in the group advising Kennedy in the Cuban crisis, some advisors perceived no problem while others perceived the Castro government as the problem. Reaching a decision as to the precise nature of the foreign problem is more difficult when the different views of various domestic factions have to be amalgamated. A decision unit with three or more members is a virtual prerequisite for problems of amalgamating different viewpoints, but size alone does not always create these problems. There was little disagreement within the United States decision unit over the problem posed by the Japanese attack on Pearl Harbor, for instance.

Strategy Search

Strategy search during the intolerable violation phase is an internal process. It is a search for a domestic coalition that can sustain a policy. Search is guided by the specific nature of the perceived problem and also by ongoing policies and existing capabilities. The focus of search at this juncture lies in the constraints raised by powerful domestic factions. This domestic focus is complete for instances in which nations drift into conflict inadvertently, for it is through ignoring the impact of a nation's actions on other nations that such drift occurs. For instances of either consciously volitional or conscious yet obligatory coercion, the domestic arena may not be the only consideration in developing a strategy, but is the focal point of strategy search. In the case of conscious obligatory coercion the conflict initiating unit is saying in effect: "We *cannot* sit idly by while the adversary takes actions of this nature." Action has become a domestic imperative, and search focuses on what lines of response can gain domestic support with only modest regard for the adversary's tolerances. It is conceivable that regard for the adversary's tolerances would weigh heavily in a case of conscious volitional coercion, but a misperception syndrome that characterizes actual episodes that approximate this type of activity is apt to downplay the necessity for considering the adversary's tolerances. This syndrome pictures the adversary as playing Chicken—a game in which players give way to demonstrations of superior strength and resolve. The adversary's preferences can be arranged in Chicken fashion so that capitulation is preferable to conflict escalation, but this preference is not necessarily held by statesmen who are confronted with bold challenges by counterparts in other nations.

Resourcefulness

One of the principles of resourcefulness discussed earlier is highly relevant to the intolerable violation phase. This is the principle of circumvention. Particularly the notion of a fait accompli is intriguing at this point in a conflict.[4] The tiny French force under Marchand suddenly appeared in the upper Nile. Under cover of quelling a local uprising the French raced to secure control of Morocco in 1911. The Japanese attempted to destroy United States naval power in the Pacific with the attack on Pearl Harbor. And this example illustrates that circumventing may be coupled with force. The Soviets closed the land access routes to Berlin, and they attempted to surreptitiously build a series of strategic installations in Cuba. All of these acts were sudden, hidden or disguised actions that appeared, at least from the standpoint of the target, to be actions that started a conflict by circumventing the target's defense of important values. But not all of these actions were perceived as conflict initiating faits accomplis by the governments that launched them. The French force at Fashoda represented such a challenge, but on the part of the French Ministry of Colonies, not the French government as a whole. In the move to secure Morocco the French definitely perceived them-

[4] George and Smoke (1974: 536–40) offer an expanded discussion of related aspects of faits accomplis.

selves to be taking advantage of a local civil war in order to reach their aim of a protectorate. But they perceived that a decade's diplomacy had essentially won them Morocco in the eyes of the only other nations legitimately involved in the Moroccan question—Italy, Britain, and Spain. The French did not perceive the Germans, or for that matter the Moroccans, as legitimate parties to this issue. The Japanese felt that they were reacting against the imperialism of the Western powers in Southeast Asia. And this imperialism, from the Japanese perspective, looked as if it would destroy the Japanese economy. The Soviets perceived that the conflict over the German question that precipitated the 1948–49 Berlin conflict was initiated by Western refusals to live up to commitments made during the last days of the war about uniform practices toward Germany. So the Soviets perceived themselves to be responding to a conflict initiated by the Western allies—particularly Britain and the United States. Soviet perceptions toward the deployment of strategic weapons in Cuba are less clear. On one hand the Soviets stressed reciprocity: they were only doing what the United States had done in similar circumstances. They were protecting an ally that was fearful of attack from the other superpower, and they were improving their deterrent position by bringing strategic weapons of limited range to forward positions. But the Soviet Union also made some effort to disguise its deployment of these weapons, and the notion of a fait accompli fits the clandestine nature of its actions.

So, from the standpoint of one party (the initiating decision unit) an act that may appear to the target as a fait accompli may actually be a blocking action—the Soviet blockade of Berlin 1948–49. Either the circumventing or the blocking principle may be blended with detouring. The Soviets did this with respect to the German question by applying pressure to a point on which the West was particularly vulnerable—Berlin. While the intentions of the party that undertakes an action are important and variations in these intentions may lead further conflict in different directions, it is also important to consider the target's perceptions. The target tends to perceive conflict initiating actions as coercive moves of the circumventing variety, and this interpretation is apt to hold whether the initiator intended a move of this nature or was only responding to a felt provocation, or even if the two parties drifted into conflict inadvertently.

Strategy Dilemmas

The strategy dilemmas of this stage vary with the consciousness of the conflict initiator. If he does not perceive his action as directed toward the nation that perceives itself as the target, then the initiator has as yet no conscious strategy with respect to the target in question. This is adaptive activity, at least in terms of the initiator's relations with the target, and there is no need at this point to carry this case further in terms of strategy dilemmas. For the conflict initiator conscious of manipulation two dilemmas may appear at this point. One of these, and an unusual problem, is the appropriateness of coercive as opposed to accommodative activity. The Germans in the Agadir crisis of 1911, for instance, could have gotten French compensation without escalating the diplomatic protest they had mounted in several European capitals. It is unclear whether the Germans could have achieved the *territorial* compensation they desired by following an accommodative strategy from late June on, but the French had accepted by this time the principle of German compensation. Coercion at this point can have the impact of creating a conflict that may become more costly in terms of both short-term risks and long-term deterioration in relations than the specific outcome sought is worth. Decisions to follow an accommodative strategy at this point might obviate the development of a severe conflict episode. But such decisions may also exacerbate conflicts. The French choice of accommodation early in the 1905–6 conflict over Morocco exacerbated this conflict in two ways. First, early accommodation rewarded and reinforced the German coercive approach, and the Germans stayed with a coercive strategy long after its productiveness was exhausted. Second, the French were burned by the failure of their early accommodative efforts, and they refused to return to accommodation in this conflict episode. Thus the Germans, who had high initial expectations, had to absorb all the later accommodation.

The second dilemma if the first decision goes, as it often does, in favor of coercion and the conflict develops further is the severity of coercion. Diplomatic history is littered with conflicts that escalated far beyond the goals either party initially perceived to be in conflict as a result of needlessly severe coercive tactics adopted by one or both parties. Yet not applying enough coercive pressure can also lead to failure to achieve objectives. This latter problem is particularly important in a case in which the conflict initiator perceives that he is responding defensively to a conflict initiated by another. Typically in this situation, a series of verbal signals—similar to those sent by Kennedy to Khrushchev during the late summer and early autumn of 1962—will have already been sent to the other party, but these signals will have been ineffective in alerting the other that the signaler considers its policy intolerable. The signaling statesman then, while still plagued with the problem of avoiding excess coercion, must be particularly careful to use a strong enough signal to get his message across this time.

These specific characteristics of interpretation patterns, decision focus, strategy search, resourcefulness, and strategy dilemmas mark the first phase of a conflict episode. This phase is more vague and often more tentative than the three that follow. The vagueness stems from the wide variety of ways in which this phase arises. The conflict initiator may do nothing new at all, but changes in the aspirations of the target—due perhaps to a change in leadership—may make another party's existing policy suddenly intolerable. Or the two parties may drift into conflict inadvertently, each failing to realize that its policy threatens the other's important values. Within the realm of conscious manipulative activity the conflict initiator—owing perhaps to the acquisition of new resources—may purposely initiate a conflict. Or, more likely, one nation may feel that another has provoked a conflict. In this case the conflict initiating statesmen will perceive themselves as resisting earlier coercion by the target. This phase is also more tentative in several senses than subsequent phases. It is often unclear during this phase that a genuine conflict of interests as opposed to mutual misunderstanding exists. Also each decision unit is apt, collectively, to be uncertain of the adversary's intentions, preferences, and objectives, and may well be unaware of its own preferences in a variety of forthcoming contingencies. Each nation has its own parochial notions of the conflict situation. But these notions are apt to be tentative in themselves, and they will almost certainly be at variance with one another.

Resistance

One aspect of the resistance phase that the conceptualization of bargaining offered in this book directs attention toward is the startling similarity between the conflict initiator and the resistor. In contrast to much strategic theory, particularly deterrence work, in which the aggressor and deterring party have different characteristics and problems, the conceptualization here stresses problems and other characteristics common to the two parties. The resistance phase of a conflict focuses on the actions of the party identified as the target in the previous phase, and denying the conflict initiator's intolerable violation is the crux of resistance activity. As such, resistance can be identical to the scenario for conflict initiation in which the initiator reacts to what he perceives to be the previous challenges of others. This potential identity reinforces the arbitrary nature of the label attached to the conflict initiating action. In fact, in many conflicts the conflict initiator and the resistor will have similar images of how a conflict has been initiated. Each perceives the other to be the initiator. A common mechanism leading to similarities across images is the drift into conflict mentioned in the discussion of intolerable violation. One nation, without considering seriously enough the implications for other nations, takes an action that a second nation perceives as intolerable. The second nation then perceives the first to have initiated a purposeful challenge and reacts in righteous indignation. This resistance strikes the first, unsuspecting nation as an act of conflict initiation. Since a strong similarity can exist between the intolerable violation and resistance phases, useful material can be developed about both by discussing the resistance phase in greater detail.

Interpretation Patterns

The perceptions of the target tend to fall into one of several general patterns, which arise as a result of differences in both personality and experience. One common pattern is to exaggerate the threatening implications of the adversary's violating move. The roots of this tendency probably lie in the anarchical character of the international system that forces nations to be ever alert to the development of threatening contingencies; the primary mechanism through which the exaggerated implications are converted into "reasonable" fears is concern with the precedent the immediate violation might hold for the future (Snyder, 1971b). The crux of the problem, as perceived by the target, is that even if the issue over which the immediate challenge is made is not worth a struggle with the adversary, the immediate issue is coupled to other issues that may become the subjects of increasingly severe and frequent challenges by this and other adversaries if a precedent of firm resistance is not set in this immediate case.

Two other reactions are less common but do occur and merit discussion. One of these constitutes in many respects the direct opposite of the syndrome considered in the preceding paragraph. Statesmen following this second pattern of thought are sometimes caught by surprise by their adversaries' actions. Rather than exaggerating the threatening implications of the adversary's actions, targets following this pattern find ways to discount the threatening implications or at least to detach the immediate instance from potential future conflict episodes. While these conclusions run in a direction opposite to those of the first syndrome, some of their roots lie in different aspects of the same image of the adversary. Typically, those who adhere to the first pattern perceive the adversary as a bully who aggressively initiates conflict episodes at what to his mind are points of weakness. These statesmen stress that the aggressor's appetite will be whetted by success and curbed by meeting forceful opposition. Statesmen who fall into the "caught by surprise" form of thought stress the cowardly side of the bully's nature. Thus they feel either that the bully is not brave enough to threaten important values or that the aggressor is primarily a bluffer or suffers from other deficiencies and can be defeated easily if he ever attacks important values. Thus in the early 1960s United States officials assumed that the Soviets would not deploy strategic weapons outside their own territory, since as consciously evil tyrants they would fear that local authorities might turn these weapons against them. Two decades earlier some United States leaders looked with bemusement on the threat of Japan. Similarly, some Israeli leaders did not take an Egyptian threat seriously in 1973 (Ben-Zvi, 1976; Shlaim, 1976).

A third perception pattern arises from an image of the adversary not shared with either of the patterns above. This pattern might be termed the "Munich syndrome," for the reactions of Western statesmen to the conflicts with Hitler during the 1930s up to and including the Munich episode are among the most obvious contemporary examples of this perception pattern. Statesmen following this pattern attempt to give the adversary some satisfaction in conflicts of interest because they view the adversary to be striving for just reforms—"the Versailles peace places Germany in an intolerable position"—or because they view a working relationship with the adversary as the least of necessary evils—"let the Germans and the Soviets, or the Chinese and the Soviets, prosper so they can eventually destroy one another." This perception pattern should not be dropped without stressing that it is not always erroneous. Nations, even adversary nations, do strive for just reforms—the Palestinians' demand for a homeland. And there is sometimes benefit in playing adversaries off against one another—Soviet détente initiatives over the past few years are often attributed at least in part to the improvement in United States–Chinese relations.

Finally, there is the possibility that the intolerable violation arises not from a change in the conflict initiator's policy but from a change in the aspirations, perceptions, or goals of the resistor. A change of this nature might be brought about by a change in leadership, as in the case of Germany in the 1930s. Changing elites created the change in British policy at the end of the nineteenth century and the beginning of this century, involving subtle shifts of emphasis between the colonial and continental realms. But sometimes a change in leadership simply reflects growing, widespread disenchantment with an existing policy. The British change of leadership in 1940 falls in this category. When an intolerable violation is created by changes in the resistor, actions designed to alter the status quo are undertaken first by the resisting party. This reverses normal (at least normal in the West) notions about how conflicts develop. More importantly, it means that the conflict initiator may have had few or no signals to alert him to the dangers of his existing policy.

Decision Focus

Strong similarities exist between the decision focus of the target's resistance and the initiator's focus in the previous phase. The focus is largely domestic in that what entails an intolerable violation—and thus a violation that demands resistance—is a domestic political issue. As May (1973) points out there is no specific rule which led the United States to react quite differently to Soviet buildups in the Caribbean and in the Mediterranean. Important political actors interpreted these challenges differently. In other words an intolerable violation is anything that gains the domestic political coalition necessary to support a reaction. A policy of resistance may be necessitated because mass public opinion will not tolerate a leadership that does not act, or it may be necessitated by the desires of a small elite group. The important point here is the arbitrary and highly domestic character of this decision. Any coalition capable of raising a strategy of resistance defines an intolerable violation.

Strategy Search

Search in this phase is similar to the search pattern of the conflict initiator in the previous phase. Search is a domestic process of striving to achieve a coalition able and willing to support a strategy. Only rarely does the search for a strategy to handle the problem proceed from a blank slate. Often there will have been some previous discussion or even previous conflict over the issues in question. The Balkan and Moroccan conflicts of the early twentieth century, the repeated challenges raised by Hitler during the interwar years, and the Berlin and Middle Eastern conflicts of the postwar period are cases in point. In some respects familiarity with the issue and relevant action alternatives eases the statesman's task. A recurring issue does not pull the statesman into an entirely unfamiliar situation. He will have the contingency plans of various government bureaucracies, the suggestions of contemporary rivals and advisors, and feedback from past attempts to deal with the situation. Yet familiarity can also foster complacency, particularly glib analyses that overlook important developments in issues over time. The Germans and Austrians overlooked the fact that the Russian leadership saw the Balkan challenge of 1914 as more severe (minimally in the sense of having Balkan challenges occur too frequently) than the previous challenges of 1908–9 and 1912–13. On the other hand, the French resistance in 1911 was based partly on misperception that failed to notice that the German Moroccan challenge of 1911 was less ambitious than the previous one of 1905–6. Familiarity with surface similarities often leads statesmen to use historical analogy loosely and poorly (Jervis, 1976). As a result they sometimes react to past rather than existing conflicts (May, 1973).

Resourcefulness

Inasmuch as the intolerable violation and resistance phases are similar, they are apt to share principles of resourcefulness. The principle of resourcefulness outlined earlier that most nearly meets the demands of this predicament is blocking, although this principle may be combined with detouring. If the adversary's conflict initiating action has been particularly successful in circumventing the resistor's defenses, compellence, similar to that used by the British in the Fashoda case, may be relevant. Blocking is a more common response, however. Blocking is a more prudent response at this stage since it offers more scope for transferring the burden of further action (perhaps violent action) and thus risk to the adversary. The Soviets blocked access to Berlin in order to get the Western allies to take their earlier promises about Germany seriously. The Germans anchored naval vessels at Agadir in order to effectively block French military occupation of southern Morocco. The United States set up a blockade of Cuba in order to block further shipments of strategic weapons to Cuba. These blocking actions have two distinct purposes. First, they carry the signal that the adversary is acting in an intolerable fashion. Second, through jeopardizing the adversary's ongoing policy by blocking its fulfillment they force the adversary from the standpoint of his own values to take some form of remedial action. So a blocking action is a signal the adversary can rarely ignore.

If the act of resistance arises from a change in the resisting state's reaction to an ongoing policy on the part of its adversary, the circumventing principle of the intolerable violation stage may be relevant. The French move to place a force at Fashoda and thus cause the British to find an established French position on the edge of their Nile territory can be analyzed in this fashion. But the French government as a whole and over time had no conscious plan to resist the British dominance in Northeast Africa in this fashion. And the lengthy time required for the French garrison to sail to Africa and wander across much of equatorial Africa, coupled with the high rate of turnover among French politicians, made the challenge a virtual echo of surprise from the past to the French government of September 1898 rather than a policy fitted to its current objectives.

Strategy Dilemmas

The major strategy dilemma of this phase involves the degree of coercive pressure. The level of coercion should not be so high as to force the adversary into a corner from which he cannot escape. On the other hand, there is a lower limit to consider. The logic of this phase demands a sharp signal that will cut through the adversary's misperception at least to the extent of warning him that he is setting out on a dangerous course. There may be a few instances in which a coercive-accommodative dilemma is relevant to this phase. Accommodation does fit with the Munich perception pattern discussed under interpretation patterns. It is conceivable that the adversary does not recognize that he is challenging the target and that he would be willing to alter his path of action to avoid crucial violations of the target's tolerances if the impact of his actions were pointed out to him in an accommodative fashion. Several problems are raised by this suggestion. First, given that the adversary has already decided to adopt what he perceives to be the benefits of a particular course of action, it may be difficult to dissuade him from his path by accommodation that promises only a partial return on his expectations. Second, offering concessions at this point may only whet his appetite. And third, the target's signals at this point are rarely the first signals the target has sent about the intolerable nature of the adversary's course of action. Usually other, milder signals have preceded the more dramatic resistance of this phase. These earlier signals either have passed unnoticed or have been misinterpreted. The failure of earlier signals, while reinforcing the need for a strong resistance signal, also adds incentive to keep the act of resistance within the upper limit of coercive pressure the adversary can tolerate. Otherwise a blind but relatively benign counterpart may be turned into an implacable adversary. Statesmen who perceive the adversary as a bully are prone to ignore this danger and to resist with an irrevocable level of coercion.

A curious aspect of the intolerable violation and resistance phases is that the conflicting parties will often perceive themselves to be in identical circumstances—aggrieved by the other's unwarranted coercion. This similarity across the conflicting parties is apt to exist regardless of variations in the consciousness of the parties or method of conflict initiation. The similarity is encapsulated in the term "mirror image" used by Osgood (1962) and others (Rapoport, 1964). Osgood argues that the mirror image can be the basis for mutual escalation or deescalation. This position is accepted here, but the position needs to be expanded and modified to make it relevant to severe conflict episodes as opposed to the cold war environment of general hostility and distrust with which Osgood dealt. When a challenge is severe enough to be resisted, the two parties are normally out of touch with one another, each perceives the other to be at fault, and a number of developments must occur before mirror images capable of sustaining accommodation or deescalation will develop. These changes comprise the crucial aspects of the confrontation phase.

Confrontation

Several works on bargaining in international conflicts (Snyder, 1972; Payne, 1970; Schelling, 1966) follow Iklé's (1964) lead in focusing on the importance of resolve in international confrontations. According to this school of thought, a statesman who can demonstrate superior resolve in conflicts with others has a crucial advantage, and much bargaining activity for these theorists goes into building a reputation for resolve and using this reputation to win conflicts. The conceptualization offered here does not ignore a statesman's ability and willingness to support his position with force. It does not, however, stress this factor to the degree that other theories do, and it considers additional matters that are pretty much ignored by theorists who emphasize resolve—for instance, the impact of misperception, the group nature of many national decisions, and the timing of coercive and accommodative efforts. The inclusion of these additional considerations makes the conceptualizational here a more complete portrayal of the activity of bargaining in international conflicts than theories that focus on resolve alone. The confrontation phase of a conflict episode is a complex affair and offers an excellent opportunity to demonstrate the importance of matters other than resolve.

The confrontation phase is distinguished from the two earlier phases in that it involves the clash of two purposefully manipulative strategies. Here a conscious conflict of interests exists. An intolerable violation has been resisted, and each party resigns itself to some form of struggle in order to obtain its goals. At the beginning of this phase the two parties are apt to be far apart in a variety of ways. Each is likely to have only a poor notion of the other's intentions, preferences, and objectives, and there are apt to be great differences in the interests perceived to be in conflict. One important similarity creates a stronger symmetry between the parties than has characterized previous phases. Each party has a policy to which important domestic factions are committed and which has so far failed to achieve its foreseen objectives. The policy that the target perceives as an intolerable violation either has been blocked or has been otherwise signaled as unacceptable to its initiator. But the resistance phase, even if successful in returning conditions to the status quo ante, is endangered by the other nation's known desire for a revision of these circumstances. There exists a stalemate consisting of incomplete strategies that express unfulfilled objectives. Tensions run high under these circumstances, but the risks imposed by the confrontation offer subtle opportunities for progress probably unachievable under less trying conditions.

Interpretation Patterns

Once mutual conscious perceptions of a conflict of interest exist, statesmen's perceptions can be divided into three general categories—hard, middle, and soft-line (Snyder and Diesing, 1977). These are broad categories that should not be used to mask the variation that exists within them. Nevertheless they are useful. Hard-liners perceive the adversary to prefer backing down to escalating a conflict. For the hard-liner the adversary is essentially a bluffer. This image of the adversary contrasts starkly with the hard-liner's self-image. Hard-liners argue that grave consequences arise from granting concessions to the adversary. This contrast points out a distinguishing feature of hard-liners—their limited empathy. The hard-liner perceives himself as standing firm in the face of the adversary's coercion and acting reasonably in the face of the adversary's accommodative actions. But for the hard-liner, the adversary works on a diametrically opposed dynamic; the adversary will draw back in the face of coercion but will take advantage of accommodative actions on the hard-liner's part. These contrasting images contribute to a preference for coercive action on the part of hard-liners. Another aspect of hard-line perceptions supports this preference. Hard-liners picture relations among nations—particularly adversaries—as being essentially conflictual. For the hard-liner adversaries are engaged in a virtually unlimited Hobbesian pursuit of power. Thus the adversary is probing the fringes of his aspirations when he "provokes" the hard-liner rather than defending his core values. And the adversary can accept a defeat on these fringes more easily than the hard-liner, who perceives himself as defending central values.

Soft-liners exhibit far more empathy for their counterparts in adversary nations than hard-liners. For the soft-liner adversary statesmen operate on principles similar to his own style of operation. The soft-liner holds that adversary statesmen are put off by harsh coercive methods that either engage additional values, thus making adversary compliance more difficult, or through provocation drive the adversary from a deliberative approach to spasm reactions. For the soft-liner coercion will be answered with coercion, but conciliatory gestures will give rise to mutual compromise efforts. The soft-liner's action preference, then, is for accommodation rather than coercion. The soft-liner's view of international relations supports his preference for accommodation based on empathy. Soft-liners acknowledge that conflict exists among nations. However, they fear first that this conflict is exaggerated by mutual misperception and second that it may be exacerbated by needlessly imprudent acts based on this misperception. Since for the soft-liner the adversary is basically like the soft-liner himself, he will be pursuing limited goals that have some claim to legitimacy. The characteristic error to this line of reasoning is to underestimate the latent conflict of interest and to assume that the conflict is largely an artificial creation of misperception and/or provoking tactics sponsored by a few troublemakers among the adversary statesmen, who are by and large reasonable fellows.

The middle-line position offers no new ingredients. Instead familiar ingredients are combined differently. Middle-liners combine some characteristics of hard-liners and other characteristics of soft-liners. At his best, then, the middle-liner brings an impressive array of insight to the management and resolution of conflict episodes. Kennedy's actions in the Cuban crisis offer an example of this conjunction of hard and soft-line skills. Kennedy used limited coercion. But he attempted to signal the Soviets that the coercion was for the support of important values and was limited to the support of specific objectives. Kennedy also shifted from coercion to accommodation once his carefully chosen coercive signals had had the desired impact of correcting Soviet misperception. At his worst, however, the middle-liner can mix strategies poorly—offer concessions in a nasty, self-defeating way or deflate the impact of coercive actions by hedging on their application. Or he can use the coercive and accommodative tactics at inappropriate times. Bülow's actions in the 1905–6 Moroccan conflict provide an example of the middle-line vacillator. Bülow was caught between a soft-liner, the Kaiser (for this instance, at least) and a hard-liner, Holstein. Bülow vacillated back and forth over time, and these conflicting influences muddled both his coercive and his accommodative efforts (Snyder, 1971b).

It is important to stress that neither hard nor soft predilections are inherently better with respect to correctly identifying conflict episodes. These two perception patterns are "gut" responses to conflict that will be coincidentally accurate or false depending on the nature of the conflict at hand. Adversaries for whom the hard-liner's bias is appropriate exist. Hitler offers an example of such a statesman. The Agadir conflict of 1911 is a classic case of the condition of exaggerated perceptions of conflict that the soft-liner assumes as a general rule. Also within individual conflict episodes the action predilections of both hard and soft-liners may be appropriate but at different points in time. Both coercion and accommodation are appropriate for most conflict episodes, but the order of application is important. Both hard and soft-liners may be insensitive to the inappropriateness of their preferences during different phases of conflict activity. The middle-line position has a theoretical advantage over both hard and soft-liners of being able to draw on the wisdom of each. But this theoretical advantage may be lost in practice, as the example of Bülow demonstrates.

One important aspect of the perceptual patterns of the confrontation phase is change that occurs during the course of the phase. At the beginning of the phase the adversaries normally have very unrealistic and often internally inconsistent perceptions of each other's intentions, preferences, and objectives. It is rare for an individual statesman's, let alone an entire decision unit's, image of the adversary to change much during the confrontation phase.[5] If the initial perception of the adversary pictures him as an expansionist power set on controlling whatever he can obtain, a conflict over a particular range of interests is unlikely to alter this image. It may even drive the image home more forcefully. What does or at least can happen as a result of the confrontation is that limitations on the adversary's aspirations with respect to this specific conflict episode become known. So while the adversary may still be every bit as discouraging or even frightful as he appeared prior to the conflict, it becomes possible to bargain with him over the specific range of interests in conflict in the current episode. As the limits to the adversary's acceptable state of affairs appear, the statesman acquires the information he needs to mold future steps of his own strategy.

Naturally, the adversary's tolerances are not the only considerations of importance here. Statesmen often enter conflicts with decision units that are collectively uncertain of their own intentions, preferences, and objectives. Even individual leaders may be uncertain what course they will follow in a particular predicament, but even if all individuals in the decision unit are personally certain, what the nation will do hinges on the mixture of preferences among the members of the decision group, the success of internal bargaining that may change the minds of some group members, and/or the results of altering the membership of the decision unit in order to bring in members with different preferences. The confrontation phase activity serves to clarify uncertainties about the course that the statesman's own nation will follow in specific contingencies. This clarification of the adversary's intentions, preferences, and objectives and of the statesman's own preferences is a mutual process. So each protagonist is making these discoveries with respect to the other and itself.

[5] The chance for change is surely greater during lengthy episodes such as the 1958–62 Berlin conflict than during a short crisis such as the Cuban affair of 1962. See Snyder and Diesing (1977) for an elaboration of this point and related issues.

Four independent possibilities exist once these uncertainties are worked out. In the first instance, each party finds it possible to make the concessions required by the other's tolerances, and activity shifts to the accommodation phase with a spirit of mutual compromise. The Cuban and Agadir cases follow this pattern. In the second instance, one party finds important substantive—although not necessarily procedural—concessions unnecessary and perhaps also impossible, while the other finds concessions both possible and necessary. Berlin 1948–49 and Fashoda follow this pattern. Here substantive accommodation is a one-sided process, although the winner in this pattern may offer procedural concessions to his adversary. In the third instance, neither party finds necessary concessions possible, but neither is willing to press the conflict further. Under these conditions each is apt to stall—perhaps for years—and a tacit although unstable settlement in place sets in. Berlin 1958–62 and the Taiwan Straits conflicts follow this pattern. In the fourth instance neither party finds it possible to make necessary concessions and the conflict explodes into a fight that, while not devoid of rules altogether, escalates far beyond the issues originally in conflict and can hardly be construed as directed toward the defense of these issues. Sarajevo and the recent Southeast Asian conflict follow this pattern. This violent struggle will eventually subside and an accommodation stage will arise, as in the three other possibilities. But the issues at this point are apt to be different from those in conflict as the episode began.[6]

Decision Focus

The confrontation marks at least a partial failure for the initial strategies of both participants. The pattern of domestic interests that created and sustained these initial strategies is now at least temporarily unable to press them through to completion. So the question around which the deliberations of the confrontation phase focus is, what is to be done about

[6] This book does not focus on expansions of conflict like that which arose from Sarajevo inasmuch as in total war among the great powers bargaining is relatively unimportant in comparison to its importance in crises (Cuba) and in military conflicts that are limited for at least one contestant (Southeast Asia). Kecskemeti (1958) deals with problems in the development of these expanded conflicts.

the failure of the existing strategy to achieve its foreseen objectives? This question focuses attention on the adversary in the external environment as opposed to the fabric of domestic politics, since this adversary presents the obstacles for the existing policy. The answers to this question can lead action in several different directions. If the changes necessary to turn an unsuccessful strategy into a successful one are perceived to be modest, a decision to make these modest changes may follow. Individual members of a decision unit may alter their positions slightly as events unfold—particularly as they learn more about the adversary's position. Or modest changes in the membership of the coalition may take place. If the changes required to turn the existing unsuccessful strategy into a successful one are perceived to be large, more drastic measures form the focus of decisions. A government that sets itself on a particular path of action and sustains international and domestic costs in the pursuit of this path rarely chooses to alter its course of action significantly. Instead new personnel—often a new government sometimes taking over by revolutionary means—effects the necessary changes. Thus the Russian revolution ended Russian involvement in the First World War. And with its policy repudiated, the Chamberlain government gave way to the Churchill government, which was more at home with a new and more appropriate policy. Johnson left office unable or unwilling to alter the course of events in Southeast Asia. Sometimes a government will simply let a situation hang suspended for a long period of time, even several years. A decision to ignore an unsatisfactory situation was adopted with respect to the German problem by Khrushchev for the last year or so of the Eisenhower administration and the first months of the Kennedy administration.

Strategy Search

As the preceding paragraph suggests, search in this phase shifts back and forth between domestic and international realms. The initial strategy is in trouble as this phase opens. So it is necessary to turn away from the source of this strategy—the structure of domestic politics—toward the source of the problem—the foreign adversary—and learn the nature of the new demands that strategy must meet. The adversary will be sending out his own signals on this matter, and few statesmen ignore these signals altogether. However, the adversary's conscious signals may well be self-serving. They may present as minimally acceptable goals matters that the adversary would concede if the issue were pressed. Some of this misrepresentation is surely conscious. But other examples may not be conscious attempts to deceive. Each decision unit in a conflict is normally uncertain as to how it will act in particular contingencies that may arise as a conflict unfolds.[7] And honest differences may exist between how a decision unit thinks it will act and how it actually acts when the contingency arises. Since the conscious signals of the adversary are unreliable, statesmen often resort to probing the adversary's position with modest actions that actually place the adversary in the position of standing firm or backing off on a particular point. This probing activity forms the crux of the goal decomposition process, which divulges to both parties the limitations of each other's requirements. This activity accomplishes two independent but necessary tasks. First, it brings the conflict out of the vague realm of principle, general hostility and distrust, or sweeping interests, and focuses the conflict on concrete interests that can be the subject of negotiation. Second, probes isolate specific, limited objectives that each party must have in order to achieve a satisfactory solution.

Once this external process is under way, search may have to turn inward again in order to find domestic combinations that will accept the changes necessitated by the adversary, and a complex interaction process develops. The demands arising from the domestic coalition are tested against the adversary's constraints. Efforts are undertaken to reduce the adversary's essential objectives. Remaining points of disagreement are brought back and run through the coalition again. The choices here—which will be discussed more thoroughly below the paragraphs on strategy dilemmas—include escalation of coercion, perhaps in conjunction with a compromise on other issues, and a lowering of objectives either through a change in the constraints of the existing coalition or through changes in the coalition's membership. The first choice shifts search back into the external arena. The second makes search once again a domestic political process. There may be several rounds of these choices during the confrontation phase.

---

[7] Jervis (1976: 54–57) dicusses a variety of amplifications of this point.

Each of four general possibilities for the confrontation phase discussed under interpretation patterns above has a characteristic search pattern. The first or mutual compromise pattern will have a rough parity between internal and external search as each party makes concessions in reaching a compromise agreement. In the second or one-sided concession case the dominant party engages primarily in external search—applying coercive measures and perhaps also procedural accommodation—in order to bring the adversary to accept the constraints imposed by the dominant nation. For the party that does most of the compromising here, search will entail lowering objectives and accepting—at least for the moment—a different and less desirable situation; so search will be largely an internal process. The third or stall possibility is essentially a case in which external search fails to turn up anything that can be dealt with through internal search. A festering sore remains but neither party is prepared for the external or internal changes that would be necessary to relieve this condition. The fourth possibility, dramatic conflict escalation, differs from the stall in that the will to press external search exists even if this search will be costly and at least temporarily broaden the conflict beyond the original issues.

Resourcefulness

No new principles of resourcefulness guide action in this phase, but new practices that follow previous guidelines come into play at this point in conflicts. An activity that sometimes develops during this phase is circumventing through stalling. This option may be used both by the party that seems to hold the advantage and by the party that appears to be losing. The two Berlin conflicts offer excellent examples of stalls on the part of both winning and losing protagonists. In the 1948–49 conflict the Soviets were in no hurry for negotiations in the weeks immediately after the blockade was imposed. They, like their United States counterparts, felt the blockade gave them the upper hand. When the airlift's potential began to be recognized, however, it was the United States that was in no hurry to discuss the German question. With the advantage of the airlift behind them, United States officials were now willing to let the Soviets endure an increasingly useless position. In the 1958–62 conflict stalling was used by Khrushchev as a dissatisfied bargainer. Khrushchev's initial efforts to deal with the Eisenhower administration ground to a halt without much progress. With his efforts blocked, Khrushchev simply stalled until a new administration came to Washington and then tried again (Diesing, 1970).

Another action of importance during this phase is the probe. Probes can follow circumventing, blocking, or even detouring and compellence guidelines. And probes may utilize force, as United States efforts in Southeast Asia show. While it is conceivable that some probes could be initiated inadvertently, most are purposeful attempts to discover the adversary's tolerances. Often these efforts serve as extensions of earlier resourcefulness. A problem these continuations sometimes face is that the initial paths may be leading nowhere, or at least only into trouble, during this phase. If actors are aware that this is happening, they may turn to detouring at this point and probe related issues in the hope of finding a more productive means of competing with the adversary. While this action cannot be categorized with certainty, the Soviet offer to withdraw its strategic weapons from Cuba if the United States would issue a noninvasion pledge certainly appears to be a detour that redefined the issues the Soviets placed in conflict. This offer focused on defense of Cuba and dropped Soviet desires for forward-based nuclear weapons. Sometimes detouring moves may be based on procedure rather than substance. Grey's suggestions for international conferences in 1912 and 1914 were procedural detours in that they were efforts to get explosive issues into a multilateral environment where less-than-enthusiastic allies could dampen the fervor of the parties at the heart of the struggles.

Strategy Dilemmas

Creating and/or discovering the limits of the adversary's tolerances is the primary strategy task of the confrontation phase. This project, if accomplished adroitly, discovers and perhaps reduces the solution characteristics essential to the adversary. Whether these characteristics are acceptable to the statesman's own nation will depend on whether the two nations' tolerances overlap or whether an intervening cushion exists between the two sets of minimal tolerances. The adversary's tolerances are ferreted out by probes that are appropriately small coercive actions or occasionally accommodative bids. Major steps should be avoided until the adversary's tolerances have been isolated with some confidence. Unless preceded by this tolerance location effort, major coercive actions carry the risk of challenging the adversary irrevocably and too severely on a crucial matter. Thus they threaten precipitating an—as yet—unnecessary escalation in violence. But not pressing hard enough leaves the problem of not discovering the adversary's actual minimal tolerances and perhaps overlooking a feasible settlement. Coercive probes carry a greater danger of the former problem, and accommodative actions at this stage are apt to create difficulties of the latter type. Most statesmen prefer coercive probes to meet the requirements or the logic of the confrontation phase adequately. Since nations enter this phase highly suspicious of one another's intentions, each side is anxious to avoid creating a dangerous impression of weakness in the eyes of the other. And a bias toward coercive probes is a wise precautionary measure at the beginning of this phase.

The four independent possibilities mentioned in the interpretation patterns section of the confrontation phase all require different strategic approaches. Gradually escalating coercion is useful for a statesman who faces an adversary for whom the issues are less important than they are for the statesman's nation and/or who cannot bring sufficient resources to bear on the conflict. Coercive measures serve several useful purposes here. First, by directing coercive efforts toward the problem at hand a statesman signals his commitment to particular situations or policies. The blockade of Cuba in 1962 and the subsequent buildup of an invasion force indicated to the Soviets that the United States leadership would not tolerate the Soviet deployment of strategic nuclear weapons in Cuba. Second, by applying coercive actions a statesman creates costs for the adversary. These costs both constitute immediate drawbacks of noncooperation for the adversary and provide indicators of the credibility of further measures. The Berlin blockade created immediate costs for the United States and other Western allies and also fears that the Soviets would use harsher tactics if necessary. Third, by undertaking coercive actions the statesman can generate a risk that conflict activity will surpass a threshold at which management becomes difficult if not impossible. That is, the statesman can practice brinkmanship that endangers both parties in an effort to coerce the adversary into acting as the statesman wishes. Hitler's bold challenges in the Rhineland and Anschluss episodes are the closest approximations in recent statecraft to this manipulation of risk principle. Gradually in this situation of asymmetrical interests and/or resources one of the parties demonstrates itself to be more serious over contested matters than the other, and the less serious party begins to look for an avenue of retreat.

A trickier situation exists when both parties to a conflict have central interests at stake and/or each is able to bring sufficient resources to bear on the conflict to block the other's success. Here neither party will back down on what is perceived as the crux of the problem even if the alternative is escalation. On the other hand, modest compromises on the fringes of the issues in conflict may be preferred by both parties to a breakdown leading to escalation. Two fundamental demands are placed on strategies in this situation. First, strategy must demonstrate commitment, but do so in a low-key fashion that limits—not necessarily avoids—provocative acts. Since the adversary is committed to certain objectives, a strategy of limited coercion cannot be expected to pressure him into backing down. Instead, the first purpose of the statesman's strategy here is to signal the adversary that he is also committed and that overlapping commitments create a contested region. Once the adversary has been provided with a clear signal of commitment the next task is to determine which aspects of the adversary's initial commitment are actually essential and which may be dropped or compromised. This determination is accomplished by probing portions of the adversary's position. Probing accomplishes two tasks. First, it may reveal concrete limits on the adversary's position. The appearance of limits is important in itself. Limits indicate that compromise initiatives will not categorically whet the adversary's appetite. Second, probing may reduce the overlap in the two parties' commitments or even eliminate the overlap entirely by coercing the adversary to accept less than he initially felt he required.

The strategy outlined for the situation of rough parity in terms of central interests and resources in the paragraph above is more conservative than the strategy outlined for the asymmetrical situation in the preceding paragraph. A symmetrical situation of central interests at stake and resources sufficient to block each other's success presents different problems than an asymmetrical situation in which one party either has less at stake or has not the resources to support its interests. The symmetrical situation is not a category of conflict in which one side or the other scores quick victories. In contrast to payoffs in the experimental Prisoner's Dilemma—the game analogue of this symmetrical situation—in which the costs of a few rounds of exploited cooperation are so trivial that they have no significant impact on the lives of the exploited experimental subjects, exploited cooperation in international conflicts sometimes threatens national survival, as has been the case for Israel. Even nations that eventually come out on top in the escalated conflicts that sometimes arise from this symmetrical pattern may, like the French after the First World War, be scarcely able to believe the terrible costs associated with victory. The essential for this symmetrical situation is to avoid the costs of disaster, not to win.

The asymmetrical situation, on the other hand, is a struggle for victory. Nations usually emerge from conflicts with clearly asymmetrical resources and/or interests winners or losers. The statesman, while he would probably like to win, must follow a strategy appropriate for the situation in which he finds himself. Pressing for victory in the symmetrical situation is apt to lead to international disaster. Here the statesman strives to win in a situation which offers no opportunity for victory. The other side will simply not allow it. The statesman who follows a cautious, disaster avoidance line of strategy from the dominant side of an asymmetrical situation suffers the costs of lost opportunities and runs different risks. He does not achieve all that he could. Here the costs are usually domestic. Hard-line or chauvinistic publics have been known to deal harshly with leaders who are reluctant to push adversaries to the wall.

Fortunately, the point of similarity between the strategies for these two situations is the initial stance of moderate firmness. No definitive yet irreversible strategy need be adopted at the outset of a conflict episode. This common stance provides an opportunity to assess the situation more carefully before branching off into definitive and often irreversible paths appropriate for different situations. The first of two crucial junctures comes at the beginning of the confrontation phase as the statesman evaluates feedback from the intolerable violation and resistance phases. If important concessions appear possible for the adversary, while concessions are not possible for the statesman's own nation, the *general* coercive pressure should be continued. These coercive measures should create immediate costs for the adversary and also fears of greater risks to come. In this situation the United States continued the blockade of Cuba, began assembling an invasion force, and warned the Soviets that it would destroy Soviet installations in Cuba if they were not withdrawn quickly. If the statesman senses that he is on the weak side of this asymmetry, the sensible action is to coast on previous firmness and to begin looking for an escape. If neither the statesman nor his adversary appear able and/or willing to make important concessions, the key is to probe *selectively* in the hope of finding a way to fit their positions together. The trick here is to find specific points of compromise—the belated and bungled German discovery in 1911 that the French would compromise on the issue of compensation but not on the territorial integrity of Morocco—which will reduce and hopefully eliminate overlap of national tolerances.

A second crucial juncture comes later in the confrontation phase. General coercive pressure or specific probes may succeed in decomposing goals and offering hope of a compromise. If this happens in an asymmetrical situation, the statesman on the stronger side of the asymmetry has the task of maintaining his firmness while offering indications both of limits on his objectives and a willingness to provide the adversary with a face-saving avenue of retreat. The statesman on the weaker side of this asymmetry has the task of eliciting the strongest sign of limited objectives possible and taking whatever gratuitous concessions are offered. In a symmetrical situation of powerfully supported central interests in which probing has been successful in discovering and forcing small compromises that leave compatible positions, a tacit solution may already exist. Or modest, mutual, and explicit compromise proposals may soon retrieve a solution.

Sometimes in these symmetrical situations the best coercive probing a statesman can devise, or at least that he can gain permission to implement, reveals an overlap of national tolerances that makes a compromise settlement impossible. In this event a statesman has essentially three options. The prudence of these three varies greatly across specific conflict instances. One option is a severe escalation of coercive pressure designed to reach a threshold at which the adversary will relax his current tolerances. The confrontation phase may require more substantial escalation than that of the earlier coercive activity. The purpose of this escalated coercion is not to find or place modest limitations on the adversary's tolerances but to change them in important ways. This approach has met with both success and failure. And the statesman's best guide for the appropriateness of this action is a strong sense of empathy—either in himself or through an advisor—with the adversary's position. As May (1973) cautions, this policy is more appropriate for circumstances in which it works in conjunction with domestic power shifts within the adversary than when it attempts to alter the tolerances of a stable group of committed adversary leaders.

A second option is the stall. The appropriateness of this option in the case of symmetrical central interests and resources is highly contingent on the escalation level reached by the time this decision point arises. If the conflict has already exploded as a result of particularly severe coercive activity (Sarajevo) or through gradual escalation of coercion (Southeast Asia), violence has already reached a level at which a stall carries severe consequences. Nations are rarely able to sustain heavy losses in the absence of foreign progress over long periods of time (Rourke, 1970). If, on the other hand, escalation has not reached a level that is difficult to maintain (Berlin, 1958–62), a stall may be a viable technique for avoiding either a costly struggle or a costly defeat. In some instances, stalls are temporary and merely postpone a conflict of interest to a later date (German Moroccan policy 1906–11), but in other cases a stall in place can offer a solution that in rough outline can eventually be accepted by both parties (Berlin, 1958–62). A stall policy is more vulnerable to shifts in the domestic coalition than other alternatives. Stalls are generally possible only when pressures for coercion *and* accommodation both exist within a decision unit. And any shift from this status can end a stall. Stalls are relevant for symmetrical cases of resources insufficient to achieve desired goals, or situations in which neither party is sufficiently interested in the stakes to escalate with recognized resources. The 1948–49 Berlin conflict was an example of such a situation for several months until the airlift, initially perceived by Western leaders as a stall, demonstrated it was a resource that could win the conflict.

The final option is to lower or shift objectives so that national tolerances no longer overlap. This action may require changing the domestic coalition that supports the present policy or convincing some elements of the existing coalition to change their tolerances. Thus strong domestic forces for accommodation will have to be present. Whether this shift in minimal tolerances can be hidden from the adversary depends both on the thoroughness of the adversary's own probing activity and the visibility of the coalition shift process. If the adversary has already pinned down the statesman's position on a tolerance that is subsequently changed, the change cannot be hidden. Nor can it be concealed if it involves a public coalition shift. The importance of concealing the shift is that, until the statesman has some indication that the adversary will not raise his aspirations, the statesman will be reluctant to reveal a willingness to relax his own tolerances. Accommodation is normally initiated in a contingent or mutual fashion.

Active accommodative action may mark the close of the confrontation phase. The boundary between this phase and the succeeding one is more subtle than for the previous transitions from phase to phase. More important than specific actions here is a change of attitude. Conflicts reach a point at which one or both parties shift their basic attitudes as a result of learning, perhaps changing and finally accepting the tolerances of the other party. Zartman (1976 and 1975) expresses this attitude shift with his notion of a mutually accepted formula that defines the crucial aspects of the solution. The point of strategy from here on is not so much to win additional major concessions as to win an agreement without causing the adversary to alter his position in important ways which violate the formula. So the initial steps toward accommodation are generally taken cautiously. One party may make an offer contingent on a sign of the other's reciprocation of good faith, as Stalin did in the 1948–49 Berlin conflict. Or a statesman may protect himself by making an offer that is unnecessarily favorable to himself and thus conceals his actual interests in order to see if the adversary is willing to reciprocate or whether he will press forward at a sign of conciliation. Kiderlen, after the failure of his initial conciliatory tactic, tried this option by proposing that Germany take virtually all of the French Congo. Or an offer may be made through an unusual channel that can be repudiated later if necessary. The approach of Alexander Fomin to John Scali in the Cuban missile crisis illustrates this technique. The task is to get a sign from the adversary that he too is ready to deal, and the accommodation phase cannot be said to begin until this signal is received.

Accommodation

The impact of the conceptualization of bargaining used in this book is sometimes less pronounced in the accommodation phase than in the previous three phases, and this decline is to be expected. By now the parties are apt to hold more accurate expectations of each other's intentions, preferences, and objectives for the immediate conflict episode. Internal and external search have identified the general area in which hope for an agreement acceptable to both parties resides, and decisions are beginning to bridge discrepancies between domestic and foreign requirements. By the end of the confrontation phase resourcefulness and the results of several strategy dilemmas have defined the specific episode at hand in terms of the relative resources available to the parties to the conflict. So some of the reasons for conceptualizing bargaining in the manner employed here have been muted; the problems central to other phases have been partially cleared up or managed. The process of accommodation that occurs after the discoveries of the previous phases—particularly the confrontation phase—resembles bargaining in economics and experimental gaming theories more closely than do the actions in the preceding three phases.

But even at this point in an international conflict episode, the similarity between bargaining in international conflicts and these other milieux is limited. Basic images of the adversary survive relatively intact, although by now some differences may have arisen between these biases and expectations about the immediate conflict episode. Powerful domestic interests are still apt to resist actions imperative from the standpoint of the international situation. Search efforts to find a settlement area may yet be too vague to be useful. Unexpected discoveries of usable options that alter the relative positions of the parties may occur, or poor handling of one of the strategy dilemmas may throw the conflict back into the confrontation phase rather than facilitating a solution. As a result of these possibilities, the conceptualization offered in this book remains useful through the accommodative phase.

The essence of the accommodation phase is agreeing on a common solution perception or formula and fitting specific details into this formula. The activity of the confrontation phase provides each party with information necessary for locating its own tolerance boundaries as well as the tolerances of the other side to the conflict. Confrontation activity also introduces incentives for creating a solution both sides can accept. With the discoveries of the confrontation phase behind them, each party holds a more realistic notion of the issues in conflict and the limits of acceptable outcomes for the adversary. These revised notions of the various parties are apt to be more similar to one another than the initial perceptions that each party held of the conflict episode. The increased similarity across national perceptions provides the basis for similar perceptions of a conflict solution. Zartman (1976 and 1975) calls this common perception a formula. The contribution of the confrontation phase is complete when a formula arises in the perceptions of conflicting parties. Although the inception of a formula marks the end of the confrontation phase, the formula is not immediately useful, and its appearance leaves two clusters of difficulties unresolved. First, the parties have to communicate their notions of the formula to one another. An attempt to signal altered perceptions of the conflict to the adversary is usually the action that opens the door for the accommodation phase. But, as Quester (1970) shows, this signaling may be difficult. The adversary may not understand the signal properly. Or, if the formula signaled is not yet to his liking, he may not want to understand the signal and so may feign missing or misunderstanding it. Second, a variety of problems remain after this communication has occurred. Important discrepancies may still exist across the solution notions of the various conflicting parties. The solution to certain issues may remain vague under the terms of a formula, and specific solutions that do not violate the formula remain to be worked out. These difficulties are handled in various ways that can be associated with different structures of interests and resources among the conflicting parties.

Interpretation Patterns

The accommodation phase marks an important shift in perceptions about the interests in conflict. New perceptions of a solution to the conflict episode develop, and these perceptions are apt to be fairly similar across the parties to the conflict. These perceptions will probably not be identical. Each party may still misperceive some of the other's tolerances, or what amounts to a detail for one may turn out to be an important formula-destroying point for the other. It is even possible that one or both parties may try to take advantage of the other's accommodation by trying to drive a new and harder bargain. These problems may force activity back to the confrontation stage. But when accommodation finally gets under way, perceptions are apt to develop along lines consistent with several predictable concession patterns.

One pattern of concession characterizes situations in which the resources the parties have succeeded in bringing to bear on the problem are asymmetrical. In contrast to suggestions in much of the strategic literature of the 1960s, statesmen do not often practice brinkmanship in these situations. If one party perceives that the other party has been successful in bringing more resources to bear, the less successful party generally gives way (Fashoda, Berlin 1948–49). The key to resolving the asymmetrical resources case is to give the party that recognizes itself as outclassed a side payment designed to take the bitterness out of defeat. The French (Fashoda) and the Soviets (Berlin 1948–49) both accepted a gesture that did nothing to change the nature of the substantive outcome but that did offer a signal of the other side's willingness to placate the pride of its adversary. The crux of this signal is an indicator that the dominant party is not out simply for all it can get. The signal offers an indication of limits on this party's objectives and places unmitigated humiliation of the weaker party beyond these objectives.

Conflicts in which the asymmetries are in the importance of the values threatened may follow a slightly different pattern of accommodation than those in which the asymmetries relate to resources. Statesmen perceive asymmetries in the importance of values (which are more subtle than asymmetries in resources) less quickly and clearly, and asymmetries in the importance of the issues do not seem to justify deviations from relatively equal settlements, as asymmetries in resources often do. Examples of cases that fall into this category include Agadir and Berlin 1958–62. By October 1911, for instance, the French and the Germans had agreed to a Moroccan accord that essentially gave Morocco to France pending a territorial exchange agreement in the Congo region. Gaining Morocco was the essential issue for the French. The principle of compensation was essential to the Germans, but no particular compensation was essential. Nevertheless, the Germans insisted on what to the French was an extraordinarily painful move of cutting the French Congo in two in order to obtain a ridiculous, narrow access strip to the Congo River. The German colonial secretary, Lindequist, was already trying to resign over what from the standpoint of the Ministry of Colonies was the folly of the Congo negotiations. The access strip, which was mostly swampland, is difficult to view as providing any concrete service to Germany.[8] Access to the Congo resulted primarily in forcing a sacrifice on the French, who had gotten exactly what they wanted in the Moroccan part of the agreement.

Situations of rough parity both in resources and in the importance of the issues at stake follow yet another accommodation pattern. In these instances parties can take advantage of changes in their perceptions that occurred during the confrontation phase. Each party has acquired some evidence that the adversary's immediate objectives (the objectives for this conflict episode) are limited. This perceptual shift erodes the previous emphasis on long-term consequences of accommodation—the precedent it might set for the future—because accommodation is now being considered in terms of specific points rather than general principles. Instead the confrontation phase has built emphasis on avoiding the consequences of further escalation, which have become more awesome as a result of the escalation of the confrontation phase. The necessary contribution that the probing activity of the confrontation phase made in locating tolerances is offset in part by the tensions of escalation that these probes invariably create. Normally, as was noted earlier, these probes do not alter a statesman's notion of the adversary's overall or long-term intentions (Snyder and Diesing, 1977). But the delineation of the limits to the adversary's objectives for this particular conflict episode—which the probes pick up—in conjunction with the increased dangers of imminent disaster also attributable to the probes shift attention away from the dire consequences of compromise and toward the dire consequences of failing to reach an agreement. In short, conditions are created by the probes that allow, even urge, a shift in emphasis from pressing further to settling the conflict.

This perceptual shift illustrates perceptual change in cases of resource and issue parity. The shift is similar to the perceptual changes that the weaker party in instances of asymmetrical resources goes through, but it does not characterize a party that comes out on top in cases of asymmetrical resources. Normally these parties are able to fulfill their substantive

---

[8] The strip did have a prominent aspect: providing access to the Congo River.

objectives—the British at Fashoda, the Germans at Munich—and a perceptual shift such as that described in the preceding paragraph is virtually irrelevant to their situation. And conflict episodes in which the parties slowly and tacitly come to accept a new and initially unsatisfactory situation—Berlin 1958–62—resemble adaptation more closely than the perceptual shift discussed here. Another instance that fails to fit the pattern of the preceding paragraph is a case such as Sarajevo, which explodes into a conflict far outdistancing the original issues at stake. In such a case accommodation, when it finally develops, may have little to do with the original issues and thus little to do with the perceptual shift of the preceding paragraph.[9] Here accommodation may come as a result of the inability to continue a military struggle because of insufficient resources (Germany in the Second World War) or of the utter folly of continuing the struggle because of its incredibly high costs (Japan in the Second World War).

Decision Focus

Decisions in the accommodation phase tend to focus on achieving a situation acceptable to both domestic factions and the foreign adversary. The domestic focus normally entails compromising on previous positions. These shifts in position will require either changes in the tolerances of various members of the decision unit or a renegotiation of the policy coalition through which the membership, or at least the status of the existing membership, changes. Sometimes a few members of the original policy coalition, even those that were particularly central to the coalition during earlier phases, will now either change their positions or lose their centrality. They may even leave the coalition altogether. This is possible because some groups necessary for escalation—the military—are not as necessary for accommodation, and since the policy needs have changed, various domestic groups are apt to shift in importance. Iklé (1971) points

---

[9] Carroll (1969: 305) observes that under circumstances of expanded conflict, obtaining objectives or victory can take on many different meanings. Victory may mean a variety of military circumstances. Or it may mean one of several relations between a party's policy aims and the outcome of the conflict episode. Victory may also be thought of as a relation between the conflicting parties, or in terms of balancing a party's gains against its losses.

out that in some instances extreme shifts occur. At the end of extensive military conflicts, national virtues of the past may become vices, and vice versa. And under these conditions whole elites may change. Generally, however, coalition leaders like to keep coalitions as intact as possible for purposes of legitimizing their actions. If the military or other groups are dropped from a coalition, a domestic bitterness such as the "stab-in-the-back" myth that plagued the Weimar Republic may develop.

Strategy Search

Search in the accommodation phase shifts back and forth again between international and domestic arenas. The focus of external search in this phase is the reconciliation of the modest differences between two generally similar views of a solution formula. External search takes the form of accommodative bids that are coupled with internal search in the form of domestic struggles about the acceptability of the adversary's counteroffers. The basis for search during this phase begins to approximate the utility maximization efforts depicted by formal and experimental theories of bargaining. Up to this point parties have attempted to assure crucial objectives. But by now what appeared crucial at the outset of the conflict has probably been redefined and assured in reduced terms through incorporation in a mutually accepted solution formula, or has been removed from the issues being contested through concessions or adaptation. So the major compromises for each conflict episode occur early in this phase as each of the parties discovers and accepts the general area of the other's revised tolerances. Within the formula provided by these tolerances the parties now begin to weigh the comparative advantages and drawbacks of several different agreement possibilities that differ only modestly from one another.

Resourcefulness

Resourcefulness, as discussed in chapter 4, involved a series of principles by which the statesman might protect his values from the actions of the adversary. Resourcefulness is then less central to the activity of the accommodation phase than it is to the other three phases, since at least the bulk of the accommodation phase comes after values still considered essential have been secured through mutual acceptance of a solution formula. Resourcefulness continues to be relevant to the accommodation phase, however, inasmuch as the formula will probably be vague on specific issues that are of considerable importance to one or another of the parties. One concern present in this phase is holding the adversary to his existing tolerances. This concern illustrates a new purpose of blocking—blocking an increase in the adversary's objectives. The statesman can solve this problem by making his own acceptance of bids contingent on the adversary's acceptance, or he can make offers through a source that can be discredited if the offer does not elicit a favorable response from the adversary. The accommodation phase has a positive aspect of acquiring values as well as protecting values from the adversary. So a second principle applied during this phase involves circumventing the adversary's defense of his values. The "Trollope ploy" used by the United States in the Cuban crisis of 1962 offers an example of a fait accompli in the form of a bid that answered Soviet accommodation initiatives by accepting a formula that circumvented Soviet defense of some of their interests (removal of United States missiles in Turkey).[10] In this phase the statesman strives for concessions that provide as favorable an outcome as the formula allows. The range of choice may be narrow and the range of benefit offered by the options may be modest in comparison to the overall settlement, but some choice usually exists even at this point in a conflict. Statesmen are sometimes able to rely on salient characteristics of solution possibilities to achieve one option over another. In 1911 the Germans picked the salience of access to the Atlantic and the Congo River over the sheer size of the Congo territorial compensation and achieved their objective against stiff French resistance.

Strategy Dilemmas

For most conflicting parties the accommodation phase opens with a decision to make important concessions, although occasionally the pro-

---

[10] The "Trollope ploy" actually was a procedural rather than a substantive maneuver. Independently Robert Kennedy offered an informal promise that the missiles in Turkey would be removed, and they were.

cess is implicit and is appropriately characterized as adaptive action. Essentially, parties determine to struggle no longer for some goals or at least some aspects of their goals. This decision occurs through the acceptance of a formula that excludes some objectives heretofore sought. In 1898 Delcassé determined to give up a foothold in the Nile basin. In 1909 the Russians accepted the Austrian annexation of Bosnia-Herzegovina. In 1911 the French accepted the principle of compensation to Germany and the Germans accepted the closure of the Moroccan question on French terms. In 1962 the Soviets accepted removal of their strategic nuclear installations in the Western Hemisphere and the United States agreed not to invade Cuba. The dominant parties in conflicts involving asymmetrical resources often escape the necessity for concessions at this point. In 1898 the British did not desert any of their objectives. The only concessions they offered were on procedural matters. In 1909 the Austrians made no concessions to the Russians at all. Austria did give Turkey some financial compensation in exchange for Bosnia-Herzegovina.

Beyond this initial accommodative step, the problem arises of whether to revert to coercion rather than to accept particular points that seem to violate the formula. This concern encapsulates many aspects of the general coercive-accommodative dilemma. Failure to find appropriate accommodative tactics will simply continue the confrontation. Yet accepting any accommodation can endanger a satisfactory solution by showing the adversary an unnecessarily weak position. This dilemma nags continually throughout the accommodation phase. Instances exist in which a reversion actually takes place—the United States Christmas bombing of 1972—or is actively considered—Kennedy's willingness to return to coercion if Khrushchev did not remove the medium-range bombers from Cuba. But by this point each side has often come to accept broad outlines of a solution that make a reversion to coercion unnecessary in the sense of defending minimal tolerance boundaries or desirable in terms of the relative costs of reverting to coercion as opposed to accepting the existing range of possible settlements. During the accommodation phase, then, each party tries to define the general formula in as favorable a set of specific provisions as possible. The idea is for each party to pick up an inexpensive concession or two that provide an attractive agreement within the boundaries of the formula.

Accommodation processes break down in some conflict episodes, and a renewed confrontation occurs. These breakdowns are unfortunate both in terms of leading to renewed conflict and in terms of making subsequent accommodation more difficult to initiate and successfully conclude. Breakdowns occur for several reasons. Sometimes breakdown occurs because accommodation is initiated prematurely, prior to mutual determination and acceptance of the other's tolerance boundaries. The Agadir conflict's June accommodation phase and to a lesser degree the Southeast Asian conflict's October "peace is at hand" episode are examples of this situation. Instances also arise in which the results of the accommodation phase seem to violate the spirit although not necessarily the letter of the formula reached in the confrontation phase. Both parties to the Agadir conflict felt this had happened to them, and the conflict, while technically resolved, fueled further and more severe conflicts among these parties due partially to dissatisfaction with the results of past conflict episodes. Finally, the nature of the formula may change—perhaps through a change in government. The French suffered this problem in 1902 in their Moroccan diplomacy with Spain. They were on the verge of concluding an agreement with the Spanish when a government with stiffer tolerances replaced the government with which the French had been negotiating.

Conclusions

The analytical chronology of conflict episodes presented in this chapter has both prescriptive and empirical concerns. It sets out action patterns that meet the demands of a dynamic situation at various points in time. Thus it sets out a sequence of prudent activity. Statesmen should consider the limited dictates of this chronology inasmuch as doing so will reduce unnecessary conflict activity and increase the chances of reaching mutually acceptable and stable solutions. Naturally, if these ends are not values for particular actors, the chronology does not prescribe useful forms of action for them. But many statesmen accept these values and intuitively follow a pattern of activity similar to one given in this chapter. In this sense the chronology is empirical in that it forms explicitly and coherently the considerations that many statesmen follow in an intuitive and sometimes haphazard fashion.

The general implication of this chapter is that the actions of parties to international conflicts follow patterns that can be anticipated by the statesman and can therefore be used as guidelines for the appropriateness of his own actions. The term "anticipated" is used in place of "predicted" purposely, since for two reasons "predicted" seems to exaggerate the service this analysis offers. First, the chronology is not specific with respect to the degree or magnitude of many patterns. While it is reasonable to anticipate that international adversaries will misperceive each other's intentions, preferences, and objectives at the outset of conflict episodes, and that accommodative actions will be more effective once this misperception has been reduced by the coercive probes of the confrontation phase, the chronology does not allow prediction of specific degrees of misperception or optimal levels of coercive and accommodative actions for specific conflict episodes. Second, the chronology includes a number of branches or alternatives at various points. For instance, the accommodation process for a case of asymmetrical resources proceeds in a different manner than it does for a case of symmetrical interests and resources. But this chronology offers no way of predicting which of these two possibilities will characterize future conflict episodes. However, it does offer some general patterns that statesmen can anticipate. Several of these that seem particularly useful in light of the problems statesmen often have in conflicts will be reviewed in this section.

One pattern involves the wide discrepancies yet curious similarities across the perceptions of protagonists at the outset of conflict episodes. Generally statesmen of various nations—even different figures within nations—see different conflicts. In 1911 German statesmen saw a conscious French affront to Germany's position in the decision council of European powers while French statesmen saw an unwarranted German intervention in a colonial region in which Germany had no legitimate interests. And the Soviets saw a grave threat requiring a solution to the German problem in the currency reform in the Western occupation zones of Germany while the United States leaders saw a reprehensible effort to snuff out political liberties in West Berlin. Each party in both instances perceived the other as initiating a conflict through unnecessary and provocative acts. It may be too much to ask that the statesman recognize and empathize with his adversary's point of view. The statesman serves a domestic audience that often has little knowledge of and little interest in the problems and viewpoints of other nations. However, since one important aspect of the bargainer's task is to work out an agreement acceptable to both this domestic audience and the foreign adversary, it is useful for the statesman as bargainer to recognize from the outset that the adversary is apt to have a different notion of the conflict and to picture himself as the aggrieved party rather than the willful initiator of an unnecessary conflict. This guidance seems so straightforward as to be superfluous. Yet the difficulty various United States administrations had in visualizing the conflict in Vietnam as a civil conflict offers a tragic example of the necessity for this guidance. Gauging accurately the importance of control of southern Vietnam to Vietnamese leaders in the North was crucial to the success of United States policy. United States officials perceived the Vietnamese in the North to be aggressively expanding their territory at the expense of another nation. United States leaders then reasoned that if this expansion—perhaps a desirable but surely not an essential goal—were made costly, the Vietnamese would desist. From the Vietnamese standpoint the struggle was to unite the nation, a core value, and United States interference simply made this essential struggle more costly.

Another pattern of particular importance relates to the impact of the manipulative, particularly coercive, actions of one party on the other. When the statesmen of one nation attempt to influence the statesmen of another by coercive actions, the pain or costs of the coercive actions are not usually borne directly by the statesmen of the nation receiving the coercion. Indirect links exist. United States bombing of northern Vietnam probably raised questions among the Vietnamese about their government's ability to protect them. And the Vietnamese leaders probably felt pain and anguish at the suffering of their people under the bombs. Yet these feelings can also backfire on the coercer. Coercion can reinforce for both those who suffer directly and their leaders the need for resisting an adversary from the other side of the world who impersonally destroys women and children. Even if the costs of coercion are transmitted from those on whom they fall to their leaders, or can be brought to bear directly on these leaders, coercion still faces difficulties. From the standpoint of the target statesman, the foreign coercer is only one source of pain. The domestic polity he serves is another (Randle, 1970). Some domestic groups are apt to be hurt by concessions to the foreign coercer.

If these groups can make life more miserable for the statesman than the foreign adversary can, the adversary's coercion is apt to be ineffective. For instance, Kennedy appears to have been at least as upset by the domestic political costs to himself and his party of the Soviet deployment of strategic nuclear weapons in Cuba as he was by the international risks of removing these weapons. In spite once again of the relative obviousness of this argument, statesmen throughout the span over which the examples cited in this essay have been drawn—1898–1973—have overestimated the efficacy of their coercion. Recent suggestions in the United States for lightning invasions of Arab oil producers are continuations of this problem.

Repeated overestimations of the efficacy of coercion emphasize more clearly than any other aspect of bargaining in international conflicts the importance of norms. Targets of coercion sometimes fail to respond as coercers anticipate because coercion is perceived by the target to violate a norm of reciprocity, equality, and/or justice. This violation becomes an additional and often an exceedingly important issue in the conflict. The British in 1898 set a fine example for others to follow by utilizing a variety of procedures—a low-key announcement of the French decision, the change of Fashoda to Kodok, and an agreement to hold a conference to discuss French concerns—to reduce violations to French notions of reciprocity and justice (Grenville, 1964: 230). Even Chamberlain, who was as reasonable with Hitler on substantive matters as a statesman can ever hope his adversary to be, was deeply concerned about the procedures used to achieve these substantive results. Chamberlain had no objection to the Sudetenland becoming part of Germany; indeed, if this development would avert a war he was eager for it. But he would accept German control only if accomplished by procedures that left his sense of justice inviolate, and Chamberlain reacted stiffly to Hitler when at one point in the Munich crisis the latter raised an argument for the necessity of German military action. The central implication to these points about coercion is that for all parties to conflict episodes strategy has two audiences— the domestic polity (and perhaps ally nations) and the foreign adversary(ies). In particular instances one of these audiences may be more important or constraining than the other, but the essence of the statesman's task in most conflict episodes is to thread his way between the obstacles presented by both audiences and so construct a solution acceptable to both. Statesmen recognize the obstacles that the interests of their own domestic polities present for them, but they have a tendency to underestimate the problems their adversaries may have in dealing with their domestic polities. A statesman is often not at liberty, as a player in an experimental game may be, to concede a point to his adversary. In the statesman's case these choices are apt to be made by a group that the statesman does not dominate.

A third topic of interest here is the need for statesmen to develop usable options from their resources. Statesmen must be able to block the adversary's pursuit of his objectives. Or they must circumvent the adversary's position and thus achieve their own objectives. Or they must be able to detour the conflict into an arena that offers them a reasonable chance of competing successfully with the adversary, or compel the adversary to give up contested values. Another possibility is to use force to destroy threats to their values. Statesmen may rely on one or more of these principles of resourcefulness to preserve their interests in the face of external threats. But statesmen must have options that transform resources or situational characteristics to serve these ends. Statesmen sometimes uncritically assume that their resources can be used to influence the actions of the adversary. In the early and middle 1960s it was difficult for many United States leaders to imagine that the tremendous resources of the United States could not influence the Vietnamese leaders to give up their nationalist struggle. Yet the resources that the United States had did not generate usable options that could influence the Vietnamese to give up their struggle.

Another pattern of particular importance deals with the sequencing of manipulation efforts. Although coercion has drawbacks, it is generally a more appropriate response to the mutual suspicion present during the early phases of a conflict episode than accommodation (Snyder and Diesing, 1977). This argument supports George's (George, Hall, and Simons, 1971) outline of using both the carrot and the stick and using them in a specific sequence. George stresses the usefulness of coercion in signaling the statesman's own determination and tolerances to his adversary. While the analysis here agrees with George on this point, it stresses an additional contribution of coercion: finding and creating specific limits on the adversary's objectives through probes. Accommodation can be more effective in eliciting a mutually acceptable solution after coercion has succeeded in replacing the vague, exaggerated perceptions of danger present at the outset of conflict episodes with a set of specific objectives that are crucial to the adversary. This sequence of coercion and then accommodation is not always easy to implement, however. An earlier section of this book emphasized that statesmen tend to have stable action preferences, and a possible weak point in George's excellent essay is that he may overestimate the degree to which statesmen in general are able to shift from coercive to accommodative action and vice versa (George, Hall, and Simons, 1971: 244). George's best illustration of such a shift is Kennedy, a middle-liner for whom such shifts are particularly easy. Either Acheson or Stevenson might have had greater difficulties accomplishing similar strategy shifts. A decision unit of hard-liners following a coercive strategy in a conflict may have difficulty in swinging around to accommodation that both grates against personal preferences and has not been appropriate for the earlier phases of the conflict. For instance, in the Cuban conflict of 1962 Acheson wanted to apply more pressure to Khrushchev once the existing pressure elicited a compromise initiative (Abel, 1966: 162). The presence of both hard and soft-liners in decision units can be useful in gaining strategy shifts at appropriate points in a conflict, although the presence of two factions can also lead to indecisiveness and even paralysis. The ability for some hard-line statesmen to recognize limitations on the adversary's objectives in the immediate conflict as the conflict progresses also provides some opportunity for a shift from coercion to accommodation. Opportunities for compromise begin to appear even for hard-line statesmen once they have recognized limitations on the adversary's objectives.

In addition to this sequence of coercion and accommodation something useful can be said about the relation between the size of concessions and the progression of time. Some parties to international conflicts make virtually no compromises of substance. Other parties make substantively significant as well as modest substantive and/or procedural concessions. In instances of this latter sort the significant compromises are apt to occur first. These compromises take place within governments at the end of the confrontation phase with the acceptance of a formula, and the compromises are communicated to the adversary early in the accommodation phase. This decision to make significant compromises is often what shifts activity from confrontation to accommodation. Two practical lessons arise from this tendency. First, once the accommodation phase is well under way, the chances of the adversary's making major concessions are pretty slim. Concessions of this nature occur with the acceptance of a new notion of a satisfactory solution (a solution formula), and this point now lies in the past. Second, pressing for additional major concessions at this point is apt to lead back to the confrontation. If the adversary has already adapted his general objectives to fit a new and improved understanding of the situation in a conciliatory effort designed to achieve a mutually acceptable solution, the appearance of pressure for additional conciliatory action is not the sort of feedback apt to generate a second significant accommodative effort.

Finally, a concluding statement about the book as a whole seems desirable. The starting point was a review of bargaining theory in economics and psychology. In these fields bargaining theory both is more highly developed than bargaining theory in the study of politics (including severe international conflicts) and asks questions fundamentally different from those most appropriate for severe international conflicts. Specifically, these theories ask for the solution point or the relationship between situational characteristics and the nature of outcomes, respectively. For bargaining in international conflicts these questions are often inappropriate. Prediction of a solution point is difficult for instances of conflict in which the parties hold different notions of the issues at stake. An issue that goes unrecognized by one of the protagonists will be resolved only coincidentally. And it is difficult to predict how successful each party will be in getting its adversaries to see the issues it sees (Kecskemeti, 1970: 113–15). In extreme cases—Lebanon, 1958—no progress is made in gaining a commonly perceived set of issues. Also, focusing on a particular dependent variable can be inappropriate for some phases of bargaining in international conflicts for which the variable is irrelevant—cooperation in the confrontation phase.

Instead this book has addressed other questions that are more practicably directed to bargaining in the context of severe international conflicts than are the foci of economic and psychological theories. These questions have dealt with the origin and impact of disparate perspectives of the interests in conflict, the stability of conflict settlements, the multiple purposes beyond international strategic interaction that conflict strategies serve, the flexibility of strategies, the nature of political choices, and the bases for compromises. In an admittedly vaguer way this book has also addressed and offered insight on matters of settlement prediction. These matters include the sorts of resources that are useful in severe international conflicts, how these resources are transformed into usable options, and when various strategies (adaptation, coercion, accommodation) are appropriate and when they are counterproductive. Answering these questions leaves, without doubt, unanswered issues about bargaining activity in international conflicts. Some of these questions are drawn from bargaining studies in other fields and are virtually unanswerable for conflicts among nations, at least with existing conceptual tools. Other questions drawn from bargaining in other arenas are simply inappropriate in this context. Still other questions, such as how misperception may be reduced or what level of coercion is useful in a particular context, are both meaningful and appropriate but have been excluded as beyond the scope of this book. Hopefully this book will offer some help in answering further questions important for understanding bargaining in international conflicts.

Bibliography

Abel, Elie. 1966. *The Missile Crisis.* New York: Bantam.

Acheson, Dean G. 1969a. Dean Acheson's version of Robert Kennedy's version of the Cuban missile crisis. *Esquire* (February): 76–77, 44, 46.

—— 1969b. *Present at the Creation: My Years in the State Department.* New York: Norton.

Adenauer, Konrad. 1968. *Erinnerungen 1955–1963, Fragmente.* Vols. 3 and 4. Stuttgart: Deutsche Verlags Anstatt.

Albertini, Luigi. 1966. *The Origins of the War of 1914.* Vol. 2. Translated and edited by Isabella M. Massey. Oxford: Oxford University Press.

Allison, Graham T. 1971. *Essence of Decision: Explaining the Cuban Missile Crisis.* Boston: Little, Brown.

Anderson, Eugene N. 1966. *The First Moroccan Crisis, 1904–06.* Hamden, Conn.: Archon.

Axelrod, Robert. 1970. *Conflict of Interest: A Theory of Divergent Goals with Applications to Politics.* Chicago: Markham.

Baldwin, David A. 1971a. Inter-nation influence revisited. *Journal of Conflict Resolution* 15 (December): 471–86.

—— 1971b. The power of positive sanctions. *World Politics* 24 (October): 19–38.

Ball, George W. 1962. Lawyers and diplomats. *Department of State Bulletin* 47 (1227): 987–91.

Barber, James D. 1977. *The Presidential Character: Predicting Performance in the White House.* 2d ed. Englewood Cliffs: Prentice-Hall.

Barlow, Ima C. 1940. *The Agadir Crisis.* Chapel Hill: University of North Carolina Press.

Barnet, Richard J. 1968. *Intervention and Revolution: The United States in the Third World.* Cleveland: World.

Barringer, Richard E. 1972. *War: Patterns of Conflict.* Cambridge: MIT Press.

Bartos, Otomar J. 1967. How predictable are negotiations? *Journal of Conflict Resolution* 11 (December): 48–96.

Baxter, George W., Jr. 1973. Prejudiced liberals: race and information effects in a two person game. *Journal of Conflict Resolution* 17 (March): 131–61.

Benton, Allan A., Harold H. Kelley, and Barry Liebling. 1972. Effects of extremity of offers and concession rates on the outcomes of bargaining. *Journal of Personality and Social Psychology* 24 (October): 73–83.

Ben-Zvi, Abraham. 1976. Hindsight and foresight: a conceptual framework for the analysis of surprise attacks. *World Politics* 28 (April): 381–95.

Bixenstine, V. Edwin, and Jacquelyn W. Gaebelein. 1971. Strategies of "real" others in eliciting cooperative choice in a Prisoner's Dilemma game. *Journal of Conflict Resolution* 15 (June): 157–66.

—— Clifford A. Levitt, and Kellogg V. Wilson. 1966. Collaboration among six persons in a Prisoner's Dilemma game. *Journal of Conflict Resolution* 10 (December): 488–96.

Bonoma, Thomas V., and James T. Tedeschi. 1973. Some effects of source behavior on target's compliance to threats. *Behavioral Science* 18 (January): 34–41.

Boulding, Kenneth E. 1962. *Conflict and Defense: A General Theory*. New York: Harper and Row.

Braithwaite, Richard B. 1955. *The Theory of Games as a Tool for the Moral Philosopher*. Cambridge: Cambridge University Press.

Braver, Sanford L., and Bruce Barnett. 1976. Effects of modeling on cooperation in a Prisoner's Dilemma game. *Journal of Personality and Social Psychology* 33 (February): 161–69.

Brown, Roger G. 1970. *Fashoda Reconsidered: The Impact of Domestic Politics on French Policy in Africa, 1893–1898*. Baltimore: Johns Hopkins University Press.

Cann, Arnie, Steven J. Sherman, and Roy Elkes. 1975. Effects of initial size and timing of a second request on compliance: the foot in the door and the door in the face. *Journal of Personality and Social Psychology* 32 (November): 774–82.

Carroll, Berenice A. 1969. How wars end: an analysis of some current hypotheses. *Journal of Peace Research* 6 (no. 4): 295–321.

Chertkoff, Jerome M., and James K. Esser. 1976. A review of experiments in explicit bargaining. *Journal of Experimental and Social Psychology* 12 (September): 464–86.

Churchill, Winston S. 1923. *The World Crisis*. Vol. 1. New York: Scribner's.

Cline, Ray S. 1974–75. Policy without intelligence. *Foreign Policy* 17 (Winter): 121–35.

Coleman, James S. 1964. *An Introduction to Mathematical Sociology*. New York: Free Press of Glencoe.

Colvin, Ian G. 1971. *The Chamberlain Cabinet: How the Meetings in 10 Downing Street, 1932–9, Led to the Second World War; Told for the First Time from the Cabinet Papers*. London: Victor Gollancz.

Conrath, David W. 1970. Experience as a factor in experimental gaming behavior. *Journal of Conflict Resolution* 14 (June): 195–202.

Cross, John G. 1969. *The Economics of Bargaining*. New York: Basic Books.

Crow, W. J., and R. C. Noel. 1965. The valid use of simulation results. Report to the Western Behavioral Sciences Institute (June).

Cyert, Richard M., and James G. March. 1963. *A Behavioral Theory of the Firm*. Englewood Cliffs: Prentice-Hall.

De Rivera, Joseph H. 1968. *The Psychological Dimension of Foreign Policy*. Columbus, Ohio: C. E. Merrill.

Deutsch, Morton. 1960a. Trust, trustworthiness and the F-scale. *Journal of Abnormal and Social Psychology* 61 (July): 138–40.

—— 1960b. The effect of motivational orientation upon trust and suspicion. *Human Relations* 13 (May): 123–40.

—— and Robert M. Krauss. 1960. The effect of threat upon interpersonal bargaining. *Journal of Abnormal and Social Psychology* 61 (September): 181–89.

—— and Roy J. Lewicki. 1970. "Locking-in" effects during a game of Chicken. *Journal of Conflict Resolution* 14 (September): 367–78.

Diesing, Paul. 1970. The (West) Berlin crisis, 1958–72. Crisis Bargaining Project, State University of New York at Buffalo Center for International Conflict Studies. Mimeographed.

—— 1971. *Patterns of Discovery in the Social Sciences*. Chicago: Aldine-Atherton.

—— 1975. Sample of messages and indices with interpretations. Crisis Bargaining Project, State University of New York at Buffalo Center for International Conflict Studies. Mimeographed.

Downs, Anthony. 1957. *An Economic Theory of Democracy*. New York: Harper and Row.

Druckman, Daniel, et al. 1976. Cultural differences in bargaining behavior: India, Argentina, and the United States. *Journal of Conflict Resolution* 20 (September): 413–52.

—— Kathleen Zechmeister, and Daniel Solomon. 1972. Determinants of bargaining behavior in a bilateral monopoly situation: opponents' concession rate and relative defensibility. *Behavioral Science* 17 (November): 514–31.

Eisenberg, Melvin A., and Michael E. Patch. 1976. Prominence as a determinant of bargaining outcomes. *Journal of Conflict Resolution* 20 (September): 523–38.

Ellsberg, Daniel. 1968. *The Theory and Practice of Blackmail*. Santa Monica: Rand.

—— 1972. *Papers on the War*. New York: Simon and Schuster.

England, J. Lynn. 1973. Mathematical models of two-party negotiations. *Behavioral Science* 18 (May): 189–97.

Esser, James K., and S. S. Komorita. 1975. Reciprocity and concession making in bargaining. *Journal of Personality and Social Psychology* 31 (May): 864–72.

Etheredge, Lloyd S. 1975. Personality and foreign policy. *Psychology Today* 8 (March): 37–41.

Fischer, Fritz. 1967. *Germany's Aims in the First World War*. New York: Norton.

Fisher, Roger. 1971. Fractionating conflict. In *Conflict: Violence and Nonviolence*, edited by Joan V. Bondurant. Chicago: Aldine-Atherton.

Frei, Daniel. 1974. The regulation of war: a paradigm for the legal approach to the control of international conflict. *Journal of Conflict Resolution* 18 (December): 620–33.

Friedman, Milton. 1953. *Essays in Positive Economics*. Chicago: Chicago University Press.

Froman, Lewis A., Jr., and Michael D. Cohen. 1970. Compromise and logroll: comparing the efficiency of two bargaining processes. *Behavioral Science* 15 (March): 180–83.

Fuchs, Kenneth. 1971. The Fashoda crisis. Crisis Bargaining Project, State University of New York at Buffalo Center for International Conflict Studies. Mimeographed.

Gelb, Leslie H. 1971. Vietnam: the system worked. *Foreign Policy* 3 (Summer): 140–67.

George, Alexander L. 1969. The operational code: a neglected approach to the study of political leaders and decision-making. *International Studies Quarterly* 13 (June): 190–222.

―――― 1972. The case for multiple advocacy in making foreign policy. *American Political Science Review* 66 (September): 751–85.

―――― David K. Hall, and William E. Simons. 1971. *The Limits of Coercive Diplomacy: Laos, Cuba, Vietnam*. Boston: Little, Brown.

―――― and Richard Smoke. 1974. *Deterrence in American Foreign Policy: Theory and Practice*. New York: Columbia University Press.

Gillis, John S., and George T. Woods. 1971. The 16PF as an indicator of performance in the Prisoner's Dilemma game. *Journal of Conflict Resolution* 15 (September): 393–402.

Gochman, Charles S. 1976. Studies of international violence. *Journal of Conflict Resolution* 20 (September): 539–59.

Gooch, George P. 1938. *Before the war: Studies in Diplomacy*. Vol. 2. London: Longmans, Green.

Gore, William J. 1964. *Administrative Decision Making: A Heuristic Model*. New York: Wiley.

Grenville, J. A. S. 1964. *Lord Salisbury and Foreign Policy: The Close of the Nineteenth Century*. London: Athlone.

Gromyko, Anatoly A. 1971. Karibskii krizis-diplomaticheskie usilia SSSR po likvidatsii krizisa. *Voprosy Istorii* (August): 121–29.

Gruder, Charles L. 1971. Relationships with opponent and partner in mixed-motive bargaining. *Journal of Conflict Resolution* 15 (September): 403–16.

Guyer, Melvin, and Anatol Rapoport. 1969. Information effects in two mixed-motive games. *Behavioral Science* 14 (November): 467–82.

――――, John Fox, and Henry Hamburger. 1973. Format effects in the Prisoner's Dilemma game. *Journal of Conflict Resolution* 17 (December): 719–44.

Haas, Ernest B. 1964. *Beyond the Nation-State: Functionalism and International Organization*. Stanford: Stanford University Press.

Halberstam, David. 1972. *The Best and the Brightest*. New York: Random House.

Halperin, Morton H. 1972. The decision to deploy the ABM: bureaucratic and domestic politics in the Johnson Administration. *World Politics* 25 (October): 62–95.

—— and Arnold Kanter, eds. 1973. *Readings in American Foreign Policy: A Bureaucratic Perspective*. Boston: Little, Brown.

Hamner, W. Clay. 1974. Effects of bargaining strategy and pressure to reach an agreement in a stalemated negotiation. *Journal of Personality and Social Psychology* 30 (October): 458–67.

Hargrove, Erwin C. 1973. Presidential personality and revisionist views of the Presidency. *American Journal of Political Science* 17 (June): 819–35.

Harris, Richard J. 1972. An interval scale classification system for all 2 × 2 games. *Behavioral Science* 17 (July): 371–83.

Hartford, Thomas, and Leonard Solomon. 1967. "Reformed sinner" and "lapsed saint" strategies in the Prisoner's Dilemma game. *Journal of Conflict Resolution* 11 (March): 104–9.

Hartmann, Frederick H. 1975. A difference in perspective. Paper delivered at the Annual Meeting of the Southwestern Political Science Association, San Antonio, Texas, March 27–29.

Hayes, Michael T. 1972. An analysis of United States decision making on Vietnam: 1945–68. Master's thesis, Indiana University.

Hilsman, Roger. 1971. *The Politics of Policy Making in Defense and Foreign Affairs*. New York: Columbia University Press.

Holsti, Kalevi J. 1970. National role conceptions in the study of foreign policy. *International Studies Quarterly* 14 (September): 233–309.

—— 1972. *International Politics: A Framework for Analysis*. 2d ed. Englewood Cliffs: Prentice-Hall.

Holsti, Ole R. 1967. Cognitive dynamics and images of the enemy: Dulles and Russia. In *Enemies in Politics*, by David J. Finlay, Ole R. Holsti, and Richard F. Fagen. Chicago: Rand-McNally.

—— 1972. *Crisis Escalation War*. Montreal: McGill–Queen's University Press.

Hosoya, Chihiro. 1968. Miscalculations in deterrent policy: Japanese-U.S. relations, 1938–41. *Journal of Peace Research* 5 (no. 2): 97–115.

Howe, Jonathan Trumbull. 1971. *Multicrises: Sea Power and Global Politics in the Missile Age*. Cambridge: MIT Press.

Iklé, Fred Charles. 1964. *How Nations Negotiate*. New York: Harper and Row.

—— 1971. *Every War Must End*. New York: Columbia University Press.

—— and Nathan Leites. 1962. Political negotiation as a process of modifying utilities. *Journal of Conflict Resolution* 6 (March): 19–28.

Janis, Irving L. 1972. *Victims of Groupthink*. Boston: Little, Brown.

Jervis, Robert. 1968. Hypotheses on misperception. *World Politics* 20 (April): 454–79.

—— 1970. *The Logic of Images in International Relations*. Princeton: Princeton University Press.

—— 1976. *Perception and Misperception in International Relations*. Princeton: Princeton University Press.

Kahn, Arnold, Joe Hottes, and William L. Davis. 1971. Cooperation and optimal responding in the Prisoner's Dilemma game: effects of sex and physical attractiveness. *Journal of Personality and Social Psychology* 17 (March): 267–79.

Kalb, Marvin I., and Bernard Kalb. 1974. *Kissinger*. Boston. Little, Brown.

Kecskemeti, Paul. 1958. *Strategic Surrender*. Stanford: Stanford University Press.

—— 1970. Political rationality and ending war. *Annals of the American Academy of Political and Social Science* 392 (November): 105–15.

Kelley, Harold H. 1965. Experimental studies of threats in interpersonal negotiations. *Journal of Conflict Resolution* 9 (March): 79–105.

—— and Anthony J. Stahelski. 1970. Social interaction basis of cooperators' and competitors' beliefs about others. *Journal of Personality and Social Psychology* 16 (September): 66–91.

Kennedy, Robert F. 1971. *Thirteen Days: A Memoir of the Cuban Missile Crisis*. New York: Norton.

Kent, George. 1967. *The Effects of Threats*. Columbus: Ohio State University Press.

Keohane, Robert O. 1971. The big influence of small allies. *Foreign Policy* 2 (Spring): 161–82.

Khrushchev, Nikita S. 1970. *Khrushchev Remembers*. Translated and edited by Strobe Talbott. Boston: Little, Brown.

—— 1974. *Khrushchev Remembers: The Last Testament*. Translated and edited by Strobe Talbott. Boston: Little, Brown.

Knorr, Klaus. 1964. Failures in national intelligence estimates: the case of the Cuban missiles. *World Politics* 16 (April): 455–67.

Knox, Robert E., and Ronald L. Douglas. 1971. Trivial incentives, marginal comprehension and dubious generalizations from Prisoner's Dilemma studies. *Journal of Personality and Social Psychology* 20 (November): 160–65.

Kohl, Wilfred L. 1975. The Nixon-Kissinger foreign policy system and U.S.-European relations: patterns of policy making. *World Politics* 28 (October): 1–43.

Komorita, S. S. 1973. Concession-making and conflict resolution. *Journal of Conflict Resolution* 17 (December): 745–62.

—— and James K. Esser. 1975. Frequency of reciprocated concessions in bargaining. *Journal of Personality and Social Psychology* 32 (October): 699–705.

Leacacos, John P. 1971–72. Kissinger's apparat. *Foreign Policy* 5 (Winter): 3–27.

Lepsius, Johannes, Albrecht Mendelssohn Bartholdy, and Friedrich Thimme, eds. 1925. *Die Grosse Politik der Europaeischen Kabinette, 1871–1914: Sammlung der Diplomatischen Akten des Auswaertigen Amtes*. Vol. 29. Berlin: Deutsche Verlagsgesellschaft fuer Politik und Geschichte.

Lieberman, Bernhardt. 1960. Human behavior in a strictly determined 3×3 matrix game. *Behavioral Science* 5 (October): 312–22.

Lindblom, Charles E. 1965. *The Intelligence of Democracy: Decision Making through Mutual Adjustment*. New York: Free Press.

Lockhart, Charles. 1973. *The Efficacy of Threats in International Interaction*

Strategies. Sage Professional Papers in International Studies, vol. 2, no. 023. Beverly Hills, Cal.: Sage.

—— 1975. The varying fortunes of incremental commitment: an inquiry into the Cuban and Southeast Asian cases. *International Studies Quarterly* 19 (March): 46–66.

—— 1977a. Problems in the management and resolution of international conflicts. *World Politics* 29 (April): 370–403.

—— 1977b. The long-term impact of conflict tactics and outcomes. Paper delivered at the Annual Meeting of the American Political Science Association, Washington, D.C., September 1–4.

Lowenthal, Abraham F. 1973. United States policy toward Latin America: "liberal," "radical" and bureaucratic perspectives. *Latin American Research Review* 8 (Fall): 3–25.

McClintock, Charles G., et al. 1963. Internationalism-isolationism, strategy of the other player, and two-person game behavior. *Journal of Abnormal and Social Psychology* 67 (December): 631–36.

Mack, Andrew J. R. 1975. Why big nations lose small wars: the politics of asymmetric conflict. *World Politics* 27 (January): 175–200.

Marquis, Donald G. 1962. Individual responsibility and group decisions involving risk. *Industrial Management Review* 3 (January): 8–23.

May, Ernest R. 1973. *"Lessons" of the Past: The Use and Misuse of History in American Foreign Policy.* New York: Oxford University Press.

Milburn, Thomas W. 1973. When do threats provoke violent responses? Paper delivered at the Annual Meeting of the International Studies Association, New York, March 14–17.

Miller, Ralph R. 1967. No play, a means of conflict resolution. *Journal of Personality and Social Psychology* 6 (June): 150–56.

Morgenthau, Hans J. 1973. *Politics among Nations: The Struggle for Power and Peace.* 5th ed. New York: Knopf.

Murdock, Clark. 1971. The Berlin blockade. Crisis Bargaining Project, State University of New York at Buffalo Center for International Conflict Studies. Mimeographed.

Nash, John F. 1950. The bargaining problem. *Econometrica* 18 (April): 155–62.

—— 1953. Two-person cooperative games. *Econometrica* 21 (January): 128–40.

Newhouse, John. 1973. *Cold Dawn: The Story of SALT.* New York: Holt, Rinehart, and Winston.

Nicolson, Harold G. 1964. *Diplomacy.* 3d ed. New York: Oxford University Press.

Nitze, Paul H. 1974–75. The strategic balance between hope and skepticism. *Foreign Policy* 17 (Winter): 136–56.

Olson, Mancur, Jr. 1965. *The Logic of Collective Action: Public Goods and the Theory of Groups.* Cambridge: Harvard University Press.

Orwant, Carol J., and Jack E. Orwant. 1970. A comparison of interpreted and abstract versions of mixed-motive games. *Journal of Conflict Resolution* 14 (March): 91–97.

194   Bibliography

Osgood, Charles E. 1962. *An Alternative to War or Surrender*. Urbana: University of Illinois Press.

Oskamp, Stuart. 1971. Effects of programmed strategies on cooperation in the Prisoner's Dilemma and other mixed-motive games. *Journal of Conflict Resolution* 15 (March): 225–57.

—— and Daniel Perlman. 1966. Effects of friendship and disliking on cooperation in a mixed-motive game. *Journal of Conflict Resolution* 10 (June): 221–26.

Park, Chang Jin. 1975. The influence of small states upon the superpowers: United States–South Korean relations as a case study, 1950–53. *World Politics* 28 (October): 97–117.

Payne, James L. 1970. *The American Threat: The Fear of War as an Instrument of Foreign Policy*. Chicago: Markham.

Pick, F. N. 1937. New light on Agadir. *Contemporary Review* 152 (September): 325–32.

Pilisuk, Marc, Barbara Brandes, and Didier van der Hove. 1976. Deceptive sounds: illicit communication in the laboratory. *Behavioral Science* 21 (November): 515–23.

—— Stewart Kiritz, and Stuart Clampitt. 1971. Undoing deadlocks of distrust: hip Berkeley students and the ROTC. *Journal of Conflict Resolution* 15 (March): 81–95.

Pruitt, Dean G. 1968. Negotiation as a form of social behavior. Technical Report no. 6 to the Office of Naval Research, Contract No. N00014–67–C–0190.

—— 1969. Reward structure and cooperation, part II. Technical Report no. 8 to the Office of Naval Research, Contract No. N00014–67–C–0190.

Quester, George H. 1970. Wars prolonged by misunderstood signals. *Annals of the American Academy of Political and Social Science* 392 (November): 30–39.

—— 1971. Missiles in Cuba, 1970. *Foreign Affairs* 49 (April): 493–506.

Raiffa, Howard. 1953. Arbitration schemes for generalized two-person games. In *Annals of Mathematics Studies*. Vol. 28, edited by Harold W. Kuhn and Albert W. Tucker. Princeton: Princeton University Press.

Randle, Robert. 1970. The domestic origins of peace. *Annals of the American Academy of Political and Social Science* 392 (November): 76–85.

Rapoport, Anatol. 1964. *Strategy and Conscience*. New York: Harper and Row.

—— 1966. *Two-person Game Theory: The Essential Ideas*. Ann Arbor: University of Michigan Press.

—— and Albert M. Chammah. 1965. *Prisoner's Dilemma: A Study in Conflict and Cooperation*. Ann Arbor: University of Michigan Press.

—— and —— 1966. *The Game of Chicken*. Ann Arbor: Mental Health Research Institute, University of Michigan.

——, Melvin Guyer, and David Gordon. 1971. A comparison of performances of Danish and American students in a "threat game." *Behavioral Science* 16 (September): 456–66.

—— and J. Perner. 1974. Testing Nash's solution of the cooperative game. In

Game Theory as a Theory of Conflict Resolution, edited by Anatol Rapoport. Boston: D. Reidel.

Raser, John R. 1966. Personal characteristics of political decision-makers: a literature review. *Peace Research Society (International), Papers* 5: 161–81.

Riker, William H., and Peter C. Ordeshook. 1973. *An Introduction to Positive Political Theory.* Englewood Cliffs: Prentice-Hall.

Rosenau, James N. 1968. Private preferences and political responsibilities. In *Quantitative International Politics: Insights and Evidence*, edited by J. David Singer. New York: Free Press.

Rourke, Francis E. 1970. The domestic scene. In *American and the World: From the Truman Doctrine to Vietnam*, by Robert E. Osgood, et al. Baltimore: Johns Hopkins University Press.

Schelling, Thomas C. 1960. *The Strategy of Conflict.* New York: Oxford University Press.

—— 1966. *Arms and Influence.* New Haven: Yale University Press.

Schmitt, Bernadotte E. 1937. *The Annexation of Bosnia 1908–09.* Cambridge: Cambridge University Press.

Schoen, Wilhelm E. 1922. *The Memoirs of an Ambassador: A Contribution to the Political History of Modern Times.* Translated by Constance Vesey. London: Allen and Unwin.

Seabury, Paul. 1967. *The Rise and Decline of the Cold War.* New York: Basic Books.

Sermat, Vello. 1967. The effect of an initial cooperative or competitive treatment upon a subject's response to conditional cooperation. *Behavioral Science* 12 (July): 301–13.

Shapley, Lloyd. S. 1953. A value for *n*-person games. In *Annals of Mathematics Studies*. Vol. 28, edited by Harold W. Kuhn and Albert W. Tucker. Princeton: Princeton University Press.

Shaw, Jerry I., and Christer Thorslund. 1975. Varying patterns of reward cooperation: effects in a Prisoner's Dilemma game. *Journal of Conflict Resolution* 19 (March): 108–22.

Sheehan, Edward R. F. 1976. Step by step in the Middle East. *Foreign Policy* 22 (Spring): 3–70.

Shlaim, Avi. 1976. Failures in national intelligence estimates: the case of the Yom Kippur War. *World Politics* 28 (April): 348–80.

Shubik, Martin. 1961. Some experimental non-zero-sum games with lack of information about the rules. Cowles Foundation Discussion Paper no. 105.

——, Gerrit Wolf, and Byron Poon. 1974. Perception of payoff structure and opponent's behavior in related matrix games. *Journal of Conflict Resolution* 18 (December): 646–54.

Simon, Herbert A. 1955. A behavioral model of rational choice. *Quarterly Journal of Economics* 69 (February): 99–108.

—— 1969. *The Sciences of the Artificial.* Cambridge: MIT Press.

Skotko, Vincent, Daniel Langmeyer, and David Lungren. 1974. Sex differences as artifact in the Prisoner's Dilemma game. *Journal of Conflict Resolution* 18 (December): 707–13.

Snyder, Glenn H. 1969. Notes on threats, commitments and "moves." Working Paper no. 2, Crisis Bargaining Project, State University of New York at Buffalo Center for International Conflict Studies. Mimeographed.

——— 1971a. "Prisoner's Dilemma" and "Chicken" models in international politics. *International Studies Quarterly* 15 (March): 66–103.

——— 1971b. The Morocco crisis of 1905–06. Crisis Bargaining Project, State University of New York at Buffalo Center for International Conflict Studies. Mimeographed.

——— 1972. Crisis bargaining. In *International Crises: Insights from Behavioral Research*, edited by Charles F. Hermann. New York: Free Press.

——— and Paul Diesing. 1977. *Conflict among Nations: Bargaining, Decision Making, and System Structure in International Crises.* Princeton: Princeton University Press.

Sorensen, Theodore C. 1965. *Kennedy.* New York: Harper and Row.

Stassen, Glen H. 1972. Individual preference versus role-constraint in policymaking: senatorial response to Secretaries Acheson and Dulles. *World Politics* 25 (October): 96–119.

Steinbruner, John D. 1974. *The Cybernetic Theory of Decision: New Dimensions of Political Analysis.* Princeton: Princeton University Press.

Stoessinger, John G. 1975. *Nations in Darkness: China, Russia, and America.* New York: Random House.

Swingle, Paul G., and Angelo Santi. 1972. Communication in non-zero-sum games. *Journal of Personality and Social Psychology* 23 (July): 54–63.

Teger, Allan T., and Dean G. Pruitt. 1967. Components of group risk taking. *Journal of Experimental Social Psychology* 3 (April): 189–205.

Terhune, Kenneth W. 1970. The effects of personality in cooperation and conflict. In *The Structure of Conflict*, edited by Paul G. Swingle. New York: Academic Press.

Thibaut, John. 1968. The development of contractual norms in bargaining: replication and variation. *Journal of Conflict Resolution* 12 (March): 102–12.

Thomson, James C., Jr. 1968. How could Vietnam happen: an autopsy. *Atlantic Monthly* 22 (April): 47–53.

Tversky, Amos. 1972. Elimination by aspects: a theory of choice. *Psychological Review* 79 (July): 281–99.

Vagts, Alfred. 1956. *Defense and Diplomacy: The Soldier and the Conduct of Foreign Relations.* New York: King's Crown Press.

Vinacke, W. Edgar. 1969. Variables in experimental games: toward a field theory. *Psychological Bulletin* 71 (April): 293–318.

——— et al. 1974. Accommodative strategy and communication in a three-person matrix game. *Journal of Personality and Social Psychology* 29 (April): 509–25.

Wall, James A., Jr. 1976. Effects of sex and opposing representatives' bargaining orientation on intergroup bargaining. *Journal of Personality and Social Psychology* 33 (January): 55–61.

Wallach, Michael A., Nathan Kogan, and Daryl J. Bem. 1962. Group influence on individual risk taking. *Journal of Abnormal and Social Psychology* 65 (August): 75–86.

Walton, Richard E., and Robert B. McKersie. 1965. *A Behavioral Theory of Labor Negotiations: An Analysis of a Social Interaction System.* New York: McGraw-Hill.

Waltz, Kenneth N. 1967. International structure, national force and the balance of world power. *Journal of International Affairs* 21 (no. 2): 215–31.

Wedge, Bryant, and Cyril Muromcew. 1963. *A View from the East.* Institute for the Study of National Behavior, Princeton University.

White, Ralph K. 1970. *Nobody Wanted War: Misperception in Vietnam and Other Wars.* Revised ed. Garden City: Doubleday.

Wichman, Harvey. 1970. Effects of isolation and communication in a two-person game. *Journal of Personality and Social Psychology* 16 (September): 114–20.

Wiegele, Thomas C. 1973. Decision-making in an international crisis: some biological factors. *International Studies Quarterly* 17 (September): 295–336.

Wilson, Warner. 1969. Cooperation and the cooperativeness of the other player. *Journal of Conflict Resolution* 13 (March): 110–17.

Winham, Gilbert R. 1977. Negotiation as a management process. *World Politics* 30 (October): 87–114.

Wohlstetter, Roberta. 1962. *Pearl Harbor: Warning and Decision.* Stanford: Stanford University Press.

Wolfers, Arnold. 1962. *Discord and Collaboration: Essays on International Politics.* Baltimore: Johns Hopkins University Press.

Wyler, Robert S., Jr. 1969. The prediction of behavior in two-person games. *Journal of Personality and Social Psychology* 13 (November): 222–38.

—— 1971. Effects of outcome matrix and partner's behavior in two-person games. *Journal of Experimental Social Psychology* 7 (March): 190–210.

Young, Oran R. 1967. *The Intermediaries: Third Parties in International Crises.* Princeton: Princeton University Press.

—— 1968. *The Politics of Force: Bargaining during International Crises.* Princeton: Princeton University Press.

Zartman, I. William. 1971. *The Politics of Trade Negotiations Between Africa and the European Economic Community: The Weak Confront the Strong.* Princeton: Princeton University Press.

—— 1974. The political analysis of negotiation: how who gets what and when. *World Politics* 26 (April): 385–99.

—— 1975. Negotiations: theory and reality. *Journal of International Affairs* 29 (Spring): 69–77.

—— 1976. Reality, image, and detail. In *The 50% Solution,* edited by I. William Zartman. Garden City: Doubleday.

Zeuthen, Frederick. 1968. *Problems of Monopoly and Economic Warfare.* New York: A. M. Kelley.

INDEX

204 Index

Pilisuk, Marc, Barbara Brandes, and Didier van der Hove: cited, 32
Players, characteristics of (games), 19–20
Policy analysis, 98–99; use of, in decision making, 69 70
Policy implementation: as source of power, 74
Poon, Byron, Martin Shubik, and Gerrit Wolf: cited, 24n
Power: policy implementation as source of, 74; effect of, 89–90; national 90–94; conventional, 100
Precedents, 95, 148–49, 173
Predictors, 18–19, 31; categories of, 19–28; strategy as, 23
Premature closure, 53; in Cuban missile crisis, 53–54
Prisoner's Dilemma (game), 14, 18–19, 20–22, 26–27, 32, 87, 166
Probes, 163, 165, 167, 173; coercive, 164, 167–68
Problem-solving orientation, 51, 124
Process theories, 32, 33–87
Projection, 49n
Prominence (in bargaining), 11
Promises, 128–29
Pruitt, Dean G.: cited, 26, 51
Psychology: bargaining theory in, 17–32

Quemoy, 114
Quester, George H.: cited, 129, 171

Raiffa, Howard: cited, 6
Rapoport, Anatol: cited, 5; and Albert M. Chammah: cited, 18n, 30
Raser, John R.: cited, 19, 31
Reciprocity, 123; in games, 23–24; and justice, 49; in Cuban missile crisis, 145
Research, experimental, 17–32; strengths and weaknesses of, 28–32; relevance of, for international conflicts, 31
Resistance, 147–54; dysfunctional, 117–18
Resolve, 154–55
Resourcefulness, 106, 107, 133; defined, 97–98; principles of, 101–6, 182; in violation of tolerance phase, 144–45; in resistance phase, 152–53; in confrontation phase, 162–63; in accommodation phase, 175–76
Resources, 89–107; and adaptive activity,

112; asymmetrical, 172–74, 177; use of, 182
Riker, William H., and Peter C. Ordeshook: cited 5
Risk taking, group, 28–29n
Rodgers, William P., 46
Role, domestic, 44–47, 57–59; impact of, on selective attention and interpretation, 69
Rosenau, James N.: cited, 47
Rostow, Walt W., and Eugene V. Rostow, 51, 53, 55
Rouvier, Pierre M., 51, 67

SALT negotiations, 64, 67, 70, 109, 126
Salisbury, Robert, Marquis of, 51, 82n
Sarajevo, 159, 168, 174
"Satisficing," 13
Saudi Arabia, 95–96
Savage, L. J., 108
Scali, John, 169
Schelling, Thomas C., 11, 21, 130; cited, 4, 5, 8, 10, 27, 57, 104, 127
Schoen, Wilhelm E., 50, 107
Schumacher, Kurt, 51, 74, 75
Search: internal, 72–76; external, 76–83; processes, 83–86; see also Strategy search
Selective attention and interpretation, 37–60
Shapley, Lloyd S.: cited 5–6
Sheehan, Edward R. F.: cited, 74n
Shubik, Martin: cited, 27; Gerrit Wolf, and Byron Poon: cited 24n
Signaling, 28, 79, 116, 147; in games, 24, 25; research on, 29–30; blocking as, 101, 152; in coercive activity, 120–21; in resistance phase, 153; in confrontation phase, 161; in accommodation phase, 171, 172
Simon, Herbert A.: cited, 4, 12, 71
Simons, William E., Alexander L. George, and David K. Hall: cited, 31, 93n, 132
Situational characteristics, 25–28, 54, 89–133
Smoke, Richard, and Alexander L. George: cited, 31
Snyder, Glenn H., 8–9; cited, 7; and Paul Diesing: cited, 21n, 34, 47, 71
Soft-liners, 155–59, 183
Solomon, Leonard, and Thomas Hartford, 24
Solution, 13, 69, 71; characteristics, 5–6,